Freedom of Expression

Fred R. Berger
University of California, Davis

Wadsworth Publishing Company
Belmont, California
A Division of Wadsworth, Inc.

Philosophy Editor: Ken King
Production Editor: Jeanne Heise
Copy Editor: Susan Weisberg

© 1980 by Wadsworth, Inc. All rights reserved. No part of this book may be reproduced, stored in a retrieval system, or transcribed, in any form or by any means, electronic, mechanical, photocopying, recording, or otherwise, without the prior written permission of the publisher, Wadsworth Publishing Company, Belmont, California 94002, a division of Wadsworth, Inc.

Printed in the United States of America
1 2 3 4 5 6 7 8 9 10—84 83 82 81 80

Library of Congress Cataloging in Publication Data
Main entry under title:

Freedom of expression.

   Bibliography: p.
   1. Freedom of speech—United States—Addresses, essays, lectures. I. Berger, Fred R., 1937-
KF4770.A75F73   342'.73'085   79-15895
ISBN 0-534-00749-X

To Liv and Daniel,
whose expressions I shall always cherish

Contents

Preface	vii
Fred R. Berger, Introduction	1
John Stuart Mill, Of the Liberty of Thought and Discussion	14
H. J. McCloskey, Liberty of Expression: Its Grounds and Limits (I)	42
D. H. Monro, Liberty of Expression: Its Grounds and Limits (II)	58
Ronald Dworkin, What Rights Do We Have?	71
Joel Feinberg, The Concept of an Absolute Constitutional Right	82
Paris Adult Theatre I v. *Slaton,* 413 U.S. 49 (1973), [Pornography and the First Amendment]	87
David A. J. Richards, The Moral Theory of Free Speech and Obscenity Law	99
Susan Brownmiller, Women Fight Back	128
Tinker v. *Des Moines Independent Community School District,* 393 U.S. 503 (1969), [Symbolic conduct and the First Amendment]	134
Fred R. Berger, Symbolic Conduct and Freedom of Speech	148
Nat Hentoff, The Enemy Within: The American Nazis and Symbolic Conduct	160
Thomas I. Emerson, Affirmative Promotion of Freedom of Expression: Radio and Television	163
Federal Communications Commission v. *Pacifica Foundation,* 438 U.S. 726 (1978), [Indecent speech, the media, and the First Amendment]	178
Thomas I. Emerson, Epilogue	200
Bibliography	205

Preface

This book surveys some of the theoretical and practical problems that arise in connection with freedom of expression. These problems involve the most fundamental issues of moral and political theory. Moreover, expression in the modern world—through the mass media—impinges on our daily lives in ways of which we are scarcely aware. The function of public expression in present-day democratic societies thus merits continued investigation. It is my hope that this book will contribute toward that investigation.

I am most grateful to Richard Wasserstrom for encouragement and editorial suggestions and criticisms that have proved invaluable. I also appreciate contributions toward the preparation of the book by Julia P. Wald, Meredith Schneider, Charlotte Honeywell, and Julie Keefer. Finally, Kenneth King, Jeanne Heise, and Peggy Meehan of Wadsworth Publishing Company have graciously provided me the benefit of their expertise in publishing, which has aided me considerably. Those frantic telephone discussions have helped to finally produce a book.

Introduction
Fred R. Berger

Freedom of expression is usually thought of as a basic political right in Western political democracy. There is no quicker way to "prove" to the modern liberal democrat that a government is not democratic, or that it is an unjust government, or that it is not a "legitimate" government, than to show that it does not permit free speech. Even governments that hold elections are denied acceptability if elections are not accompanied by liberty of discussion and freedom for expression of views contrary to the government's.

Because we presuppose the value of free speech as fundamental, however, too little thought is given to the grounds of that value and to what weight that value has when, inevitably, it comes in conflict with other values that we cherish.

Academic philosophy in recent years has come to have a vigorous interest in issues of contemporary moral and social significance. The morality of abortion, civil disobedience, preferential treatment of minorities and women, war, and so on, have received considerable attention in the literature. This is not true of the subject of freedom of expression. Though very good work (some of which is included in this volume) has been done, the issues the subject poses have hardly been touched in the philosophy literature.

However, freedom of expression is no less a source of problems for us today than it was in the past. Though we agree widely that it is part of our heritage as a "free and democratic people," we disagree considerably over the basis of free speech rights and over the practical implications of accepting free expression.

Indeed, not only are most of the traditional problems still with us—for example, whether to suppress expression by those thought dangerous, such as Nazis, or to suppress pornography—but the technology that has created new free speech problems—the electronic and mass-print media—tend to exacerbate the old difficulties. The dangerous tendency of "bad" speech may be greatly increased in today's world.

In this introduction I shall try to outline these issues and some of the major positions that have been taken on them. In addition, as discussion invariably leads to questions concerning the legal implementation of freedom of speech, I shall seek to provide the reader with an understanding of some of the relevant legal doctrines that have arisen in the United States. It should be clear from the readings that this volume represents only a portion of the problems and views that are associated with the subject.

I. The Philosophical Issues

The central philosophical issues concern the nature of and justification for the right of free expression. The philosophical arguments for free expression generally take two forms: utilitarian or consequentialist, and nonconsequentialist. (I shall use the terms *utilitarian* and *consequentialist* interchangeably.) Utilitarian arguments appeal to the consequences of recognizing free speech as its justification. John Stuart Mill, one of the founders of the utilitarian tradition, gave such a justification in his enormously influential book *On Liberty*. Mill maintained the general thesis that society may rightfully interfere with the freedom of an individual only to prevent harm to others and only if the conduct interfered with "directly" affects others. Though this principle appears to permit suppression of speech, at least when the expression is deemed harmful, Mill argued that "human beings should be free to form opinions, and to express their opinions without reserve." Mill's argument for this proposition (which is reprinted in this book) appeals to the role of free inquiry in discovering the truth and for testing propositions for the truth. Mill's presumption was that rational discovery and verification of the truth have great importance for human well-being, and freedom of expression makes an indispensable contribution to this end.

A related consequentialist argument stresses the special contribution of free speech to democratic political life and values. In a democracy, citizens participate in their own governance. Each member, at least as an elector, exercises a political role, which entails special rights and duties. But that role cannot be properly fulfilled without the freedom to express one's own views, to criticize those of others and of government officials, and to have access to the opinions of others. Freedom of expression, then, makes a crucial contribution to democratic political life, and is justified on this ground.[1]

[1]Such a view is found in the works of Alexander Meiklejohn. See *Political Freedom: The Constitutional Power of the People* (New York: Harper & Row, 1948, 1960); and "The First Amendment Is an Absolute," in *The Supreme Court Review 1961*, ed. P. Kurland (Chicago: University of Chicago Press, 1962), pp. 245–66.

Finally, we should mention consequentialist views that reflect either philosophical skepticism or philosophical pragmatism with regard to the concept of truth. The skeptical approach questions the idea of an "objective" truth and regards free speech as a practical and useful way of dealing with the lack of objective standards. The pragmatic view regards the truth as the result of free inquiry or as that which tends to emerge from a continuing process of questioning, testing, and debate. On this view, there can be no absolutely settled truth, and the acquisition of whatever warranted claims we have presupposes a free "marketplace of ideas."

Arguments that justify free expression by its consequences seem to many critics to have the weakness that, in particular cases or classes of cases, the relevant utilities may favor suppression of speech. In the article included in this volume, H. J. McCloskey exploits this weakness and attempts to show that Mill's argument fails to provide grounds for Mill's strong principle of noninterference. He tries to show that the utilities in fact justify more interferences with speech than Mill recognized in his theoretical statement. Moreover, he argues, the interferences Mill and other liberals permit show that no strong principle of the type Mill held can be defended; only the circumstances of the case can dictate when, and in what form, interference with speech is justified.

The article by D. H. Monro is a response to McCloskey's. Monro points to aspects of Mill's position that he claims McCloskey either overlooks or misinterprets. He also tries to show that Mill's principle does justify the interferences with speech that he recognized without opening the door to all the interferences for which McCloskey argues. Monro also suggests that for a utilitarian, who justifies free speech by its consequences, a fairly strict principle of noninterference is justified, even though in particular cases utility may not be obviously served. This is so because of the inherent disutilities of suppressing speech, the difficulties of evaluating the possible dangers of speech, and the constant threat of the abuse of the censorship power. The very attempt to avoid the dangers in a particular case runs risks that are not worth the effort.

Many critics hold that the appeal to consequences represents a radical misunderstanding of the right of free expression. Though there are certainly good consequences from free expression, the right is not based on that fact but is a moral demand governments must recognize whether or not the general welfare is furthered. Traditionally, this view was associated with a general moral theory known as *natural law* theory, according to which there are certain rights that all persons have by virtue of being persons. These rights can be discovered by reason, just as the laws of nature can be discovered by scientists. Usually, these positions are tied to a metaphysical view about the nature of reality and especially to belief in God as the author of natural and moral law. Though contemporary writers not in a religious tradition would not hold to the metaphysical underpinnings of natural law theory, and would avoid much of its terminology, many critics of utilitarianism do contend that there are rights all persons possess inherently, which can be discovered by the process of analyzing basic concepts of morality or basic moral principles, or which can be justified by appeal to such principles.

In his essay "What Rights Do We Have?" Ronald Dworkin argues for such a position. He rejects the notion that there is a right to freedom as such as the source of the right of free speech. And he denies that a basic right against government can be adequately defended on consequentialist grounds. However, Dworkin argues that we do have a right to basic liberties, including free expression, which is derived from a right all persons have to be treated as equals. To violate a basic right is wrong not because it will have bad consequences but because such a violation in and of itself demeans us as persons deserving of equal concern and respect.

A somewhat different nonconsequentialist view, which has been elaborated by John Rawls, is used by David A. J. Richards in "The Moral Theory of Free Speech and Obscenity Law." In Rawls' view, basic political rights are not justified by appeal to consequences, nor may they be overridden in order to further the general welfare.[2] Rawls has argued for a comprehensive theory of justice that holds that principles of justice can be discovered by consideration of what principles for regulating their basic social structure a group of people would adopt if they were coming together to form a society. Rawls imposes the condition that the persons are not to know what positions in society they will occupy. Such a procedure, Rawls argues, would represent a fair choice of principles, and so he labels the conception *justice as fairness*. He goes on to argue that, given the constraints of the principles of justice that would be selected, such persons would further choose the protections of basic political rights, including that of free speech.

It may be that these two main approaches are not as far apart as they might appear. Though Mill defended free expression as contributing to the discovery of truth, later sections of *On Liberty* argue for individuality, self-development, and autonomy as important constituents of happiness. Moreover, in his essay "Utilitarianism," he held that human beings require certain sorts of things to make them happy—those things that go to make up human dignity. In addition, Mill outlined a theory of rights as social protections for the prime constituents of happiness. This opens the door to at least a partial reconciliation of the two positions. Freedom of speech could be defended as a basic right on the grounds of its necessary connection with a fundamental aspect of human well-being, not to be overridden for lesser utilities. Ordinary case-by-case calculations of utility might be rejected because of the special importance of freedom and dignity, and because the utility of having rights would be lost.[3]

One of the most outstanding aspects of the functioning of free speech in the United States is the fact that it is administered primarily through the Supreme Court. Aside from the practical issues to be taken up later, the role of the Supreme Court gives rise to profound issues in the philosophy of constitutional government.

---

[2]Rawls' theory is found in his important work, *A Theory of Justice* (Cambridge, Mass.: Harvard University Press, 1971).

[3]David Lyons has presented an interpretation of Mill's theory of justice and morality that gives a strong role for rights that cannot be overridden merely in order to maximize the general welfare. See his "Human Rights and the General Welfare," *Philosophy and Public Affairs* VI (Winter 1977), pp. 113–29. I have given a somewhat different analysis of Mill on justice, with a similar conclusion, in "John Stuart Mill on Justice and Fairness," *Canadian Journal of Philosophy*, suppl. vol. V, (September 1979).

Constitutional rights are guarantees *against* government. And an individual's constitutional right cannot, presumably, be violated on the ground that society as a whole would be better off by violating it. In a democracy, the government is ultimately responsible to the majority of the citizens. Legislators, then, can be thought of as agents of the majority, but the Supreme Court is not an elected body. If, however, the Court is the protector of political rights, it can exercise this protection only through the device of declaring unconstitutional laws that are passed by the legislature. Such an exercise of power, not sanctioned by or responsible to the popular will, is thus thought by many critics to be essentially undemocratic. Some defenders of the Court admit this undemocratic character but uphold the exercise of such power as a necessary check on democracy. Other defenders hold a different conception of constitutional democracy, in which what is crucial to democracy is meaningful participation in the community's political life. Majority rule is thus a secondary value, democratic *because* of its guarantee of participation. But if it is the capacity to participate that is central, then the devices of participation—the ballot, free speech, freedom to assemble, and so on—must be protected even from majorities. Thus, the court is seen as playing a central role in guaranteeing the democratic character of political life.

Unfortunately, truly fundamental issues in the philosophy of constitutional government have been somewhat ignored by philosophers. Though there are exceptions, most of the debate has been conducted in the Court itself, and among legal scholars.[4] This book includes one selection that explores issues in the philosophy of constitutional government—Joel Feinberg's essay "The Concept of an Absolute Constitutional Right." Freedom of expression has sometimes been held to be an "absolute" right. Without arguing either side of that controversy, Feinberg assays the philosophical question of what it might *mean* to assert the existence of an absolute right.

II. The Practical Issues

The practical issues that are posed for the concrete realization of freedom of expression are numerous, and the selections in the text represent a sampling, designed to give readers a sense of the nature of these debates.

That limitations must be placed on speech, nearly everyone agrees. Mill upheld the state's right to suppress incitements to riot. Today, legislation that suppresses slander and libel and that enforces truth-in-advertising has been held constitutional. The question then arises as to whether other expression may be interdicted on grounds of its potential harmfulness. The free speech rights of

---

[4]A very good exchange on these issues is to be found in two important Supreme Court cases in the early 1940s: Minersville School District v. Gobitis, 310 U.S. 586 (1940); and West Virginia State Board of Education v. Barnette, 319 U.S. 624 (1943). It is clear that, in these "flag-salute" cases, competing judicial philosophies of the kinds I have described played a role in the decisions. Study of these cases makes an excellent introduction to political and legal philosophy.

revolutionaries have had tenuous protection in the courts of the United States, and many persons today would gladly suppress freedom of expression for racists and Nazis on the ground that their speech poses dangers to minorities.

It should be noted that this ground for suppression—that the speech activities are dangerous—is distinct from another ground, which contends that racist or sexist speech and pornography are immoral, and thus can rightfully be suppressed. The debate on these issues has not kept these claims separate, and the resulting discussion has been confused. The Supreme Court addressed the pornography question in an important case represented here, *Paris Adult Theatre I*. In this case, the Court reasserted a long-standing position that obscene material has no protected status under the First Amendment. Moreover, it held that there are legitimate interests requiring protection from pornographic materials. Quoting a well-known law professor, Alexander Bickel, the Court referred to the "style and quality of life" that, presumably, pornography freed of censorship would threaten. However, Bickel's statement is not especially clear or well thought out. Does it claim that pornography is likely to produce harmful effects on people, or merely that it will lead to conceptions of social relations that society (at least the majority) now regards as immoral? (Note that neither the Court nor Bickel attempted to show that pornography *is* immoral.) The Court seems to have interpreted the claim as causal, that is, as holding that bad effects will be produced, but it conceded that this cannot be proved. Rather than step in and exercise the judicial power to overrule the judgment of the legislature, the Court affirmed the right of the state to judge that such effects are likely.

David A. J. Richards criticizes this decision of the Court. Richards outlines a theory of the First Amendment based on a Rawls-like conception of justice. After a searching analysis of the nature of pornography, he argues that the Court's reasoning in *Paris Adult Theatre* cannot be accepted. Bickel's argument is subjected to criticism, and Richards points out that the Court's handling of the issue of evidence is "disingenuous," because there is virtually no evidence of the bad effects that are feared. To allow suppression of speech in such cases is to give support to irrational legislation.

Also included in this volume is a selection from Susan Brownmiller's book *Against Our Will*, which is an important contribution to our understanding of sexism and rape. In "Women Fight Back," she outlines a view on pornography that has become popular with some (though not all) feminists. Brownmiller attacks pornography as antifemale: It is designed to humiliate women. Her argument for suppression has two parts (though she may not recognize them as distinct). Her first claim, that pornography contributes to a "cultural ideology" that promotes rape, is causal in nature. Her other argument, which has rarely been recognized or dealt with, sees pornography as essentially degrading toward women, much as Nazi propaganda degraded Jews. Respect for persons is undercut by tolerance of such expressions, and such tolerance is wrong for that reason. Pornography, in this view, is a kind of group defamation, which can be suppressed on that ground, whether or not it incites to rape or has other bad effects.

In Nat Hentoff's brief discussion of the free speech rights of Nazis, a partial response to a position like Brownmiller's is given. The case of Nazis desiring to march into the predominantly Jewish community of Skokie, Illinois, captured national attention. The American Civil Liberties Union, which supported the Nazis, lost many members as a result. Hentoff argues that Skokie's attempt to suppress the march was probably unconstitutional. (The courts agreed.) Moreover, he claims that freedom of speech is "indivisible"; in other words, the grounds urged for suppressing Nazis can be urged against other groups in similar circumstances. Although this is certainly the beginning of a treatment of the problem of hateful, degrading expression, it is not a complete response. The fact is that freedom of speech has not proved *so* indivisible; we have been able to isolate classes of cases—for example, libelous speech—in which the nature of the speech has been a basis for suppression. On the other hand, it cannot be said that the proponents of censorship in these cases have presented a general theory and criterion that would assure us that only truly immoral expression would be suppressed. Indeed, the history of the pornography controversy shows how difficult defining such criteria can be.

In this article, Hentoff describes the display of the swastika as "symbolic speech." This is a reference to a First Amendment classification that came to have great significance for the civil rights movement and the anti-Vietnam War movement. The issues raised have not been completely resolved even today. The Supreme Court has recognized the significance of nonverbal means of expression. In the *Barnette* flag-salute case, for example, the Court said:

> *There is no doubt that, in connection with the pledges, the flag salute is a form of utterance. Symbolism is a primitive but effective way of communicating ideas. The use of an emblem or flag to symbolize some system, idea, institution, or personality, is a short cut from mind to mind. . . . Here it is the State that employs a flag as a symbol of adherence to government as presently organized. It requires the individual to communicate by word and sign his acceptance of the political ideas it thus bespeaks. Objection to this form of communication when coerced is an old one, well known to the framers of the Bill of Rights.* (West Virginia State Board of Education *v.* Barnette, 319 U.S. 624, 632–33 [1943].)

The *Tinker* case reprinted in this book shows the Court once again affirming that symbolic conduct—in this case the wearing of black armbands by students in school as a war protest—enjoys First Amendment protection. (The case also involves important, though much neglected, issues concerning the free speech rights of children.) No one, however, would want to hold that *all* symbolic conduct, under *any* circumstances, should be given legal protection. The Court has grappled with the difficulties posed, but it has not settled on a definitive set of doctrines. In several draft-card burning cases, for example, the Court refused First Amendment protection to this symbolic activity on grounds that many observers find difficult to square with the reasoning in the *Tinker* case. In my article,

"Symbolic Conduct and Freedom of Speech," I argue that the difficulties posed by symbolic conduct cannot be resolved if the Court insists on treating symbolic conduct as fundamentally different from "pure" speech and entitled to lesser protection. I argue for criteria that are inspired by the old "clear and present danger" test, which can be applied to all speech. In one form or another, these criteria have been espoused by the Court and thus enjoy prior judicial understanding and application.

Finally, contemporary society presents us with a range of practical free speech issues that derive from the presence of modern technology—radio, television, the mass-print media. The public mind is to some extent the captive of the mass media, and the implications for freedom of expression are enormous. I shall list just some of the problems that law in this area must confront. First is the problem of guaranteeing access to the media, which are controlled by relatively few persons, who represent wealthy, entrenched economic interests and for whom the media are primarily a source of income and power. To the extent that meaningful political and social communications are dependent on the capacity to effectively reach an audience, the organization of media control must give any First Amendment advocate pause. In addition, even when those in the media are doing their jobs well, there is the danger of an overreach of power. Should the media be free to reveal anything whatever about the private lives of public officials or of their business dealings? Is there a public "right to know" that overrides the interests in privacy of officials? On a different level, we might question the right of the media to publish government secrets. In the Pentagon Papers case there seemed a strong public interest in the materials and a weak government claim of a national interest in secrecy. But what if circumstances had been different? Suppose that some significant national or military interest was, in fact, substantially endangered by the publication of the documents. And what role, if any, ought the courts to play in adjusting these interests?

There are other ways in which the work of media reporters can conflict with the rights of private individuals. It is plausible that the rights of free expression encompass a public right to know, and that reporters can guarantee their access to information only (or best) if they can protect their sources of information and the information itself. But what if that information is needed by a defendant at trial? Does the public's right to know, interpreted in the way described, override the right of an individual to a fair trial? And finally, there is the question of whether the public has a right to influence or control the stream of programming that dominates the airwaves. Objectives to violence and sex on television are familiar, as are citizen campaigns to reduce them. Other concerns may be even more significant. Though these issues have been insufficiently discussed, a plausible case can be made that media programming reflects and fosters racism and sexism by displaying and endorsing demeaning, secondary-status roles for minorities and women. By television's preponderance of depictions that merely reflect existing racist, sexist social patterns, a limited, essentially unjust vision of human relationships is endorsed as "normal." However, effective ways of combatting this sort of negative influence appear to present grave difficulties for First Amendment theory.

The problems posed by the media are difficult and numerous, and the literature is vast. I have chosen to include a selection by Thomas I. Emerson, one of the foremost legal authorities on the First Amendment, in which he seeks to outline the sorts of problems and legal principles that the Supreme Court has addressed. This is an area of much litigation, and Emerson's discussion may become quickly dated. (Indeed, there are some authorities who believe the *Red Lion* case, on which Emerson places great reliance, has already fallen somewhat into the background, and Congress may change the laws that define the powers of the Federal Communications Commission.) His discussion should, however, stimulate an understanding of the problems and promote discussion of the relevant principles.

The final Supreme Court case that is reprinted here, *Federal Communications Commission v. Pacifica Foundation*, represents to some commentators a retreat by the Court from the position that "government cannot control the content of individual expression, or normally try to purify the system, or favor one person over another," to use Thomas Emerson's words. George Carlin's "Filthy Words" monologue—about words that cannot be used on radio and television—had been broadcast over a radio station operated by the Pacifica Foundation in New York City. The Federal Communications Commission received a complaint and subsequently issued an order to the effect that such broadcasts might be subject to "administrative sanctions." The Supreme Court upheld the constitutionality of this order. Some of the issues raised in the case are narrow (e.g., whether the "indecent" is limited to the "obscene"), and the Court's position might be recast in terms of "nuisance" theory. Nonetheless, much of the Court's position can be taken to affirm the right of government to control speech on the airwaves that is *not* (for constitutional purposes) obscene or generally unprotected on grounds of its content and social value. Justice Brennan, dissenting, interpreted the Court in this way, as did Justices Powell and Blackmun (who concurred in the Court's disposition of the case).

III. Legal Doctrines

The history of the First Amendment probably comes as a shock to most lay persons. We assume the Supreme Court can declare unconstitutional laws passed at any level of government that interfere with free expression. But the Amendment itself says that *Congress* may pass no law abridging freedom of speech. The authority for the broader sweep of the Court's power derives from the Fourteenth Amendment, adopted in 1868, which forbids any state from "[abridging the] privileges or immunities of citizens of the United States; nor shall any State deprive any person of life, liberty, or property, without due process of law." It was not until 1925 that the Court held that the Fourteenth Amendment "incorporates" the First Amendment and, thus, that the Court's purview extends to the acts of the states and local governments. This means that significant First Amendment doctrine is largely the result of little more than fifty years of Court discussion. The history of this period is a history of competing, supplementary, and clarificatory "doctrines," designed to accord with judicial philosophies and the exigencies of free speech problems. These cannot be explored in detail here, but the reader will be well served to have a brief description of some of the most important doctrines designed for dealing with significant cases:

1. *No prior restraint.* The doctrine of "no prior restraint," one of the most consistently applied principles in First Amendment decision-making, says that expression may not be restrained or censored prior to its issuance. The doctrine has near-universal acceptance,[5] and some legal historians believe that the prime purpose of the Founders in writing the First Amendment was to incorporate this doctrine, already a part of the common law (largely the work of English judges), into the American system.

2. *Bad tendency test.* This doctrine was also a carry-over from the common law, and it was employed by some members of the Supreme Court in the early part of this century. This doctrine held that expression may be punished if it has a "reasonable tendency" to produce such evils as corrupting public morals, inciting to crime, or disturbing the peace. Because no immediate, likely effect must be shown, the test clearly provided little protection to freedom of expression and has fallen out of favor.

3. *Clear and present danger test.* The rule of "clear and present danger" was first articulated by Justice Holmes as part of a dissenting opinion in 1919. (The case was *Schenck* v. *United States*, 249 U.S. 47 [1919].) It was developed and employed by Holmes and Justice Brandeis in subsequent cases and acquired wide acceptance in the Court into the 1940s. In essence, the test prohibits punishment of speech unless it occurs in a context in which it poses a serious, "substantive," and immediate danger that Congress or the states have a right to protect against. Thus, falsely shouting "Fire!" in a crowded theater (to use the famous example) might be punished because it is so closely linked to subsequent harmful action. The rule seems to capture the notion that, where speech is harmful, the remedy is further speech, but where the harm is likely to be great and occurs in circumstances that present no further opportunity for speech, the law may step in. During the 1950s, the Cold War scare that infected all American institutions undermined the "clear and present danger" doctrine. The threat of communism was not perceived as immediate, but it was sufficiently terrifying that many persons thought suppression was justified. (The most famous case involving this fear was *Dennis* v. *United States*, 341 U.S. 494 [1951].)

4. *Preferred freedoms.* If clear and present danger had an inauspicious beginning (as part of a dissent), this was even more true of the doctrine of "preferred freedoms," which was first stated in a footnote to a case that would be little remembered except for the footnote. (The case was *U.S.* v. *Carolene Products Co.*, 304 U.S. 144 [1938].) "Preferred freedom" doctrine holds that the First Amendment gives a special role to freedom of expression that does not permit

---

[5]Even the dissenters in the Pentagon Papers case, who would have permitted restraining publication of the papers by the New York Times, recognized that great weight had to be given the doctrine. See United States *v.* New York Times, 403 U.S. 713 (1971).

"dubious intrusions" by government on speech. Legislation that interferes with speech must undergo special scrutiny. Whereas legislation must normally be presumed constitutional even if there is a rational connection between the legislation and the prevention of an evil, in the case of free speech interests, "only the gravest abuses, endangering paramount interests," permit intervention by the state. Though sometimes thought of as an additional rule to clear and present danger, it was usually held in conjunction with that doctrine, and may be thought of as a justification, or even as a presupposition, of clear and present danger.

5. *Ad hoc balancing of interests.* The "balancing of interests" test developed largely as a reaction to the clear and present danger rule. Some judges felt that it was too vague, others that it was too strict, and still others held that it permitted the Court to overrule Congressional decisions more readily than a nonelective body should. These justices have felt that each case must be decided on its own merits, with the interests at stake weighed and balanced in each case. Some form of balancing has been the predominant doctrine in the Court in recent years. Presumably, the individual's interest in free expression would be given great weight; however, in the hands of judicial conservatives, great deference is given to the supposed balancing already done by the legislature. Moreover, the interest any individual has in free speech in a particular circumstance all too easily appears insignificant in comparison with large-scale social interests that government action seeks to protect. Many liberals regard this approach as a retreat from the Constitution entirely.

6. *Absolutism.* An "absolutist" position represents another extreme—that the Constitution "means what it says," that there can be *no* abridgment of free speech. Put this way, the position invites a caricature—that there may be no interference with speech—that is easily shown to be silly. But absolutists have always conceded that speech that is inseparable from action may be interfered with, and the circumstances of the public forum—the time, place, and (perhaps) the manner of speech—may be regulated to guarantee all a fair chance and as long as content is not suppressed and may get a hearing. With the death of Justice Black and the departure of Justice Douglas, the Court appears to have lost its only absolutists, and, some would say, its strongest defenders of freedom of expression.

In addition to the employment of general doctrines that represent judicial First Amendment philosophies, there are also a number of special criteria that have developed in Supreme Court cases for dealing with particular cases. For example, legislation that is designed to achieve some legitimate governmental function might be too broadly phrased or too broad in scope, thus posing unnecessary dangers to free expression. In order to maintain sanitation in the streets, for example, a city could not forbid distribution of handbills (which could present a littering problem). A more narrowly drawn statute would, say, levy a fine for littering, thus getting more directly at the activity in which the state's legitimate interest lies. Similar to the "over-breadth" test is the requirement that legislation must not be so vague that officials can use that legislation to suppress legitimate speech. Laws are sometimes, then, held to be "void for vagueness." In addition, the Court has sometimes been concerned with the effects or impact of legislation and has sometimes held laws to be unconstitutional because in practice they could have a "chilling effect" on communication. This can happen, for example, when a law results in making persons fearful of prosecution if they engage in communications of certain kinds. These and other such tests have a significant role in First Amendment cases, and are all referred to in the cases in this book.

IV. Some Final Concerns

The book ends with an "Epilogue" that Professor Emerson wrote to his monumental work, *The System of Freedom of Expression*. His book is an extensive survey of First Amendment theory and practice, together with Emerson's own First Amendment theory. In the "Epilogue," he addresses issues raised by critics of free speech as practiced in contemporary liberal democracies. The most influential of these critics has been Herbert Marcuse, in an essay entitled "Repressive Tolerance"[6] (which, unfortunately, could not be reprinted in this volume). Marcuse appears to accept Mill's rationale for free expression, in particular Mill's view that it is required for discovery of the truth, which is needed for improving human welfare. However, he points out that Mill's theory of freedom is meant to apply to a society of rational beings capable of being improved by free discussion. This presupposition is not fulfilled, Marcuse contends, in modern society. The structure of liberal states concentrates economic and political power and thus places the primary media of expression in the control of an entrenched Establishment. The public forum is monopolized from the outset, and the public mind is indoctrinated by the overwhelming one-sidedness of public instruction. One's picture of the world is manipulated through the control that the established economic and political order wield. In this context, tolerance for any sort of view can be allowed, because the public has predigested its views and cannot sift truth from falsehood. Every idea, no matter how evil or repressive, arrives on an equal footing in the "objective" media. It is a "preformed mentality" that chooses, however. Thus, reporting pro and con assessments of the FBI, while seemingly neutral, is really prejudiced, as the public mind is disposed favorably toward Establishment institutions. In such a system, which permits "the systematic moronization of children and adults alike," *effective* dissent is impossible, even if all points of view may be expressed. Though present barriers to truly free discussion are "weak and pleasant enough" in comparison with totalitarian regimes, the tolerance that takes place in the modern liberal democracy is "repressive" toward effective dissent in its overall effect.

Others have commented on the way the media can control and influence the public mind. One critic, Jerry Mander, has published a book that explores the unique features of television—both the structure of industry control as well as

---

[6]Herbert Marcuse, "Repressive Tolerance," in R. P. Wolff, B. Moore, and H. Marcuse, *A Critique of Pure Tolerance* (Boston: Beacon Press, 1965), pp. 81–123.

features of the medium itself—that result in a narrowing of mental vision, a constricted view of the world, and an incapacity to deal intelligently with reality.[7]

These critics have proposed extreme solutions. Marcuse, though recognizing the impracticality of the proposal, argues for a "discriminating tolerance," in which the imbalance of views on the Right is countered by restraining the freedom of "aggressive, regressive, destructive forces." Marcuse realizes that this "solution" presupposes the political ascendance of dissenters to the Establishment. Mander, in his attack on television, concludes that the structure of control and the nature of the beast make significant reform impossible. He thus advocates the elimination of television.

Regardless of one's attitude toward these suggested solutions, or toward these critics' assessments of the problems, there can be little doubt that they pose difficulties that call for a rethinking of freedom of expression and its justification and meaningful realization in the modern world.

[7]Jerry Mander, *Four Arguments for the Elimination of Television* (New York: William Morrow, 1978).

Of the Liberty of Thought and Discussion

John Stuart Mill

The time, it is to be hoped, is gone by when any defence would be necessary of the "liberty of the press" as one of the securities against corrupt or tyrannical government. No argument, we may suppose, can now be needed, against permitting a legislature or an executive, not identified in interest with the people, to prescribe opinions to them, and determine what doctrines or what arguments they shall be allowed to hear. This aspect of the question, besides, has been so often and so triumphantly enforced by preceding writers, that it needs not be specially insisted on in this place. Though the law of England, on the subject of the press, is as servile to this day as it was in the time of the Tudors, there is little danger of its being actually put in force against political discussion, except during some temporary panic, when fear of insurrection drives ministers and judges from their propriety;[1] and, speaking generally, it is not, in constitutional countries, to be

---

[1] These words had scarcely been written, when, as if to give them an emphatic contradiction, occurred the Government Press Prosecutions of 1858. That ill-judged interference with the liberty of public discussion has not, however, induced me to alter a single word in the text, nor has it at all weakened my conviction that, moments of panic excepted, the era of pains and penalties for political discussion has, in our own country, passed away. For, in the first place, the prosecutions were not persisted in; and, in the second, they were never, properly speaking, political prosecutions. The offence charged was not that of criticizing institutions, or the acts of persons or rulers, but of circulating what was deemed an immoral doctrine, the lawfulness of Tyrannicide.

If the arguments of the present chapter are of any validity, there ought to exist the fullest liberty of professing and discussing, as a matter of ethical conviction, any doctrine, however

apprehended, that the government, whether completely responsible to the people or not, will often attempt to control the expression of opinion, except when in doing so it makes itself the organ of the general intolerance of the public. Let us suppose, therefore, that the government is entirely at one with the people, and never thinks of exerting any power of coercion unless in agreement with what it conceives to be their voice. But I deny the right of the people to exercise such coercion, either by themselves or by their government. The power itself is illegitimate. The best government has no more title to it than the worst. It is as noxious, or more noxious, when exerted in accordance with public opinion, than when in opposition to it. If all mankind minus one, were of one opinion, and only one person were of the contrary opinion, mankind would be no more justified in silencing that one person, than he, if he had the power, would be justified in silencing mankind. Were an opinion a personal possession of no value except to the owner; if to be obstructed in the enjoyment of it were simply a private injury, it would make some difference whether the injury was inflicted only on a few persons or on many. But the peculiar evil of silencing the expression of an opinion is, that it is robbing the human race; posterity as well as the existing generation; those who dissent from the opinion, still more than those who hold it. If the opinion is right, they are deprived of the opportunity of exchanging error for truth: if wrong, they lose, what is almost as great a benefit, the clearer perception and livelier impression of truth, produced by its collision with error.

It is necessary to consider separately these two hypotheses, each of which has a distinct branch of the argument corresponding to it. We can never be sure that the opinion we are endeavoring to stifle is a false opinion; and if we were sure, stifling it would be an evil still.

First: the opinion which it is attempted to suppress by authority may possibly be true. Those who desire to suppress it, of course deny its truth; but they are not infallible. They have no authority to decide the question for all mankind, and exclude every other person from the means of judging. To refuse a hearing to an opinion, because they are sure that it is false, is to assume that *their* certainty is the same thing as *absolute* certainty. All silencing of discussion is an assumption of infallibility. Its condemnation may be allowed to rest on this common argument, not the worse for being common.

Unfortunately for the good sense of mankind, the fact of their fallibility is

---

immoral it may be considered. It would, therefore, be irrelevant and out of place to examine here, whether the doctrine of Tyrannicide deserves that title. I shall content myself with saying, that the subject has been at all times one of the open questions of morals; that the act of a private citizen in striking down a criminal, who, by raising himself above the law, has placed himself beyond the reach of legal punishment or control, has been accounted by whole nations, and by some of the best and wisest of men, not a crime, but an act of exalted virtue; and that, right or wrong, it is not of the nature of assassination, but of civil war. As such, I hold that the instigation to it, in a specific case, may be a proper subject of punishment, but only if an overt act has followed, and at least a probable connection can be established between the act and the instigation. Even then, it is not a foreign government, but the very government assailed, which alone, in the exercise of self-defence can legitimately punish attacks directed against its own existance.

far from carrying the weight in their practical judgment, which is always allowed to it in theory; for while every one well knows himself to be fallible, few think it necessary to take any precautions against their own fallibility, or admit the supposition that any opinion, of which they feel very certain, may be one of the examples of the error to which they acknowledge themselves to be liable. Absolute princes, or others who are accustomed to unlimited deference, usually feel this complete confidence in their own opinions on nearly all subjects. People more happily situated, who sometimes hear their opinions disputed, and are not wholly unused to be set right when they are wrong, place the same unbounded reliance only on such of their opinions as are shared by all who surround them, or to whom they habitually defer: for in proportion to a man's want of confidence in his own solitary judgment, does he usually repose, with implicit trust, on the infallibility of "the world" in general. And the world, to each individual, means the part of it with which he comes in contact; his party, his sect, his church, his class of society: the man may be called, by comparison, almost liberal and large-minded to whom it means anything so comprehensive as his own country or his own age. Nor is his faith in this collective authority at all shaken by his being aware that other ages, countries, sects, churches, classes, and parties have thought, and even now think, the exact reverse. He devolves upon his own world the responsibility of being in the right against the dissentient worlds of other people; and it never troubles him that mere accident has decided which of these numerous worlds is the object of his reliance, and that the same causes which make him a Churchman in London, would have made him a Buddhist or a Confucian in Pekin. Yet it is as evident in itself, as any amount of argument can make it, that ages are no more infallible than individuals; every age having held many opinions which subsequent ages have deemed not only false but absurd; and it is as certain that many opinions, now general, will be rejected by future ages, as it is that many, once general, are rejected by the present.

The objection likely to be made to this argument, would probably take some such form as the following. There is no greater assumption of infallibility in forbidding the propagation of error, than in any other thing which is done by public authority on its own judgment and responsibility. Judgment is given to men that they may use it. Because it may be used erroneously, are men to be told that they ought not to use it at all? To prohibit what they think pernicious, is not claiming exemption from error, but fulfilling the duty incumbent on them, although fallible, of acting on their conscientious conviction. If we were never to act on our opinions, because those opinions may be wrong, we should leave all our interests uncared for, and all our duties unperformed. An objection which applies to all conduct, can be no valid objection to any conduct in particular. It is the duty of governments, and of individuals, to form the truest opinions they can; to form them carefully, and never impose them upon others unless they are quite sure of being right. But when they are sure (such reasoners may say), it is not conscientiousness but cowardice to shrink from acting on their opinions, and allow doctrines which they honestly think dangerous to the welfare of mankind, either in this life or in another, to be scattered abroad without restraint, because other people, in less enlightened times, have persecuted opinions now believed to be true. Let us take care, it may be said, not to make the same mistake: but governments and nations have made mistakes in other things, which are not denied to be fit subjects for the exercise of authority: they have laid on bad taxes, made unjust wars. Ought we therefore to lay on no taxes, and, under whatever provocation, make no wars? Men, and governments, must act to the best of their ability. There is no such thing as absolute certainty, but there is assurance sufficient for the purposes of human life. We may, and must, assume our opinion to be true for the guidance of our own conduct: and it is assuming no more when we forbid bad men to pervert society by the propagation of opinions which we regard as false and pernicious.

I answer, that it is assuming very much more. There is the greatest difference between presuming an opinion to be true, because, with every opportunity for contesting it, it has not been refuted, and assuming its truth for the purpose of not permitting its refutation. Complete liberty of contradicting and disproving our opinion, is the very condition which justifies us in assuming its truth for purposes of action; and on no other terms can a being with human faculties have any rational assurance of being right.

When we consider either the history of opinion, or the ordinary conduct of human life, to what is it to be ascribed that the one and the other are no worse than they are? Not certainly to the inherent force of the human understanding; for, on any matter not self-evident, there are ninety-nine persons totally incapable of judging of it, for one who is capable; and the capacity of the hundredth person is only comparative; for the majority of the eminent men of every past generation held many opinions now known to be erroneous, and did or approved numerous things which no one will now justify. Why is it, then, that there is on the whole a preponderance among mankind of rational opinions and rational conduct? If there really is this preponderance—which there must be, unless human affairs are, and have always been, in an almost desperate state—it is owing to a quality of the human mind, the source of everything respectable in man either as an intellectual or as a moral being, namely, that his errors are corrigible. He is capable of rectifying his mistakes, by discussion and experience. Not by experience alone. There must be discussion, to show how experience is to be interpreted. Wrong opinions and practices gradually yield to fact and argument: but facts and arguments, to produce any effect on the mind, must be brought before it. Very few facts are able to tell their own story, without comments to bring out their meaning. The whole strength and value, then, of human judgment, depending on the one property, that it can be set right when it is wrong, reliance can be placed on it only when the means of setting it right are kept constantly at hand. In the case of any person whose judgment is really deserving of confidence, how has it become so? Because he has kept his mind open to criticism of his opinions and conduct. Because it has been his practice to listen to all that could be said against him; to profit by as much of it as was just, and expound to himself, and upon occasion to others, the fallacy of what was fallacious. Because he has felt, that the only way in which a human being can make some approach to knowing the whole of a subject, is by hearing what can be said about it by persons of every variety of opinion, and studying all modes in which it can be looked at by every character of mind. No wise man ever acquired his wisdom in any mode but this; nor is it in the nature of human intellect to become wise in any other manner. The steady habit of correcting and completing his own opinion by collating it with those of others, so far from causing doubt and hesitation in carrying it into practice, is the only stable foundation for a just reliance on it: for, being cognizant of all that can, at least obviously, be said against him, and having taken up his position against all gainsayers—knowing that he has sought for objections and difficulties, instead of avoiding them, and has shut out no light which can be thrown upon the subject from any quarter—he has a right to think his judgment better than that of any person, or any multitude, who have not gone through a similar process.

It is not too much to require that what the wisest of mankind, those who are best entitled to trust their own judgment, find necessary to warrant their relying on it, should be submitted to by that miscellaneous collection of a few wise and many foolish individuals, called the public. The most intolerant of churches, the Roman Catholic Church, even at the canonization of a saint, admits, and listens patiently to, a "devil's advocate." The holiest of men, it appears, cannot be admitted to posthumous honors, until all that the devil could say against him is known and weighed. If even the Newtonian philosophy were not permitted to be questioned, mankind could not feel as complete assurance of its truth as they now do. The beliefs which we have most warrant for, have no safeguard to rest on, but a standing invitation to the whole world to prove them unfounded. If the challenge is not accepted, or is accepted and the attempt fails, we are far enough from certainty still; but we have done the best that the existing state of human reason admits of; we have neglected nothing that could give the truth a chance of reaching us: if the lists are kept open, we may hope that if there be a better truth, it will be found when the human mind is capable of receiving it; and in the mean time we may rely on having attained such approach to truth, as is possible in our own day. This is the amount of certainty attainable by a fallible being, and this the sole way of attaining it.

Strange it is, that men should admit the validity of the arguments for free discussion, but object to their being "pushed to an extreme"; not seeing that unless the reasons are good for an extreme case, they are not good for any case. Strange that they should imagine that they are not assuming infallibility, when they acknowledge that there should be free discussion on all subjects which can possibly be *doubtful,* but think that some particular principle or doctrine should be forbidden to be questioned because it it *so certain,* that is, because *they are certain* that it is certain. To call any proposition certain, while there is any one who would deny its certainty if permitted, but who is not permitted, is to assume that we ourselves, and those who agree with us, are the judges of certainty, and judges without hearing the other side.

In the present age—which has been described as "destitute of faith, but terrified at scepticism,"—in which people feel sure, not so much that their opinions are true, as that they should not know what to do without them—the claims of an opinion to be protected from public attack are rested not so much on its truth, as on its importance to society. There are, it is alleged, certain beliefs, so useful, not to say indispensable to well-being, that it is as much the duty of governments to uphold those beliefs, as to protect any other of the interests of society. In a case of such necessity, and so directly in the line of their duty, something less than infallibility may, it is maintained, warrant, and even bind, governments, to act on their own opinion, confirmed by the general opinion of mankind. It is also often argued, and still oftener thought, that none but bad men would desire to weaken these salutary beliefs; and there can be nothing wrong, it is thought, in restraining bad men, and prohibiting what only such men would wish to practise. This mode of thinking makes the justification of restraints on discussion not a question of the truth of doctrines, but of their usefulness; and flatters itself by that means to escape the responsibility of claiming to be an infallible judge of opinions. But those who thus satisfy themselves, do not perceive that the assumption of infallibility is merely shifted from one point to another. The usefulness of an opinion is itself matter of opinion: as disputable, as open to discussion and requiring discussion as much, as the opinion itself. There is the same need of an infallible judge of opinions to decide an opinion to be noxious, as to decide it to be false, unless the opinion condemned has full opportunity of defending itself. And it will not do to say that the heretic may be allowed to maintain the utility or harmlessness of his opinion, though forbidden to maintain its truth. The truth of an opinion is part of its utility. If we would know whether or not it is desirable that a proposition should be believed, is it possible to exclude the consideration of whether or not it is true? In the opinion, not of bad men, but of the best men, no belief which is contrary to truth can be really useful: and can you prevent such men from urging that plea, when they are charged with culpability for denying some doctrine which they are told is useful, but which they believe to be false? Those who are on the side of received opinions, never fail to take all possible advantage of this plea; you do not find *them* handling the question of utility as if it could be completely abstracted from that of truth: on the contrary, it is, above all, because their doctrine is "the truth," that the knowledge or the belief of it is held to be so indispensable. There can be no fair discussion of the question of usefulness, when an argument so vital may be employed on one side, but not on the other. And in point of fact, when law or public feeling do not permit the truth of an opinion to be disputed, they are just as little tolerant of a denial of its usefulness. The utmost they allow is an extenuation of its absolute necessity, or of the positive guilt of rejecting it.

In order more fully to illustrate the mischief of denying a hearing to opinions because we, in our own judgment, have condemned them, it will be desirable to fix down the discussion to a concrete case; and I choose, by preference, the cases which are least favorable to me—in which the argument against freedom of opinion, both on the score of truth and on that of utility, is considered the strongest. Let the opinions impugned be the belief in a God and in a future state, or any of the commonly received doctrines of morality. To fight the battle on such ground, gives a great advantage to an unfair antagonist; since he will be sure to say (and many who have no desire to be unfair will say it internally), Are these the doctrines which you do not deem sufficiently certain to be taken under the protection of law? Is the belief in a God one of the opinions, to feel sure of which, you hold to be assuming infallibility? But I must be permitted to observe, that it is not the feeling sure of a doctrine (be it what it may) which I call an assumption of infallibility. It is the undertaking to decide that question *for others*, without allowing them to hear what can be said on the contrary side. And I denounce and reprobate this pretension not the less, if put forth on the side of my most solemn convictions. However positive any one's persuasion may be, not only of the falsity, but of the pernicious consequences—not only of the pernicious consequences, but (to adopt expressions which I altogether condemn) the immorality and impiety of an opinion; yet if, in pursuance of that private judgment, though backed by the public judgment of his country or his contemporaries, he prevents the opinion from being heard in its defence, he assumes infallibility. And so far from the assumption being less objectionable or less dangerous because the opinion is called immoral or impious, this is the case of all others in which it is most fatal. These are exactly the occasions on which the men of one generation commit those dreadful mistakes, which excite the astonishment and horror of posterity. It is among such that we find the instances memorable in history, when the arm of the law has been employed to root out the best men and the noblest doctrines; with deplorable success as to the men, though some of the doctrines have survived to be (as if in mockery) invoked, in defence of similar conduct towards those who dissent from *them*, or from their received interpretation.

Mankind can hardly be too often reminded, that there was once a man named Socrates, between whom and the legal authorities and public opinion of his time, there took place a memorable collision. Born in an age and country abounding in individual greatness, this man has been handed down to us by those who best knew both him and the age, as the most virtuous man in it; while *we* know him as the head and prototype of all subsequent teachers of virtue, the source equally of the lofty inspiration of Plato and the judicious utilitarianism of Aristotle, "i maëstri di color che sanno," the two headsprings of ethical as of all other philosophy. This acknowledged master of all the eminent thinkers who have since lived—whose fame, still growing after more than two thousand years, all but outweighs the whole remainder of the names which make his native city illustrious—was put to death by his countrymen, after a judicial conviction, for impiety and immorality. Impiety, in denying the gods recognized by the State; indeed his accuser asserted (see the "Apologia") that he believed in no gods at all. Immorality, in being, by his doctrines and instructions, a "corruptor of youth." Of these charges the tribunal, there is every ground for believing, honestly found him guilty, and condemned the man who probably of all then born had deserved best of mankind, to be put to death as a criminal.

To pass from this to the only other instance of judicial iniquity, the mention of which, after the condemnation of Socrates, would not be an anti-climax: the event which took place on Calvary rather more than eighteen hundred years ago. The man who left on the memory of those who witnessed his life and conversation, such an impression of his moral grandeur, that eighteen subsequent centuries have done homage to him as the Almighty in person, was ignominiously put to death, as what? As a blasphemer. Men did not merely mistake their benefactor; they mistook him for the exact contrary of what he was, and treated him as that prodigy of impiety, which they themselves are now held to be, for their treatment of him. The feelings with which mankind now regard these lamentable transactions, especially the later of the two, render them extremely unjust in their judgment of the unhappy actors. These were, to all appearance, not bad men—not worse than men commonly are, but rather the contrary; men who possessed in a full, or somewhat more than a full measure, the religious, moral, and patriotic feelings of their time and people: the very kind of men who, in all times, our own included, have every chance of passing through life blameless and respected. The high-priest who rent his garments when the words were pronounced, which, according to all the ideas of his country, constituted the blackest guilt, was in all probability quite as sincere in his horror and indignation, as the generality of respectable and pious men now are in the religious and moral sentiments they profess; and most of those who now shudder at his conduct, if they had lived in his time, and been born Jews, would have acted precisely as he did. Orthodox Christians who are tempted to think that those who stoned to death the first martyrs must have been worse men than they themselves are, ought to remember that one of those persecutors was Saint Paul.

Let us add one more example, the most striking of all, if the impressiveness of an error is measured by the wisdom and virtue of him who falls into it. If ever any one, possessed of power, had grounds for thinking himself the best and most enlightened among his contemporaries, it was the Emperor Marcus Aurelius. Absolute monarch of the whole civilized world, he preserved through life not only the most unblemished justice, but what was less to be expected from his Stoical breeding, the tenderest heart. The few failings which are attributed to him, were all on the side of indulgence: while his writings, the highest ethical product of the ancient mind, differ scarcely perceptibly, if they differ at all, from the most characteristic teachings of Christ. This man, a better Christian in all but the dogmatic sense of the word, than almost any of the ostensibly Christian sovereigns who have since reigned, persecuted Christianity. Placed at the summit of all the previous attainments of humanity, with an open, unfettered intellect, and a character which led him of himself to embody in his moral writings the Christian ideal, he yet failed to see that Christianity was to be a good and not an evil to the world, with his duties to which he was so deeply penetrated. Existing society he knew to be in a deplorable state. But such as it was, he saw, or thought he saw, that it was held together and prevented from being worse, by belief and reverence of the received divinities. As a ruler of mankind, he deemed it his duty not to suffer society to fall in pieces; and saw not how, if its existing ties were removed, any others could be formed which could again knit it together. The new religion openly aimed at dissolving these ties: unless, therefore, it was his duty to adopt that religion, it seemed to be his duty to put it down. Inasmuch then as the theology of Christianity did not appear to him true or of divine origin; inasmuch as this strange history of a crucified God was not credible to him, and a system which purported to rest entirely upon a foundation to him so wholly unbelievable, could not be foreseen by him to be that renovating agency which, after all abatements, it has in fact proved to be; the gentlest and most amiable of philosophers and rulers, under a solemn sense of duty, authorized the persecution of Christianity. To my mind this is one of the most tragical facts in all history. It is a bitter thought, how different a thing the Christianity of the world might have been, if the Christian faith had been adopted as the religion of the empire under the auspices of Marcus Aurelius instead of those of Constantine. But it would be equally unjust to him and false to truth, to deny, that no one plea which can be urged for punishing anti-Christian teaching, was wanting to Marcus Aurelius for punishing, as he did, the propagation of Christianity. No Christian more firmly believes that Atheism is false, and tends to the dissolution of society, than Marcus Aurelius believed the same things of Christianity; he who, of all men then living, might have been thought the most capable of appreciating it. Unless any one who approves of punishment for the promulgation of opinions, flatters himself that he is a wiser and better man than Marcus Aurelius—more deeply versed in the wisdom of his time, more elevated in his intellect above it—more earnest in his search for truth, or more single-minded in his devotion to it when found—let him abstain from that assumption of the joint infallibility of himself and the multitude, which the great Antoninus made with so unfortunate a result.

Aware of the impossibility of defending the use of punishment for restraining irreligious opinions, by any argument which will not justify Marcus Antoninus, the enemies of religious freedom, when hard pressed, occasionally accept this consequence, and say, with Dr. Johnson, that the persecutors of Christianity were in the right; that persecution is an ordeal through which truth ought to pass, and always passes successfully, legal penalties being, in the end, powerless against truth, though sometimes beneficially effective against mischievous errors. This is a form of the argument for religious intolerance, sufficiently remarkable not to be passed without notice.

A theory which maintains that truth may justifiably be persecuted because persecution cannot possibly do it any harm, cannot be charged with being intentionally hostile to the reception of new truths; but we cannot commend the generosity of its dealing with the persons to whom mankind are indebted for them. To discover to the world something which deeply concerns it, and of which it was previously ignorant; to prove to it that it had been mistaken on some vital point of temporal or spiritual interest, is as important a service as a human being can render to his fellow-creatures, and in certain cases, as in those of the early Christians and of the Reformers, those who think with Dr. Johnson believe it to have been the most precious gift which could be bestowed on mankind. That the authors of such splendid benefits should be requited by martyrdom; that their reward should be to be dealt with as the vilest of criminals, is not, upon this theory, a deplorable error and misfortune, for which humanity should mourn in sackcloth and ashes, but the normal and justifiable state of things. The propounder of a new truth, according to this doctrine, should stand, as stood, in the legislation of the Locrians, the proposer of a new law, with a halter round his neck, to be instantly tightened if the public assembly did not, on hearing his reasons, then and there adopt his proposition.

People who defend this mode of treating benefactors, cannot be supposed to set much value on the benefit; and I believe this view of the subject is mostly confined to the sort of persons who think that new truths may have been desirable once, but that we have had enough of them now.

But, indeed, the dictum that truth always triumphs over persecution, is one of those pleasant falsehoods which men repeat after one another till they pass into commonplaces, but which all experience refutes. History teems with instances of truth put down by persecution. If not suppressed forever, it may be thrown back for centuries. To speak only of religious opinions: the Reformation broke out at least twenty times before Luther, and was put down. Arnold of Brescia was put down. Fra Dolcino was put down. Savonarola was put down. The Albigeois were put down. The Vaudois were put down. The Lollards were put down. The Hussites were put down. Even after the era of Luther, wherever persecution was persisted in, it was successful. In Spain, Italy, Flanders, the Austrian empire, Protestantism was rooted out; and, most likely, would have been so in England, had Queen Mary lived, or Queen Elizabeth died. Persecution has always succeeded, save where the heretics were too strong a party to be effectually persecuted. No reasonable person can doubt that Christianity might have been extirpated in the Roman empire. It spread, and became predominant, because the persecutions were only occasional, lasting but a short time, and separated by long intervals of almost undisturbed propagandism. It is a piece of idle sentimentality that truth, merely as truth, has any inherent power denied to error, of prevailing against the dungeon and the stake. Men are not more zealous for truth than they often are for error, and a sufficient application of legal or even of social penalties will generally succeed in stopping the propagation of either. The real advantage which truth has, consists in this, that when an opinion is true, it may be extinguished once, twice, or many times, but in the course of ages there will generally be found persons to rediscover it, until some one of its reappearances falls on a time when from favorable circumstances it escapes persecution until it has made such head as to withstand all subsequent attempts to suppress it.

It will be said, that we do not now put to death the introducers of new opinions: we are not like our fathers who slew the prophets, we even build sepulchres to them. It is true we no longer put heretics to death; and the amount of penal infliction which modern feeling would probably tolerate, even against the most obnoxious opinions, is not sufficient to extirpate them. But let us not flatter ourselves that we are yet free from the stain even of legal persecution. Penalties for opinion, or at least for its expression, still exist by law; and their enforcement is not, even in these times, so unexampled as to make it at all incredible that they may some day be revived in full force. In the year 1857, at the summer assizes of the county of Cornwall, an unfortunate man,[2] said to be of unexceptionable conduct in all relations of life, was sentenced to twenty-one months imprisonment, for uttering, and writing on a gate, some offensive words concerning Christianity.

---

[2]Thomas Pooley, Bodmin Assizes, July 31, 1857. In December following, he received a free pardon from the Crown.

Within a month of the same time, at the Old Bailey, two persons, on two separate occasions,[3] were rejected as jurymen, and one of them grossly insulted by the judge and by one of the counsel, because they honestly declared that they had no theological belief; and a third, a foreigner,[4] for the same reason, was denied justice against a thief. This refusal of redress took place in virtue of the legal doctrine, that no person can be allowed to give evidence in a court of justice, who does not profess belief in a God (any god is sufficient) and in a future state; which is equivalent to declaring such persons to be outlaws, excluded from the protection of the tribunals; who may not only be robbed or assaulted with impunity, if no one but themselves, or persons of similar opinions, be present, but any one else may be robbed or assaulted with impunity, if the proof of the fact depends on their evidence. The assumption on which this is grounded, is that the oath is worthless, of a person who does not believe in a future state; a proposition which betokens much ignorance of history in those who assent to it (since it is historically true that a large proportion of infidels in all ages have been persons of distinguished integrity and honor); and would be maintained by no one who had the smallest conception how many of the persons in greatest repute with the world, both for virtues and for attainments, are well known, at least to their intimates, to be unbelievers. The rule, besides, is suicidal, and cuts away its own foundation. Under pretence that atheists must be liars, it admits the testimony of all atheists who are willing to lie, and rejects only those who brave the obloquy of publicly confessing a detested creed rather than affirm a falsehood. A rule thus self-convicted of absurdity so far as regards its professed purpose, can be kept in force only as a badge of hatred, a relic of persecution; a persecution, too, having the peculiarity, that the qualification for undergoing it, is the being clearly proved not to deserve it. The rule, and the theory it implies, are hardly less insulting to believers than to infidels. For if he who does not believe in a future state, necessarily lies, it follows that they who do believe are only prevented from lying, if prevented they are, by the fear of hell. We will not do the authors and abettors of the rule the injury of supposing, that the conception which they have formed of Christian virtue is drawn from their own consciousness.

These, indeed, are but rags and remnants of persecution, and may be thought to be not so much an indication of the wish to persecute, as an example of that very frequent infirmity of English minds, which makes them take a preposterous pleasure in the assertion of a bad principle, when they are no longer bad enough to desire to carry it really into practice. But unhappily there is no security in the state of the public mind, that the suspension of worse forms of legal persecution, which has lasted for about the space of a generation, will continue. In this age the quiet surface of routine is as often ruffled by attempts to resuscitate past evils, as to introduce new benefits. What is boasted of at the present time as the revival of religion, is always, in narrow and uncultivated minds, at least as much the revival of bigotry; and where there is the strong permanent leaven of intolerance in the feelings of a people, which at all times abides in the middle

---

[3]George Jacob Holyoake, August 17, 1857; Edward Truelove, July, 1857.
[4]Baron de Gleichen, Marlborough Street Police Court, August 4, 1857.

classes of this country, it needs but little to provoke them into actively persecuting those whom they have never ceased to think proper objects of persecution.[5] For it is this—it is the opinions men entertain, and the feelings they cherish, respecting those who disown the beliefs they deem important, which makes this country not a place of mental freedom. For a long time past, the chief mischief of the legal penalties is that they strengthen the social stigma. It is that stigma which is really effective, and so effective is it, that the profession of opinions which are under the ban of society is much less common in England, than is, in many other countries, the avowal of those which incur risk of judicial punishment. In respect to all persons but those whose pecuniary circumstances make them independent of the good will of other people, opinion, on this subject, is as efficacious as law; men might as well be imprisoned, as excluded from the means of earning their bread. Those whose bread is already secured, and who desire no favors from men in power, or from bodies of men, or from the public, have nothing to fear from the open avowal of any opinions, but to be ill-thought of and ill-spoken of, and this it ought not to require a very heroic mould to enable them to bear. There is no room for any appeal *ad misericordiam* in behalf of such persons. But though we do not now inflict so much evil on those who think differently from us, as it was formerly our custom to do, it may be that we do ourselves as much evil as ever by our treatment of them. Socrates was put to death, but the Socratic philosophy rose like the sun in heaven, and spread its illumination over the whole intellectual firmament. Christians were cast to the lions, but the Christian Church grew up a stately and spreading tree, overtopping the older and less vigorous growths, and stifling them by its shade. Our merely social intolerance, kills no one, roots out no opinions, but induces men to disguise them, or to abstain from any active effort for their diffusion. With us, heretical opinions do not perceptibly gain, or even lose, ground in each decade or generation; they never blaze out far and wide, but continue to smoulder in the narrow circles of thinking and studious persons among whom they

---

[5]Ample warning may be drawn from the large infusion of the passions of a persecutor, which mingled with the general display of the worst parts of our national character on the occasion of the Sepoy insurrection. The ravings of fanatics or charlatans from the pulpit may be unworthy of notice; but the heads of the Evangelical party have announced as their principle, for the government of Hindoos and Mahomedans, that no schools be supported by public money in which the Bible is not taught, and by necessary consequence that no public employment be given to any but real or pretended Christians. An Under-Secretary of State, in a speech delivered to his constituents on the 12th of November, 1857, is reported to have said: "Toleration of their faith" (the faith of a hundred millions of British subjects), "the superstition which they called religion, by the British Government, had had the effect of retarding the ascendency of the British name, and preventing the salutary growth of Christianity. . . . Toleration was the great corner-stone of the religious liberties of this country; but do not let them abuse that precious word toleration. As he understood it, it meant the complete liberty to all, freedom of worship, *among Christians, who worshipped upon the same foundation.* It meant toleration of all sects and denominations of *Christians who believed in the one mediation.*" I desire to call attention to the fact, that a man who has been deemed fit to fill a high office in the government of this country, under a liberal Ministry, maintains the doctrine that all who do not believe in the divinity of Christ are beyond the pale of toleration. Who, after this imbecile display can indulge the illusion that religious persecution has passed away never to return?

originate, without ever lighting up the general affairs of mankind with either a true or a deceptive light. And thus is kept up a state of things very satisfactory to some minds, because, without the unpleasant process of fining or imprisoning anybody, it maintains all prevailing opinions outwardly undisturbed, while it does not absolutely interdict the exercise of reason by dissentients afflicted with the malady of thought. A convenient plan for having peace in the intellectual world, and keeping all things going on therein very much as they do already. But the price paid for this sort of intellectual pacification, is the sacrifice of the entire moral courage of the human mind. A state of things in which a large portion of the most active and inquiring intellects find it advisable to keep the genuine principles and grounds of their convictions within their own breasts, and attempt, in what they address to the public, to fit as much as they can of their own conclusions to premises which they have internally renounced, cannot send forth the open, fearless characters, and logical, consistent intellects who once adorned the thinking world. The sort of men who can be looked for under it, are either mere conformers to commonplace, or time-servers for truth whose arguments on all great subjects are meant for their hearers, and are not those which have convinced themselves. Those who avoid this alternative, do so by narrowing their thoughts and interest to things which can be spoken of without venturing within the region of principles, that is, to small practical matters, which would come right of themselves, if but the minds of mankind were strengthened and enlarged, and which will never be made effectually right until then; while that which would strengthen and enlarge men's minds, free and daring speculation on the highest subjects, is abandoned.

Those in whose eyes this reticence on the part of heretics is no evil, should consider in the first place, that in consequence of it there is never any fair and thorough discussion of heretical opinions; and that such of them as could not stand such a discussion, though they may be prevented from spreading, do not disappear. But it is not the minds of heretics that are deteriorated most, by the ban placed on all inquiry which does not end in the orthodox conclusions. The greatest harm done is to those who are not heretics, and whose whole mental development is cramped, and their reason cowed, by the fear of heresy. Who can compute what the world loses in the multitude of promising intellects combined with timid characters, who dare not follow out any bold, vigorous, independent train of thought, lest it should land them in something which would admit of being considered irreligious or immoral? Among them we may occasionally see some man of deep conscientiousness, and subtile and refined understanding, who spends a life in sophisticating with an intellect which he cannot silence, and exhausts the resources of ingenuity in attempting to reconcile the promptings of his conscience and reason with orthodoxy, which yet he does not, perhaps, to the end succeed in doing. No one can be a great thinker who does not recognize, that as a thinker it is his first duty to follow his intellect to whatever conclusions it may lead. Truth gains more even by the errors of one who, with due study and preparation, thinks for himself, than by the true opinions of those who only hold them because they do not suffer themselves to think. Not that it is solely, or chiefly, to form great thinkers, that freedom of thinking is required. On the contrary, it is as much, and even more indispensable, to enable average human beings to attain the mental stature which they are capable of. There have been, and may again be, great individual thinkers, in a general atmosphere of mental slavery. But there never has been, nor ever will be, in that atmosphere, an intellectually active people. Where any people has made a temporary approach to such a character, it has been because the dread of heterodox speculation was for a time suspended. Where there is a tacit convention that principles are not to be disputed; where the discussion of the greatest questions which can occupy humanity is considered to be closed, we cannot hope to find that generally high scale of mental activity which has made some periods of history so remarkable. Never when controversy avoided the subjects which are large and important enough to kindle enthusiasm, was the mind of a people stirred up from its foundations, and the impulse given which raised even persons of the most ordinary intellect to something of the dignity of thinking beings. Of such we have had an example in the condition of Europe during the times immediately following the Reformation; another, though limited to the Continent and to a more cultivated class, in the speculative movement of the latter half of the eighteenth century; and a third, of still briefer duration, in the intellectual fermentation of Germany during the Goethian and Fichtean period. These periods differed widely in the particular opinions which they developed; but were alike in this, that during all three the yoke of authority was broken. In each, an old mental despotism had been thrown off, and no new one had yet taken its place. The impulse given at these three periods has made Europe what it now is. Every single improvement which has taken place either in the human mind or in institutions, may be traced distinctly to one or other of them. Appearances have for some time indicated that all three impulses are well-nigh spent; and we can expect no fresh start, until we again assert our mental freedom.

Let us now pass to the second division of the argument, and dismissing the supposition that any of the received opinions may be false, let us assume them to be true, and examine into the worth of the manner in which they are likely to be held, when their truth is not freely and openly canvassed. However unwillingly a person who has a strong opinion may admit the possibility that his opinion may be false, he ought to be moved by the consideration that however true it may be, if it is not fully, frequently, and fearlessly discussed, it will be held as a dead dogma, not a living truth.

There is a class of persons (happily not quite so numerous as formerly) who think it enough if a person assents undoubtingly to what they think true, though he has no knowledge whatever of the grounds of the opinion, and could not make a tenable defence of it against the most superficial objections. Such persons, if they can once get their creed taught from authority, naturally think that no good, and some harm, comes of its being allowed to be questioned. Where their influence prevails, they make it nearly impossible for the received opinion to be rejected wisely and considerately, though it may still be rejected rashly and ignorantly; for to shut out discussion entirely is seldom possible, and when it once gets in, beliefs not grounded on conviction are apt to give way before the slightest semblance of an argument. Waiving, however, this possibility—assuming that the true opinion abides in the mind, but abides as a prejudice, a belief independent of, and proof against, argument—this is not the way in which truth ought to be held by a rational being. This is not knowing the truth. Truth, thus held, is but one superstition the more, accidentally clinging to the words which enunciate a truth.

If the intellect and judgment of mankind ought to be cultivated, a thing which Protestants at least do not deny, on what can these faculties be more appropriately exercised by any one, than on the things which concern him so much that it is considered necessary for him to hold opinions on them? If the cultivation of the understanding consists in one thing more than in another, it is surely in learning the grounds of one's own opinions. Whatever people believe, on subjects on which it is of the first importance to believe rightly, they ought to be able to defend against at least the common objections. But, some one may say, "Let them be *taught* the grounds of their opinions. It does not follow that opinions must be merely parroted because they are never heard controverted. Persons who learn geometry do not simply commit the theorems to memory, but understand and learn likewise the demonstrations; and it would be absurd to say that they remain ignorant of the grounds of geometrical truths, because they never hear any one deny, and attempt to disprove them." Undoubtedly: and such teaching suffices on a subject like mathematics, where there is nothing at all to be said on the wrong side of the question. The peculiarity of the evidence of mathematical truths is, that all the argument is on one side. There are no objections, and no answers to objections. But on every subject on which difference of opinion is possible, the truth depends on a balance to be struck between two sets of conflicting reasons. Even in natural philosophy, there is always some other explanation possible of the same facts; some geocentric theory instead of heliocentric, some phlogiston instead of oxygen; and it has to be shown why that other theory cannot be the true one: and until this is shown, and until we know how it is shown, we do not understand the grounds of our opinion. But when we turn to subjects infinitely more complicated, to morals, religion, politics, social relations, and the business of life, three-fourths of the arguments for every disputed opinion consist in dispelling the appearances which favor some opinion different from it. The greatest orator, save one, of antiquity, has left it on record that he always studied his adversary's case with as great, if not with still greater, intensity than even his own. What Cicero practised as the means of forensic success, requires to be imitated by all who study any subject in order to arrive at the truth. He who knows only his own side of the case, knows little of that. His reasons may be good, and no one may have been able to refute them. But if he is equally unable to refute the reasons on the opposite side; if he does not so much as know what they are, he has no ground for preferring either opinion. The rational position for him would be suspension of judgment, and unless he contents himself with that, he is either led by authority, or adopts, like the generality of the world, the side to which he feels most inclination. Nor is it enough that he should hear the arguments of adversaries from his own teachers, presented as they state them, and accompanied by what they offer as refutations. That is not the way to do justice to the arguments, or bring them into real contact with his own mind. He must be able to hear them from persons who actually believe them; who defend them in earnest, and do their very utmost for them. He must know them in their most plausible and persuasive form; he must feel the whole force of the difficulty which the true view of the subject has to encounter and dispose of; else he will never really possess himself of the portion of truth which meets and removes that difficulty. Ninety-nine in a hundred of what are called educated men are in this condition; even those who can argue fluently for their opinions. Their conclusion may be true, but it might be false for anything they know: they have never thrown themselves into the mental position of those who think differently from them, and considered what such persons may have to say; and consequently they do not, in any proper sense of the word, know the doctrine which they themselves profess. They do not know those parts of it which explain and justify the remainder; the considerations which show that a fact which seemingly conflicts with another is reconcilable with it, or that, of two apparently strong reasons, one and not the other ought to be preferred. All that part of the truth which turns the scale, and decides the judgment of a completely informed mind, they are strangers to; nor is it ever really known, but to those who have attended equally and impartially to both sides, and endeavored to see the reasons of both in the strongest light. So essential is this discipline to a real understanding of moral and human subjects, that if opponents of all important truths do not exist, it is indispensable to imagine them, and supply them with the strongest arguments which the most skillful devil's advocate can conjure up.

  To abate the force of these considerations, an enemy of free discussion may be supposed to say, that there is no necessity for mankind in general to know and understand all that can be said against or for their opinions by philosophers and theologians. That it is not needful for common men to be able to expose all the misstatements or fallacies of an ingenious opponent. That it is enough if there is always somebody capable of answering them, so that nothing likely to mislead uninstructed persons remains unrefuted. That simple minds, having been taught the obvious grounds of the truths inculcated on them, may trust to authority for the rest, and being aware that they have neither knowledge nor talent to resolve every difficulty which can be raised, may repose in the assurance that all those which have been raised have been or can be answered, by those who are specially trained to the task.

  Conceding to this view of the subject the utmost that can be claimed for it by those most easily satisfied with the amount of understanding of truth which ought to accompany the belief of it; even so, the argument for free discussion is no way weakened. For even this doctrine acknowledges that mankind ought to have a rational assurance that all objections have been satisfactorily answered; and how are they to be answered if that which requires to be answered is not spoken? Or how can the answer be known to be satisfactory, if the objectors have no opportunity of showing that it is unsatisfactory? If not the public, at least the philosophers and theologians who are to resolve the difficulties, must make themselves familiar with those difficulties in their most puzzling form; and this cannot be accomplished unless they are freely stated, and placed in the most advantageous light which they admit of. The Catholic Church has its own way of dealing with this embarrassing problem. It makes a broad separation between those who can be permitted to receive its doctrines on conviction, and those who must accept them on trust. Neither, indeed, are allowed any choice as to what they will accept; but the clergy, such at least as can be fully confided in, may admissibly and meritoriously make themselves acquainted with the arguments of opponents, in order to answer them, and may, therefore, read heretical books; the laity, not unless by special permission, hard to be obtained. This discipline recognizes a knowledge of the enemy's case as beneficial to the teachers, but finds means, consistent with this, of denying it to the rest of the world: thus giving to the élite more mental culture, though not more mental freedom, than it allows to the mass. By this device it succeeds in obtaining the kind of mental superiority which its purposes require; for though culture without freedom never made a large and liberal mind, it can make a clever *nisi prius* advocate of a cause. But in countries professing Protestantism, this resource is denied; since Protestants hold, at least in theory, that the responsibility for the choice of a religion must be borne by each for himself, and cannot be thrown off upon teachers. Besides, in the present state of the world, it is practically impossible that writings which are read by the instructed can be kept from the uninstructed. If the teachers of mankind are to be cognizant of all that they ought to know, everything must be free to be written and published without restraint.

If, however, the mischievous operation of the absence of free discussion, when the received opinions are true, were confined to leaving men ignorant of the grounds of those opinions, it might be thought that this, if an intellectual, is no moral evil, and does not affect the worth of the opinions, regarded in their influence on the character. The fact, however, is, that not only the grounds of the opinion are forgotten in the absence of discussion, but too often the meaning of the opinion itself. The words which convey it, cease to suggest ideas, or suggest only a small portion of those they were originally employed to communicate. Instead of a vivid conception and a living belief, there remain only a few phrases retained by rote; or, if any part, the shell and husk only of the meaning is retained, the finer essence being lost. The great chapter in human history which this fact occupies and fills, cannot be too earnestly studied and meditated on.

It is illustrated in the experience of almost all ethical doctrines and religious creeds. They are all full of meaning and vitality to those who originate them, and to the direct disciples of the originators. Their meaning continues to be felt in undiminished strength, and is perhaps brought out into even fuller consciousness, so long as the struggle lasts to give the doctrine or creed an ascendency over other creeds. At last it either prevails, and becomes the general opinion, or its progress stops; it keeps possession of the ground it has gained, but ceases to spread further. When either of these results has become apparent, controversy on the subject flags, and gradually dies away. The doctrine has taken its place, if not as a received opinion, as one of the admitted sects or divisions of opinion: those who hold it have generally inherited, not adopted it; and conversion from one of these doctrines to another, being now an exceptional fact, occupies little place in the thoughts of their professors. Instead of being, as at first, constantly on the alert either to defend themselves against the world, or to bring the world over to them, they have subsided into acquiescence, and neither listen, when they can help it, to arguments against their creed, nor trouble dissentients (if there be such) with arguments in its favor. From this time may usually be dated the decline in the living power of the doctrine. We often hear the teachers of all creeds lamenting the difficulty of keeping up in the minds of believers a lively apprehension of the truth which they nominally recognize, so that it may penetrate the feelings, and acquire a real mastery over the conduct. No such difficulty is complained of while the creed is still fighting for its existence: even the weaker combatants then know and feel what they are fighting for, and the difference between it and other doctrines; and in that period of every creed's existence, not a few persons may be found, who have realized its fundamental principles in all the forms of thought, have weighed and considered them in all their important bearings, and have experienced the full effect on the character, which belief in that creed ought to produce in a mind thoroughly imbued with it. But when it has come to be an hereditary creed, and to be received passively, not actively—when the mind is no longer compelled, in the same degree as at first, to exercise its vital powers on the questions which its belief presents to it, there is a progressive tendency to forget all of the belief except the formularies, or to give it a dull and torpid assent, as if accepting it on trust dispensed with the necessity of realizing it in consciousness, or testing it by personal experience; until it almost ceases to connect itself at all with the inner life of the human being. Then are seen the cases, so frequent in this age of the world as almost to form the majority, in which the creed remains as it were outside the mind, encrusting and petrifying it against all other influences addressed to the higher parts of our nature; manifesting its power by not suffering any fresh and living conviction to get in, but itself doing nothing for the mind or heart, except standing sentinel over them to keep them vacant.

To what an extent doctrines intrinsically fitted to make the deepest impression upon the mind may remain in it as dead beliefs, without being ever realized in the imagination, the feelings, or the understanding, is exemplified by the manner in which the majority of believers hold the doctrines of Christianity. By Christianity I here mean what is accounted such by all churches and sects—the maxims and precepts contained in the New Testament. These are considered sacred, and accepted as laws, by all professing Christians. Yet it is scarcely too much to say that not one Christian in a thousand guides or tests his individual conduct by reference to those laws. The standard to which he does refer it, is the custom of his nation, his class, or his religious profession. He has thus, on the one hand, a collection of ethical maxims, which he believes to have been vouchsafed to him by infallible wisdom as rules for his government; and on the other, a set of everyday judgments and practices, which go a certain length with some of those maxims, not so great a length with others, stand in direct opposition to some, and are, on the whole, a compromise between the Christian creed and the interests and suggestions of worldly life. To the first of these standards he gives his homage; to the other his real allegiance. All Christians believe that the blessed are the poor and humble, and those who are ill-used by the world; that it is easier for a camel to pass through the eye of a needle than for a rich man to enter the kingdom of heaven; that they should judge not, lest they be judged; that they should swear not at all; that they should love their neighbor as themselves; that if one take their cloak, they should give him their coat also; that they should take no thought for the morrow; that if they would be perfect, they should sell all that they have and give it to the poor. They are not insincere when they say that they believe these things. They do believe them, as people believe what they have always heard lauded and never discussed. But in the sense of that living belief which regulates conduct, they believe these doctrines just up to the point to which it is usual to act upon them. The doctrines in their integrity are serviceable to pelt adversaries with; and it is understood that they are to be put forward (when possible) as the reasons for whatever people do that they think laudable. But any one who reminded them that the maxims require an infinity of things which they never even think of doing, would gain nothing but to be classed among those very unpopular characters who affect to be better than other people. The doctrines have no hold on ordinary believers—are not a power in their minds. They have an habitual respect for the sound of them, but no feeling which spreads from the words to the things signified, and forces the mind to take *them* in, and make them conform to the formula. Whenever conduct is concerned, they look round for Mr. A and B to direct them how far to go in obeying Christ.

Now we may be well assured that the case was not thus, but far otherwise, with the early Christians. Had it been thus, Christianity never would have expanded from an obscure sect of the despised Hebrews into the religion of the Roman empire. When their enemies said, "See how these Christians love one another" (a remark not likely to be made by anybody now), they assuredly had a much livelier feeling of the meaning of their creed than they have ever had since. And to this cause, probably, it is chiefly owing that Christianity now makes so little progress in extending its domain, and after eighteen centuries, is still nearly confined to Europeans and the descendants of Europeans. Even with the strictly religious, who are much in earnest about their doctrines, and attach a greater amount of meaning to many of them than people in general, it commonly happens that the part which is thus comparatively active in their minds is that which was made by Calvin, or Knox, or some such person much nearer in character to themselves. The sayings of Christ coexist passively in their minds, producing hardly any effect beyond what is caused by mere listening to words so amiable and bland. There are many reasons, doubtless, why doctrines which are the badge of a sect retain more of their vitality than those common to all recognized sects, and why more pains are taken by teachers to keep their meaning alive; but one reason certainly is, that the peculiar doctrines are more questioned, and have to be oftener defended against open gainsayers. Both teachers and learners go to sleep at their post, as soon as there is no enemy in the field.

The same thing holds true, generally speaking, of all traditional doctrines—those of prudence and knowledge of life, as well as of morals or religion. All languages and literatures are full of general observations on life, both as to what it is, and how to conduct oneself in it; observations which everybody knows, which everybody repeats, or hears with acquiescence, which are received as truisms, yet of which most people first truly learn the meaning, when experience, generally of a painful kind, has made it a reality to them. How often, when smarting under some unforeseen misfortune or disappointment, does a person call to mind some proverb or common saying, familiar to him all his life, the meaning of which, if he had ever before felt it as he does now, would have saved him from the calamity. There are indeed reasons for this, other than the absence of discussion: there are many truths of which the full meaning *cannot* be realized, until personal experience has brought it home. But much more of the meaning even of these would have been understood and what was understood would have been far more deeply impressed on the mind, if the man had been accustomed to hear it argued *pro* and *con* by people who did understand it. The fatal tendency of mankind to leave off thinking about a thing when it is no longer doubtful, is the cause of half their errors. A contemporary author has well spoken of "the deep slumber of a decided opinion."

But what! (it may be asked) Is the absence of unanimity an indispensable condition of true knowledge? Is it necessary that some part of mankind should persist in error, to enable any to realize the truth? Does a belief cease to be real and vital as soon as it is generally received—and is a proposition never thoroughly understood and felt unless some doubt of it remains? As soon as mankind have unanimously accepted a truth, does the truth perish within them? The highest aim and best result of improved intelligence, it has hitherto been thought, is to unite mankind more and more in the acknowledgment of all important truths: and does the intelligence only last as long as it has not achieved its object? Do the fruits of conquest perish by the very completeness of the victory?

I affirm no such thing. As mankind improve, the number of doctrines which are no longer disputed or doubted will be constantly on the increase: and the well-being of mankind may almost be measured by the number and gravity of the truths which have reached the point of being uncontested. The cessation, on one question after another, of serious controversy, is one of the necessary incidents of the consolidation of opinion; a consolidation as salutary in the case of true opinions, as it is dangerous and noxious when the opinions are erroneous. But though this gradual narrowing of the bounds of diversity of opinion is necesssary in both senses of the term, being at once inevitable and indispensable, we are not therefore obliged to conclude that all its consequences must be beneficial. The loss of so important an aid to the intelligent and living apprehension of a truth, as is afforded by the necessity of explaining it to, or defending it against, opponents, though not sufficient to outweigh, is no trifling drawback from the benefit of its universal recognition. Where this advantage can no longer be had, I confess I should like to see the teachers of mankind endeavoring to provide a substitute for it; some contrivance for making the difficulties of the question as present to the learner's consciousness, as if they were pressed upon him by a dissentient champion, eager for his conversion.

But instead of seeking contrivances for this purpose, they have lost those they formerly had. The Socratic dialectics, so magnificently exemplified in the dialogues of Plato, were a contrivance of this description. They were essentially a negative discussion of the great questions of philosophy and life, directed with consummate skill to the purpose of convincing any one who had merely adopted the commonplaces of received opinion, that he did not understand the subject —that he as yet attached no definite meaning to the doctrines he professed; in order that, becoming aware of his ignorance, he might be put in the way to attain a stable belief, resting on a clear apprehension both of the meaning of doctrines and of their evidence. The school disputations of the Middle Ages had a somewhat similar object. They were intended to make sure that the pupil understood his own opinion, and (by necessary correlation) the opinion opposed to it, and could enforce the grounds of the one and confute those of the other. These last-mentioned contests had indeed the incurable defect, that the premises appealed to were taken from authority, not from reason; and, as a discipline to the mind, they were in every respect inferior to the powerful dialectics which formed the intellects of the "Socratici viri": but the modern mind owes far more to both than it is generally willing to admit, and the present modes of education contain nothing which in the smallest degree supplies the place either of the one or of the other. A person who derives all his instruction from teachers or books, even if he escape the besetting temptation of contenting himself with cram, is under no compulsion to hear both sides; accordingly it is far from a frequent accomplishment, even among thinkers, to know both sides; and the weakest part of what everybody says in defence of his opinion, is what he intends as a reply to antagonists. It is the fashion of the present time to disparage negative logic—that which points out weaknesses in theory or errors in practice, without establishing positive truths. Such negative criticism would indeed be poor enough as an ultimate result; but as a means to attaining any positive knowledge or conviction worthy the name, it cannot be valued too highly; and until people are again systematically trained to it, there will be few great thinkers, and a low general average of intellect, in any but the mathematical and physical departments of speculation. On any other subject no one's opinions deserve the name of knowledge, except so far as he has either had forced upon him by others, or gone through of himself, the same mental process which would have been required of him in carrying on an active controversy with opponents. That, therefore, which when absent, it is so indispensable, but so difficult, to create, how worse than absurd is it to forego, when spontaneously offering itself! If there are any persons who contest a received opinion, or who will do so if law or opinion will let them, let us thank them for it, open our minds to listen to them, and rejoice that there is some one to do for us what we otherwise ought, if we have any regard for either the certainty or the vitality of our convictions, to do with much greater labor for ourselves.

It still remains to speak of one of the principal causes which make diversity of opinion advantageous, and will continue to do so until mankind shall have entered a stage of intellectual advancement which at present seems at an incalculable distance. We have hitherto considered only two possibilities: that the received opinion may be false, and some other opinion, consequently, true; or that, the received opinion being true, a conflict with the opposite error is essential to a clear apprehension and deep feeling of its truth. But there is a commoner case than either of these; when the conflicting doctrines, instead of being one true and the other false, share the truth between them; and the nonconforming opinion is needed to supply the remainder of the truth, of which the received doctrine embodies only a part. Popular opinions, on subjects not palpable to sense, are often true, but seldom or never the whole truth. They are a part of the truth; sometimes a greater, sometimes a smaller part, but exaggerated, distorted, and disjoined from the truths by which they ought to be accompanied and limited. Heretical opinions, on the other hand, are generally some of these suppressed and neglected truths, bursting the bonds which kept them down, and either seeking reconciliation with the truth contained in the common opinion, or fronting it as enemies, and setting themselves up, with similar exclusiveness, as the whole truth. The latter case is hitherto the most frequent, as, in the human mind, one-sidedness has always been the rule, and many-sidedness the exception. Hence, even in revolutions of opinion, one part of the truth usually sets while another rises. Even progress, which ought to superadd, for the most part only substitutes one partial and incomplete truth for another; improvement consisting chiefly in this, that the new fragment of truth is more wanted, more adapted to the needs of the time, than that which it displaces. Such being the partial character of prevailing opinions, even when resting on a true foundation; every opinion which embodies somewhat of the portion of truth which the common opinion omits, ought to be considered precious, with whatever amount of error and confusion that truth may be blended. No sober judge of human affairs will feel bound to be indignant because those who force on our notice truths which we should otherwise have overlooked, overlook some of those which we see. Rather, he will think that so long as popular truth is one-sided, it is more desirable than otherwise that unpopular truth should have one-sided asserters too; such being usually the most energetic, and the most likely to compel reluctant attention to the fragment of wisdom which they proclaim as if it were the whole.

Thus, in the eighteenth century, when nearly all the instructed, and all those of the uninstructed who were led by them, were lost in admiration of what is called civilization, and of the marvels of modern science, literature, and philosophy, and while greatly overrating the amount of unlikeness between the men of modern and those of ancient times, indulged the belief that the whole of the difference was in their own favor; with what a salutary shock did the paradoxes of Rousseau explode like bombshells in the midst, dislocating the compact mass of one-sided opinion, and forcing its elements to recombine in a better form and with additional ingredients. Not that the current opinions were on the whole farther from the truth than Rousseau's were; on the contrary, they were nearer to it; they contained more of positive truth, and very much less of error. Nevertheless there lay in Rousseau's doctrine, and has floated down the stream of opinion along with it, a considerable amount of exactly those truths which the popular opinion wanted; and these are the deposit which was left behind when the flood subsided. The superior worth of simplicity of life, the enervating and demoralizing effect of the trammels and hypocrisies of artificial society, are ideas which have never been entirely absent from cultivated minds since Rousseau wrote; and they will in time produce their due effect, though at present needing to be asserted as much as ever, and to be asserted by deeds, for words, on this subject, have nearly exhausted their power.

In politics, again, it is almost a commonplace, that a party of order or stability, and a party of progress or reform, are both necessary elements of a healthy state of political life; until the one or the other shall have so enlarged its mental grasp as to be a party equally of order and of progress, knowing and distinguishing what is fit to be preserved from what ought to be swept away. Each of these modes of thinking derives its utility from the deficiencies of the other; but it is in a great measure the opposition of the other that keeps each within the limits of reason and sanity. Unless opinions favorable to democracy and to aristocracy, to property and to equality, to coöperation and to competition, to luxury and to abstinence, to sociality and individuality, to liberty and discipline, and all the other standing antagonisms of practical life, are expressed with equal freedom, and enforced and defended with equal talent and energy, there is no chance of both elements obtaining their due; one scale is sure to go up, and the other down. Truth, in the great practical concerns of life, is so much a question of the reconciling and combining of opposites, that very few have minds sufficiently capacious and impartial to make the adjustment with an approach to correctness, and it has to be made by the rough process of a struggle between combatants fighting under hostile banners. On any of the great open questions just enumerated, if either of the two opinions has a better claim than the other, not merely to be tolerated, but to be encouraged and countenanced, it is the one which happens at the particular time and place to be in a minority. That is the opinion which, for the time being, represents the neglected interests, the side of human well-being which is in danger of obtaining less than its share. I am aware that there is not, in this country, any intolerance of differences of opinion on most of these topics. They are adduced to show, by admitted and multiplied examples, the universality of the fact, that only through diversity of opinion is there, in the existing state of human intellect, a chance of fair play to all sides of the truth. When there are persons to be found, who form an exception to the apparent unanimity of the world on any subject, even if the world is in the right, it is always probable that dissentients have something worth hearing to say for themselves, and that truth would lose something by their silence.

It may be objected, "But *some* received principles, especially on the highest and most vital subjects, are more than half-truths. The Christian morality, for instance, is the whole truth on that subject, and if any one teaches a morality which varies from it, he is wholly in error." As this is of all cases the most important in practice, none can be fitter to test the general maxim. But before pronouncing what Christian morality is or is not, it would be desirable to decide what is meant by Christian morality. If it means the morality of the New Testament, I wonder that any one who derives his knowledge of this from the book itself, can suppose that it was announced, or intended, as a complete doctrine of morals. The Gospel always refers to a preëxisting morality, and confines its precepts to the particulars in which that morality was to be corrected, or superseded by a wider and higher; expressing itself, moreover, in terms most general, often impossible to be interpreted literally, and possessing rather the impressiveness of poetry or eloquence than the precision of legislation. To extract from it a body of ethical doctrine, has never been possible without eking it out from the Old Testament, that is, from a system elaborate indeed, but in many respects barbarous, and intended only for a barbarous people. St. Paul, a declared enemy to this Judaical mode of interpreting the doctrine and filling up the scheme of his Master, equally assumes a preëxisting morality, namely, that of the Greeks and Romans; and his advice to Christians is in a great measure a system of accommodation to that; even to the extent of giving an apparent sanction to slavery. What is called Christian, but should rather be termed theological, morality, was not the work of Christ or the Apostles, but is of much later origin, having been gradually built up by the Catholic Church of the first five centuries, and though not implicitly adopted by moderns and Protestants, has been much less modified by them than might have been expected. For the most part, indeed, they have contented themselves with cutting off the additions which had been made to it in the Middle Ages, each sect supplying the place by fresh additions, adapted to its own character and tendencies. That mankind owe a great debt to this morality, and to its early teachers, I should be the last person to deny; but I do not scruple to say of it, that it is, in many important points, incomplete and one-sided, and that unless ideas and feelings, not sanctioned by it, had contributed to the formation of European life and character, human affairs would have been in a worse condition than they now are. Christian morality (so called) has all the characters of a reaction; it is, in great part, a protest against Paganism. Its ideal is negative rather than positive; passive rather than active; Innocence rather than Nobleness; Abstinence from Evil, rather than energetic Pursuit of Good: in its precepts (as has been well said) "thou shalt not" predominates unduly over "thou shalt." In its horror of sensuality, it made an idol of asceticism, which has been gradually compromised away into one of legality. It holds out the hope of heaven and the threat of hell, as the appointed and appropriate motives to a virtuous life: in this falling far below the best of the ancients, and doing what lies in it to give to human morality an essentially selfish character, by disconnecting each man's feelings of duty from the interests of his fellow-creatures, except so far as a self-interested inducement is offered to him for consulting them. It is essentially a doctrine of passive obedience; it inculcates submission to all authorities found established; who indeed are not to be actively obeyed when they command what religion forbids, but who are not to be resisted, far less rebelled against, for any amount of wrong to ourselves. And while, in the morality of the best Pagan nations, duty to the State holds even a disproportionate place, infringing on the just liberty of the individual; in purely Christian ethics, that grand department of duty is scarcely noticed or acknowledged. It is in the Koran, not the New Testament, that we read the maxim—"A ruler who appoints any man to an office, when there is in his dominions another man better qualified for it, sins against God and against the State." What little recognition the idea of obligation to the public obtains in modern morality, is derived from Greek and Roman sources, not from Christian; as, even in the morality of private life, whatever exists of magnanimity, high-mindedness, personal dignity, even the sense of honor, is derived from the purely human, not the religious part of our education, and never could have grown out of a standard of ethics in which the only worth, professedly recognized, is that of obedience.

I am as far as any one from pretending that these defects are necessarily inherent in the Christian ethics, in every manner in which it can be conceived, or that the many requisites of a complete moral doctrine which it does not contain, do not admit of being reconciled with it. Far less would I insinuate this of the doctrines and precepts of Christ himself. I believe that the sayings of Christ are all, that I can see any evidence of their having been intended to be; that they are irreconcilable with nothing which a comprehensive morality requires; that everything which is excellent in ethics may be brought within them, with no greater violence to their language than has been done to it by all who have attempted to deduce from them any practical system of conduct whatever. But it is quite consistent with this, to believe that they contain, and were meant to contain, only a part of the truth; that many essential elements of the highest morality are among the things which are not provided for, nor intended to be provided for in the recorded deliverances of the Founder of Christianity, and which have been entirely thrown aside in the system of ethics erected on the basis of those deliverances by the Christian Church. And this being so, I think it a great error to persist in attempting to find in the Christian doctrine that complete rule for our guidance, which its author intended it to sanction and enforce, but only partially to provide. I believe, too, that this narrow theory is becoming a grave practical evil, detracting greatly from the value of the moral training and instruction, which so many well-meaning persons are now at length exerting themselves to promote. I much fear that by attempting to form the mind and feelings on an exclusively religious type, and discarding those secular standards (as for want of a better name they may be called) which heretofore coexisted with and supplemented the Christian ethics, receiving some of its spirit, and infusing into it some of theirs, there will result, and is even now resulting, a low, abject, servile type of character, which, submit itself as it may to what it deems the Supreme Will, is incapable of rising to or sympathizing in the conception of Supreme Goodness. I believe that other ethics than any which can be evolved from exclusively Christian sources, must exist side by side with Christian ethics to produce the moral regeneration of mankind; and that the Christian system is no exception to the rule, that in an imperfect state of the human mind, the interests of truth require a diversity of opinions. It is not necessary that in ceasing to ignore the moral truths not contained in Christianity, men should ignore any of those which it does contain. Such prejudice, or oversight, when it occurs, is altogether an evil; but it is one from which we cannot hope to be always exempt, and must be regarded as the price paid for an inestimable good. The exclusive pretension made by a part of the truth to be the whole, must and ought to be protested against, and if a reactionary impulse should make the protestors unjust in their turn, this one-sidedness, like the other, may be lamented, but must be tolerated. If Christians would teach infidels to be just to Christianity, they should themselves be just to infidelity. It can do truth no service to blink the fact, known to all who have the most ordinary acquaintance with literary history, that a large portion of the noblest and most valuable moral teaching has been the work, not only of men who did not know, but of men who knew and rejected, the Christian faith.

I do not pretend that the most unlimited use of the freedom of enunciating all possible opinions would put an end to the evils of religious or philosophical sectarianism. Every truth which men of narrow capacity are in earnest about, is sure to be asserted, inculcated, and in many ways even acted on, as if no other truth existed in the world, or at all events none that could limit or qualify the first. I acknowledge that the tendency of all opinions to become sectarian is not cured by the freest discussion, but is often heightened and exacerbated thereby; the truth which ought to have been, but was not, seen, being rejected all the more violently because proclaimed by persons regarded as opponents. But it is not on the impassioned partisan, it is on the calmer and more disinterested by-stander, that this collision of opinions works its salutary effect. Not the violent conflict between parts of the truth, but the quiet suppression of half of it, is the formidable evil: there is always hope when people are forced to listen to both sides; it is when they attend only to one that errors harden into prejudices, and truth itself ceases to have the effect of truth, by being exaggerated into falsehood. And since there are few mental attributes more rare than that judicial faculty which can sit in intelligent judgment between two sides of a question, of which only one is represented by an advocate before it, truth has no chance but in proportion as every side of it, every opinion which embodies any fraction of the truth, not only finds advocates, but is so advocated as to be listened to.

We have now recognized the necessity to the mental well-being of mankind (on which all their other well-being depends) of freedom of opinion, and freedom of the expression of opinion, on four distinct grounds; which we will now briefly recapitulate.

First, if any opinion is compelled to silence, that opinion may, for aught we can certainly know, be true. To deny this is to assume our own infallibility.

Secondly, though the silenced opinion be an error, it may, and very commonly does, contain a portion of truth; and since the general or prevailing opinion on any subject is rarely or never the whole truth, it is only by the collision of adverse opinions that the remainder of the truth has any chance of being supplied.

Thirdly, even if the received opinion be not only true, but the whole truth; unless it is suffered to be, and actually is, vigorously and earnestly contested, it will, by most of those who receive it, be held in the manner of a prejudice, with little comprehension or feeling of its rational grounds. And not only this, but, fourthly, the meaning of the doctrine itself will be in danger of being lost, or enfeebled, and deprived of its vital effect on the character and conduct: the dogma becoming a mere formal profession, inefficacious for good, but cumbering the ground, and preventing the growth of any real and heartfelt conviction from reason or personal experience.

Before quitting the subject of freedom of opinion, it is fit to take some notice of those who say, that the free expression of all opinions should be permitted, on condition that the manner be temperate, and do not pass the bounds of fair discussion. Much might be said on the impossibility of fixing where these supposed bounds are to be placed; for if the test be offence to those whose opinion is attacked, I think experience testifies that this offence is given whenever the attack is telling and powerful, and that every opponent who pushes them hard, and whom they find it difficult to answer, appears to them, if he shows any strong feeling on the subject, an intemperate opponent. But this, though an important consideration in a practical point of view, merges in a more fundamental objection. Undoubtedly the manner of asserting an opinion, even though it be a true one, may be very objectionable, and may justly incur severe censure. But the principal offences of the kind are such as it is mostly impossible, unless by accidental self-betrayal, to bring home to conviction. The gravest of them is, to argue sophistically, to suppress facts or arguments, to misstate the elements of the case, or misrepresent the opposite opinion. But all this, even to the most aggravated degree, is so continually done in perfect good faith, by persons who are not considered, and in many other respects may not deserve to be considered, ignorant or incompetent, that it is rarely possible on adequate grounds conscientiously to stamp the misrepresentation as morally culpable; and still less could law presume to interfere with this kind of controversial misconduct. With regard to what is commonly meant by intemperate discussion, namely, invective, sarcasm, personality, and the like, the denunciation of these weapons would deserve more sympathy if it were ever proposed to interdict them equally to both sides; but it is only desired to restrain the employment of them against the prevailing opinion: against the unprevailing they may not only be used without general disapproval, but will be likely to obtain for him who uses them the praise of honest zeal and righteous indignation. Yet whatever mischief arises from their use, is greatest when they are employed against the comparatively defenceless; and whatever unfair advantage can be derived by any opinion from this mode of asserting it, accrues almost exclusively to received opinions. The worse offence of this kind which can be committed by a polemic, is to stigmatize those who hold the contrary opinion as bad and immoral men. To calumny of this sort, those who hold any unpopular opinion are peculiarly exposed, because they are in general few and uninfluential, and nobody but themselves feels much interest in seeing justice done them; but this weapon is, from the nature of the case, denied to those who attack a prevailing opinion: they can neither use it with safety to themselves, nor, if they could, would it do anything but recoil on their own cause. In general, opinions contrary to those commonly received can only obtain a hearing by studied moderation of language, and the most cautious avoidance of unnecessary offence, from which they hardly ever deviate even in a slight degree without losing ground: while unmeasured vituperation employed on the side of the prevailing opinion, really does deter people from professing contrary opinions, and from listening to those who profess them. For the interest, therefore, of truth and justice, it is far more important to restrain this employment of vituperative language than the other; and, for example, if it were necessary to choose, there would be much more need to discourage offensive attacks on infidelity, than on religion. It is, however, obvious that law and authority have no business with restraining either, while opinion ought, in every instance, to determine its verdict by the circumstances of the individual case; condemning every one, on whichever side of the argument he places himself, in whose mode of advocacy either want of candor, or malignity, bigotry, or intolerance of feeling manifest themselves; but not inferring these vices from the side which a person takes, though it be the contrary side of the question to our own: and giving merited honor to every one, whatever opinion he may hold, who has calmness to see and honesty to state what his opponents and their opinions really are, exaggerating nothing to their discredit, keeping nothing back which tells, or can be supposed to tell, in their favor. This is the real morality of public discussion; and if often violated, I am happy to think that there are many controversialists who to a great extent observe it, and a still greater number who conscientiously strive towards it.

Liberty of Expression: Its Grounds and Limits (I)

H. J. McCloskey

I. Introduction

The problem to which I address myself in this paper is:[1] Is it possible to set out a principle which satisfactorily defines the legitimate limits to the State's and society's interference with freedom of expression? That is, can those interferences which are necessary and desirable be indicated in some simple, general way, for example, in terms of some such principle as "Interference with freedom of expression is justified only when harm is thereby prevented"? An aspect of this problem therefore consists in determining whether there can be satisfactory, convincing grounds for accepting any such principle as a basis for political action. It will involve asking whether the arguments with which liberals have supported their demand for freedom of expression are adequate, and if not, whether other, more satisfactory grounds are available on which a defence of this kind of principle may be based.

Many liberals, including J. S. Mill, have sought to devise a principle—e.g. the self- and other-regarding principle—which indicates the legitimate limits of interference with freedom of action. However, such principles aim simply to

From "Liberty of Expression: Its Grounds and Limits (I);" *Inquiry*, XIII (Autumn 1970), pp. 219-37. Reprinted by permission of the publisher, Universitetsforlaget, Oslo, Norway.

[1] In this paper I am concerned to elaborate upon arguments and issues discussed in my "Some Arguments for a Liberal Society," *Philosophy*, Vol. XLIII (1968), No. 166.

indicate the limits of interference with action, not speech and expression, although speech and expression are other-regarding actions which could therefore reasonably be construed as falling under these principles. Mill obviously did not wish to set the same limits to freedom of expression as to other kinds of action. Consider, for instance, the first footnote in Chapter 2 of *On Liberty*. There Mill argued for the "fullest liberty of professing and discussing . . . any doctrine." Further, the whole tone of the discussion in that chapter, and not simply the footnote, suggests that Mill was concerned to argue for unlimited freedom of expression. Had that not been his intention, it would be extraordinary that he did not examine both the possible grounds for those interferences which were necessary and legitimate, and also how these exceptions would lead to modifying and qualifying his arguments. Yet, clearly, unlimited freedom of expression is not defensible, and Mill himself implicitly acknowledged this when, for example, in a casual aside at the beginning of Chapter 3 of *On Liberty* he noted one type of legitimate restriction, observing:

> No one pretends that actions should be as free as opinions. On the contrary, even opinions lose their immunity when the circumstances in which they are expressed are such as to constitute their expression a positive instigation to some mischievous act. An opinion that corn-dealers are starvers of the poor, or that private property is robbery, ought to be unmolested when simply circulated through the press, but may justly incur punishment when delivered orally to an excited mob assembled before the house of a corn-dealer, or when handed about among the same mob in the form of a placard. (p. 114, Everyman ed.)

Further, by implication, Mill allowed other exceptions. In Chapter 5, he allowed as legitimate, interference with acts (and, in consistency, utterances) which are indecent, offensive, or breaches of good manners. He also observed:

> Whatever it is permitted to do, it must be permitted to advise to do. The question is doubtful only when the instigator derives a personal benefit from his advice; when he makes it his occupation, for subsistence or pecuniary gain, to promote what society and the State consider to be an evil. (p. 154)

Since Mill acknowledged that the State may act to protect the individual against force and fraud, he was also committed to banning the means to fraud, e.g. fraudulent advertising. (This latter qualification admits of many interesting, varied applications.) Thus, whilst appearing to argue for unlimited freedom of expression, Mill both explicitly and implicitly, in a rather *ad hoc*, unsystematic way, allowed interferences, not all of which—e.g. those concerning persuasive enticements to evil acts, indecent, offensive speech—would be acceptable to a thoughtful liberal today. His comments therefore do little to forward the search for a principle setting out limits to interferences with liberty of expression. I suggest that what is true of Mill is true of other notable liberal philosophers. If their writings are examined, it will be found that no clear, determinate, plausible principles or theories are set out indicating what are, and what are not, legitimate interferences with liberty of expression and discussion.

On the other hand, if we look at the kinds of restrictions which liberals of today seem to accept as necessary and even as adequate, we should probably find that some such principle as the following is accepted: "Liberty of expression should be left unrestricted except for the sake of protecting liberty, ensuring fair trials and legal hearings, preventing libel, defamation, fraud, or incitement to riotous behavior." The latter two grounds, fraud and riotous behavior, may provide grounds for more interferences than some should like, but most liberals today accept the need for protection against fraudulent advertising and inflammatory utterances which stir up destructive rioting. Even though our (Australian) libel laws are stricter than those of other liberal democratic societies, and even though the restricting of freedom for the sake of freedom, is open to unfair and dishonest application, the other accepted limitations are obviously liberal-inspired. My concern in this paper is to show that even this qualified principle is not acceptable as a guide to political action, and that just as all the attempts to delimit legitimate interferences with action in terms of some one simple principle such as the self- and other-regarding principle come to grief when the necessities of political and social life are considered (Mill, for example, saw that it may be right to coerce individuals engaged in purely self-regarding acts into helping others and rendering services to the community), so too, all attempts similarly to delimit freedom of expression must fail, and in such a way as to reveal the limitations of many of the arguments with which it has been defended. This may best be shown by an examination of the main arguments which have been urged in support of freedom of expression.

II. Mill's Infallibility Argument

Probably the most important of Mill's arguments is the infallibility argument, both because of its intrinsic character and because its premise and conclusion underlie many other important arguments. Mill's formulation runs:

> *The opinion which it is attempted to suppress by authority may possibly be true. Those who desire to suppress it, of course deny its truth; but they are not infallible. They have no authority to decide the question for all mankind, and exclude every other person from the means of judging. To refuse a hearing to an opinion because they are sure that it is false, is to* assume *their certainty is the same thing as* absolute *certainty. All silencing of discussion is an assumption of infallibility. Its condemnation may be allowed to rest on this common argument, not the worse for being common. (p. 79)*

A vital, supplementary part of the argument runs:

> *There is the greatest difference between presuming an opinion to be true, because, with every opportunity for contesting it, it has not been refuted,*

and assuming its truth for the purpose of not permitting its refutation. Complete liberty of contradicting and disproving our opinion is the very condition which justifies us in assuming its truth for the purposes of action; and on no other terms can a being with human faculties have any rational assurance of being right. (p. 81)

Later I shall contend that many other arguments for freedom of expression draw heavily upon this argument. Briefly to anticipate my later arguments: The argument against censorship, that the evils which result from making the expression of certain views a crime are greater than the evils which censorship may prevent, derives great strength from the often unstated suggestion that the suppressed views may well be true. If the censors were indeed infallible, this argument would lose much of its force. Further, the argument from respecting persons, that to coerce a person and deny him the right to express his beliefs or to hear opposed beliefs of others, is largely thought to be wrong, because the coercers may be wrong. Could they be known to be infallibly right, we may well have doubts whether the same lack of respect was involved. This is why using social pressure to silence the fool who believes the earth to be flat is not a serious breach of the morality of respecting persons; nor do we regard it as involving a serious lack of respect to silence the dangerous individual who encourages her foolish friends to take sizeable doses of arsenic to improve their complexions. To suppress the expression of all but one view, and thereby to manipulate the mass of the people into accepting what may be a false belief, smacks of lack of respect for them as persons in a way and to a degree that similar coercion of the same people in respect of the true view does not. Hence the claims made in the infallibility argument reinforce and underlie the usual formulation of the argument for liberty of expression from the duty to respect persons.

The infallibility argument therefore is doubly important. It also has the virtue of being able, without great amendment, to accommodate two of the desired exceptions, the banning of inflammatory speech, and restrictions for the sake of fair trials. The former restricts expression *via* one avenue, whilst the latter is a temporary, short-term restriction. However, a number of points need to be made concerning the scope and validity of the argument.

1. Mill urged this argument in support of his demand for tolerance in those spheres in which intolerance most commonly prevailed, namely, in the spheres of religion, morality, politics, and taste. If we could determine the truth in these areas with certainty, the argument would have no application. Equally, the very relevance of the argument depends on the assumption that theories and beliefs about these matters admit of truth or falsity, i.e. that cognitivist accounts of religious, moral, and political utterances—and, it would seem, expressions of personal tastes—are true. If religious, moral, and political beliefs do not admit of truth, this argument would be completely irrelevant as far as freedom of expression of such beliefs was concerned.

The infallibility argument depends on the claim that there are factual beliefs, beliefs which admit of truth or falsity, which are such that we can never know with certainty whether they are true. This claim is now widely challenged, although not by myself, and the impossibility of testing, in principle and in practice, the truth or falsity of beliefs in those areas in which intolerance is most commonly practised, is now widely accepted as a ground for denying the cognitivity of the utterances expressing these so-called beliefs, and, by implication, the relevance of this argument. It is true that the argument could be recast as one of a significantly different character, namely, that whilst religious, moral, political, and aesthetic utterances, and expressions of taste, have no truth values, intolerance of such views is unjustified simply because the intolerance cannot lay claim to a basis in truth. This is a possible, although a very different and weaker argument, and one which would derive its appeal from the evils of intolerance. By contrast, Mill's infallibility argument draws its strength from the double claim that intolerance may rob the world of a belief which may be both true and valuable by means which involve evils. Mill deems the former to be so vastly more important a consideration that he neglects in this context even to mention the latter.

2. Taken in isolation and without regard for other arguments for liberty, this argument expresses a very qualified liberalism, suggesting as it does, not that we have the right to say whatever we will, whether right or wrong, but simply that, since we may be right and the censor wrong, we ought to be accorded freedom of expression. Thus, if its premise, that there is no infallible knowledge, is mistaken, the argument would provide no grounds for according freedom of expression to false beliefs.

3. For it to establish an absolute right of expression, it must rest on what I suggest is an inflated, indefensible valuation of true belief. It would involve claiming that no matter what the consequences of expressing a view, no matter how much harm was done, what evils and injustices resulted, *the mere possibility* that the belief may be true would justify according it absolute freedom of expression. The truth is not of such overriding importance as this. If, alternatively, the argument is used to support a qualified right to freedom of expression, i.e. if it is acknowledged that there are goods and values other than true belief which may override the claims of true belief, goods and values such as human happiness, justice, respect for persons, then the proponents of the argument would be obliged to allow many more grounds for restricting freedom of expression than noted either by Mill or in the contemporary liberal principle as set out earlier in this paper.

4. The argument proceeds from *the assumption* that we do not possess infallible knowledge, or at least, cannot possess it in the absence of rational discussion of the various alternative views. Yet our willingness to accept the limitations on freedom of expression in respect of libellous and defamatory statements rests *in part* on our belief that in these areas we can reach conclusions of a high degree of probability concerning which views are true. (They also rest in part on a preparedness to limit liberty of expression to prevent this kind of harm, it being implied that we can know with confidence or certainty that harm is being done.) Thus the argument will have to be modified to allow that there are some matters about which the truth is ascertainable, some concerning which it is not ascertainable. Since all parties to the dispute except the proponents of this

argument agree on this, but disagree about where to draw the line, this modification has the effect of rendering the argument of much less value as a practical guide. It will not do to say that where empirical verification is possible, the truth can be known, for Mill and those who use the argument would wish to keep open the question of what constitutes sound empirical verification. That the admission that there are areas in which the truth can be known with certainty is a damaging one is evident from the fact that many, for example, Roman Catholics and others, whose intolerance Mill was opposing, lay claim to infallible knowledge concerning various matters of faith and morals. Indeed, much of their intolerance in the past, in keeping with the spirit of Mill's argument, has been directed at protecting these allegedly infallible beliefs. It is hard to see how any single, specific claim to infallible knowledge in such matters can be shown to be mistaken. Further, many, besides orthodox Roman Catholics, make this claim; and their claims are not always implausible. I myself feel no sense of immodesty or arrogance in laying claim to the infallible knowledge in morals that the sadistic torture of unwanted children by frustrated parents is gravely evil; nor do I see how my claim can be shown to be mistaken.

5. The argument rests on the further claim that intolerance involves denying *mankind* the truth or what may be the truth. A number of distinctions need to be drawn here. Denying expression to a view is something very different from, and less than, persecuting all members of a community until they outwardly profess agreement with the desired view. Mill's opponents in this argument are those who advocate denial of free expression to false views, not persecution of holders of such views. Secondly, restriction of freedom of expression is a matter which admits of degrees. A view may be denied free expression in the marketplace but be unrestricted elsewhere—on the Yarra bank, in newspapers, learned journals, and the like. There are some views which we might deem it desirable to express in an article such as this but which might well be dangerous in a TV program, and vice versa, and hence be inclined to deny expression in one medium but not in the other. Mill, in expounding this argument, claims that any restriction at all of freedom of expression involves depriving mankind of the truth or of what may be the truth. This is not so. For rulers of one country to suppress a true view as false is not to deprive mankind of the truth. Often the view suppressed is that which is protected by intolerance in another country. At most, the suppression of a true view in Australia deprives *some* Australians of that truth; their number will depend on the nature of the truth, the degree of the intolerance, and the number of Australians who travel abroad. No amount of denial of freedom of expression and discussion would destroy the beliefs that fires burn and are hot. Similarly, as long as pain, suffering, and moral evil exist, some people at least must continue to engage in reflection about the existence of an all-perfect being. With moral and other normative beliefs, restriction of expression and discussion may well be more successful. This may also be true of detailed religious beliefs, where the publication of the religious writings is necessary for individuals to know or even to entertain the doctrine, e.g. the death and resurrection of Christ. Thus, even were all beliefs fallible, it would not be true that intolerance would always involve the risk of

depriving mankind or even all members of a community of the truth. It all depends on the nature of the truths concerned, the intellectual and moral character of the community, and the nature and extent of the intolerance, i.e. whether it is restricted to public speeches, TV, newspapers, learned journals, etc.

6. Equally important, intolerance need not involve a claim to infallible knowledge. Often it proceeds on the basis of probabilities. Consider our intolerance of libellous and defamatory statements. Sometimes we can ascertain the truth, but much of the time the judge and jury must proceed on the basis of probabilities. Yet such intolerance is desirable for the sake of human happiness, human dignity, and the truth itself. Secondly, it may be known that the view which is denied expression is true, but it nonetheless be seen as essential that the State take a stand on the issue for the sake of goods such as human happiness, welfare, justice, or respect for persons. Mill, in effect, concedes this in his discussion of the public expression of the view that corn-dealers are starvers of the poor. Thus, if missionaries were to become very effective in their anti-contraception propaganda in India, arousing fears in Hindu women or causing them to believe that contraception was morally evil, and thereby aggravating the problems posed by over-population, the government of India might reasonably decide to restrict such teaching, partially by limiting their expression to inside Roman Catholic churches, or more generally, for the sake of goods such as human happiness, self-development, individuality, and the like, i.e. liberal goods, *and this without necessarily thereby claiming the teaching to be false.* Similarly, in an unstable community, the rulers, without laying any claim to be infallible, may need to back their criminal laws with laws making it a crime to encourage others to break those laws they deem to be morally unjustified. Thus the advocacy of treason, racial and religious killing, theft and sabotage of private property, may have to be made crimes, whether or not the legislator believes the views on which the acts would rest, to be true. This is so, because in such cases tolerance may result in disorder, and a lessening of goods such as happiness, human welfare, and justice. Such situations and such divided societies are not mere logical possibilities.

It may be replied that Mill had anticipated this objection, that true beliefs may cause harm, in arguing that the claim that a view may be suppressed because pernicious also involves a claim to infallible knowledge. However, the claim that the public expression and discussion of a belief leads to harm is obviously different from the claim that the belief is morally pernicious. Mill, and any reasonable political theorist, must acknowledge that we can make well-founded judgments about the harmful effects of actions, speeches, articles, and books. Thus, if it were to be found that the publishing of the true figures concerning Negro crime rates in the U.S.A. in respect of murder and rape incited mob violence and opposition to poverty relief measures, it would be reasonable for enlightened legislators to consider *temporarily* restricting the publication of these figures. The legislators would, of course, need to weigh up the evils of suppressing the truth, and of setting what could become a dangerous precedent, against the harm, misery, and injustice prevented. Thus, the conclusion to be drawn from this argument must be modified to acknowledge that it may be right and necessary to suppress the expression of a true view, to prevent harm. Not all views, the public expression of which leads to harm, may legitimately be denied freedom of expression. Rather, the harm done or prevented, has to be weighed against the truth lost, and the harm involved and risks incurred in suppressing, even temporarily, the truth. Here probabilities will have to be weighed, and for this reason, it will commonly be the case that the more immediate, direct, harmful effects will constitute stronger grounds for intolerance than less direct, more remote, harmful effects.

7. Mill suggests that we are not entitled to suppress a belief because it is morally pernicious or noxious, e.g. we are not entitled to suppress the public expression of the view that it is a good thing for parents to beat their unwanted children, because we may be mistaken about the perniciousness or noxious character of the view denied expression. This, I suggest, is a completely untenable claim. If, as must be allowed, the public expression of true beliefs may be restricted to prevent harm such as the suffering and deaths of innocent people, it must even more obviously be allowed that those beliefs which, because of their intrinsic character, foster such harm, must also be denied freedom of expression. This is, in effect, part of the earlier argument concerning intolerance in racially, religiously, or politically divided communities.

Clearly, with legislation designed to curtail free expression when its consequences are likely to be harmful, lovers of liberty may well disagree concerning when and what legislation is justified. The British Race Relations Act can be construed as such legislation (and also, as it has been, as an attempt to improve the moral tone of a community), and when construed in the former way, there is room for disagreement as to its justification when first introduced, and whether it should have been introduced earlier or later, in a more, or a less, stringent form.

Mill pressed the same general argument from the fallibility of beliefs in a special form, namely, that many views are partially true and partially false, and hence, that intolerance may involve a loss of true knowledge. Mill had expressed this view in his essays on Bentham and Coleridge. He believed, and no doubt correctly, that his contention had wide application. In many areas, especially that of political philosophy, different theories contain different truths. However, the same limitations, qualifications, and objections which hold against the argument in its general form hold against this version of it. Further, the partial truths version is open to the objection that in many areas the concept of a partial truth does not have application, e.g. concerning the existence of an all-perfect being.

All that can reasonably be concluded from Mill's argument, I suggest, is that intolerance of expression should not be applied recklessly or thoughtlessly, that the risk of intolerance depriving some of the opportunity of knowing what may be a true belief be taken into account when assessing the case for or against freedom of expression. This in turn suggests that note be taken of the reasonableness of the grounds on which the belief is based, the seriousness of the objections to it, the urgency or otherwise of the need for intolerance, together with the possibility or otherwise of achieving the goods and preventing the evils in ways which involve less risk of loss of true belief. It enjoins the minimum restrictions on freedom of expression compatible with achieving worthwhile ends. Mill's argument therefore has validity as a warning that censors may interfere on inadequate grounds, and with views which ought not to be the objects of interference. However, it does not establish an absolute right to freedom of expression, nor do the exceptions which must be allowed fall only into those categories noted in what I represented as being "a contemporary liberal principle of liberty of expression." The argument points to the value of true belief, but it must be qualified by the need to protect such goods and values as human happiness and welfare, individuality, self-development, justice, fraternity, respect for persons, to mention only the more important of the relevant values.

III. Arguments Which Appeal To the Claim That Our Beliefs Are Fallible

The arguments discussed in this section involve an appeal to what is claimed in the infallibility argument, namely that our beliefs are indeed fallible.

1. "The evils of censorship outweigh the evils it lessens." A special version, or an aspect, of this argument stresses in particular the evils which result from according undue power to the State, and from the misuse and even deliberate abuse of this power by human legislators and censors. It will be useful, however, to consider the argument in its more general form first. Clearly, in its more general form, the argument is a much stronger one if it is associated with the infallibility argument, and if the latter can successfully be defended against the criticisms I have pressed against it. Here I wish first to separate the two arguments, and then to consider them when conjoined with one another.

Let us therefore suppose that our legislators banned only the expression and discussion of false and evil beliefs. Would the denial of such freedom of expression involve more evils than the evils prevented? I suggest that it is by no means clear that it would do so. If the truth could be ascertained in religion, morality, and politics, and only the true views were accorded freedom of expression, there would be great gains. More people would believe what is true, more would know and do what they ought, there would be fewer harmful, dangerous political experiments, and there would be a redirection of human intellectual endeavors in so far as there would simply be the need to explain and present the reasons for the true views and against false theories, but no need to waste time and energy, as now, in combating plausible propaganda in favor of false theories. Thus, instead of false and evil views being propagated in such a way as to result in evil actions—views such as that the taking of innocent life, infliction of unnecessary suffering, lying to and cheating one's enemies or racial "inferiors" are right, and the like—we should have the free and reasoned expression of true views. That there would be very substantial gains to balance against any losses if freedom of expression could be restricted only to true views becomes more evident if less controversial areas and theories are considered. What would be lost and what gained if freedom of expression were denied to flat earth theories, dangerous and false medical theories, falsehoods about the effects of cigarette smoking, the pill, or fluoridation of drinking water? Among the new evils introduced by censorship of false beliefs would be the evil of rendering the rebel who insisted on expressing his beliefs a criminal, or at least a violator of the law. However, if intolerance has the vast, far-reaching effects it is usually claimed to have, it could reasonably be expected that there would be a continually diminishing number of such rebels. Other possible evils would include those of abuse of power by the police and magistrates, but this would occur only if false beliefs were accorded free expression and true views denied expression. By contrast, the gains could be immense. Besides the gains in true belief, and in more people coming rightly to direct their moral and political endeavors, impediments to the attaining of happiness and to effective self-development would be removed, and lives would come to be more wisely planned on the basis of genuine knowledge. Relevant here is the fact that, in respect of many matters, what is important is that we know the truth and not the reasons upon which it is based. It is valuable for me to know that arsenic is poisonous, the earth a sphere, whether or not I know the scientific theories which explain these facts or on which they are based. Suppression of false propaganda would prevent the public being misinformed, without in any way restricting their access to knowledge of the grounds on which the true beliefs rest.

In fact, as was acknowledged in the discussion of the infallibility argument, it is impossible, once censorship is accepted, to restrict it to views which can be known with certainty to be false. Legislators and censors are fallible, and sometimes corruptible, people; hence they may and do, once accorded the power, censor when they are not entitled to, i.e. when there is a distinct possibility that the view denied expression is true, and its expression results in no evils. Relevant here is the much quoted, if only roughly accurate, liberal generalization, "To the pure, all things are impure." This fact results in a good deal of misdirected, unnecessary censorship, censorship which prevents no real evils but which involves the loss of real goods and the causing of serious harm to individuals. Much censorship in Australia, for example, is evidently of this kind. Indeed, in view of the absence of worthwhile scientific evidence that pornography has bad effects, such as resulting in anti-social behavior, it is probable that the intolerance of pornography in Australia is censorship of this kind; it denies individuals harmless pleasures and renders them violators of the law. Again, the old, hackneyed, but vitally important liberal argument, that each is the best judge and guardian of his own interests, because he is more interested in the matter and has more access to the relevant facts than others, is sufficiently true to make fallible censorship sometimes at least deprive individuals of relevant knowledge of which they, as guardians of their own destiny, could make good use. However, the individual is not always the best judge and guardian of his own interests; and control of propaganda can protect as well as harm him. What its effects will be will depend on the rationality, character, gullibility or otherwise of the persons involved, and the wisdom, integrity, and liberality of the censor, to mention only some of the relevant factors. I suggest, therefore, that the argument from the evils of censorship is strong in so far as it rests on an appeal to the fact on which the infallibility argument rests, namely, that people commonly believe to be indubitably true, propositions and theories which are false. When assessed in the light of the qualifications indicated in the discussion of the infallibility argument, I suggest that it simply brings out the need for caution in controlling freedom of expression, and in encouraging legislators to contemplate such restrictions.

It would now be useful to consider in more detail those other goods and evils claimed to be affected by restrictions on freedom of expression. The relevant goods and evils are: the goods of vitally and rationally held beliefs; the evil of forcing the consciences of those silenced; the evils of suppressing individuality and restricting self-development; the evil of showing lack of respect for persons; the evil of impeding progress.

2. "The vitality and liveliness of a belief is dependent on the freedom to express and discuss it." Mill's statement of this argument runs:

> *However unwillingly a person who has a strong opinion may admit the possibility that his opinion may be false, he ought to be moved by the consideration that, however true it may be, if it is not fully, frequently, and fearlessly discussed, it will be held as a dead dogma, and not a living truth. (p. 95)*

This argument is empirically false. Many factors bear on the vitality and liveliness of beliefs, among them whether the belief has or has not been denied free expression. However, tolerance and intolerance have varying effects. Tolerance may result in a belief ceasing to matter to those who have fought for the right to express it; and intolerance may make a little cared-for belief matter desperately. (Consider the Irish.) Some of our most vitally held beliefs have never been fully, fearlessly, and frequently discussed in the community in which I live—beliefs such as that the infliction of needless suffering on children and animals is evil. Some of the most passionately held views, e.g. concerning the immorality of incest and masturbation, are seldom discussed. Certainly, I have never seen the pros and cons discussed in any popular newspaper, nor have I heard persons who believe in the moral desirability of masturbation and incest presenting their points of view on TV. In brief, the effects of tolerance and intolerance on the vitality of beliefs are variable and depend on many factors. By and large, a thoughtful intolerance would seem not to be dangerous to the vitality of a belief.

3. "Freedom of expression and discussion are necessary for rational as opposed to superstitious belief." Mill rightly contends that where there is intolerance of opposed views, there is a real danger of beliefs coming to be accepted without argument being offered in their support, and hence of their being held in a manner akin to superstitions or prejudices. However, this is simply a possible, not a necessary danger. How seriously it should be taken as a danger depends on the kind of truth it is. It is not necessary for the arguments, if any, in support of false mathematical and factual beliefs, e.g. that a square may have 5 angles, $2+2=6$, that cyanide is not poisonous, that lemons are sweet, to be known and examined for the relevant true beliefs to be held as rational beliefs and not as mere superstitions or

prejudices. With many beliefs on the other hand—and these include those about which Mill was most concerned, namely basic moral, political, and aesthetic beliefs which concern, for instance, values and principles, freedom, respect for life, for persons, etc.—whilst it is true that rational considerations capable of influencing the intellect are available, it is not true that such beliefs are open to rational *testing*. There are other beliefs again—and these include many philosophical and religious beliefs—which are such that it is possible to indicate the reasons upon which they are based and the objections from opposed views without allowing exponents of these opposed views freedom to express them; hence here the favored views may also be held as rationally grounded views, and not as mere prejudices or superstitions. The dangers to which this argument points are those of laziness and dishonesty—the protectors of the true view may become too lazy to offer reasons for it or to offer reasons for the favored view honestly. This argument, like the previous ones, is an ideal utilitarian argument. It appeals to the value of rationality and of rationally held beliefs. If, as has been argued, intolerance can be applied without loss of rational backing for the favored view, to that extent this argument leaves the case against intolerance untouched.

4. "It is evil to force consciences." Suppression of free expression and discussion may involve coercing persons into abstaining from doing what they believe they ought to do. However, by contrast with coercion of action, it less commonly involves forcing a person to do what he believes to be morally evil. To prevent someone from doing what he believes he ought to do is clearly undesirable. Nonetheless, it is a feature of all law that it may involve this. Where what is prevented is believed indubitably to be gravely evil—e.g. murder, cruelty, assault—we have no qualms. Hence, could we be certain that the view to be propagated as a matter of conscience was false, we should have few qualms. It is when there is uncertainty, or even a real possibility that the belief is true, that this lack of respect for the so-called right of conscience is thought to be a serious evil. It then becomes a failure to show respect for the person as a person, i.e. as a responsible moral agent.

5. "Intolerance involves lack of respect for persons." This argument too, derives much of its strength from the fact of human fallibility, and hence from the fact that the belief that is denied expression may be true. To deny freedom of expression to a true view, or even to one which may be true, is to show lack of respect for the expounder of the belief and for his possible audience. Depending on the belief, this lack of respect may be considerable. Suppressing information which has an important bearing on how individuals may plan their lives when the information may well be true, is a grave affront to the possible audience as well as to the person wishing to impart the information. On the other hand, where the view seeking free expression can be known to be false, or even probably false, there may be lack of respect in allowing its expression. An extreme case would be the successfully persuasive advocacy of sadistic murder; a less extreme case would be that concerning the taking of drugs. If it comes to be shown that cannabis and L.S.D. are seriously harmful, then not to suppress the advocacy by teen-age idols of experimenting with them may well involve lack of respect for persons. So too, with

racialist propaganda. (In the case of drugs, it could well be, as I have heard it argued, that respect for persons dictates allowing the jazz musician to take the drug if he finds this essential for development of his art, but denying him the right freely to commend drug-taking to his public.) Thus, concern for persons as persons will sometimes dictate tolerance, sometimes intolerance, of expression of beliefs. A very relevant consideration will be the certainty or degree of probability of the belief.

6. "It is evil to suppress individuality and self-development." For various reasons, freedom of expression has a very important bearing on self-development. Without scope for free expression and discussion we should be greatly restricted in our power to bring about the legislative changes necessary to permit or assist individuals in their self-development. Thus without scope for free expression it is certain that the recent British law sanctioning homosexuality would never have been passed, though such a law clearly has very important implications in respect of self-development for many people. However, we should note here that free discussion, particularly of the careless, thoughtless kind which is so frequent in Western Democracies, may lead to very undesirable changes. It was in the context of free and careless discussion that abortion (1803) was made a crime in Great Britain and that the Comstock Law (1873) was passed in the U.S.A. Thus freedom of expression may lead to legislative reforms which aid self-development, but it may also result in severe restrictions. Its value depends on *who* uses it and *how*.

Freedom of expression bears upon self-development in many other ways too. It is necessary for man *qua* thinker. Thus, it is vitally necessary for the individuality and self-development of those, including scholars and scientists, whose callings involve rational enquiry, that there be free expression and discussion. It is also valuable to man *qua* rational being, for the presence of conflicting ideas will usually force individuals to think out their own views to a degree not necessary in the absence of freedom of expression, although it must be recognized that *men are not fully nor purely rational beings,* and that some are more rational than others. Further, freedom of expression and discussion are valuable in that they may provide knowledge and thereby awaken individuals to avenues of self-development of which they might well otherwise be unaware. This is well illustrated by the history of the fight by advocates of birth-control for freedom of expression. Thus freedom of expression is an essential condition for certain avenues of self-development, and it provides a context in which important human capacities are likely to be developed. This may be the case even if the views denied expression were always false ones, for, in spite of Plato's hopes and the practices of many religious groups, philosophy and many other avenues of self-development need a context of freedom of expression and discussion.

However, this argument from individuality and self-development is often overstated, as can best be shown by the following considerations. First, were only false beliefs to be denied expression, not only would there be important compensating goods to weigh against any goods that were lost, but much could be done to mitigate such loss. For example, in denying free expression to false beliefs one would be contributing to a diminution in the making of wrong, self-frustrating choices; and individuals would be protected from persuasive enticements to bad development while remaining free to be self-motivating and self-developing. The loss of stimulation to thinking in general and to the planning of one's own life due to the absence of any clash of ideas could be countered, to some extent, by a controlled Platonic dialectic. It is important, secondly, to remember again that human beings are only partially rational, as even Mill, in his less sanguine moments, acknowledged. Thus the author of *On Liberty* had written in the *Principles of Political Economy*:

> *The prospect of the future depends on the degree in which they (the laboring classes) can be made rational beings. There is no reason to believe that prospect other than hopeful. (Bk. IV, Ch. 7, p. 763, Toronto ed.)*

Mill nonetheless wished to accord these imperfectly rational men the fullest freedom of discussion, at least in part, in the name of individuality and self-development. People are not fully rational. They are open to manipulation, influence by propaganda, and in general exposed to the skills of those who have an interest in influencing their thoughts and actions. Society is not a philosophical society in which members cultivate the virtues of fairness and open-mindedness in attending to and assessing the various views advanced. Rather, it is a jungle in which some make it their interest to prey on the intellectual and moral weaknesses of others, and in which most of us need protection in some areas, for we are neither wise nor rational enough to protect ourselves all of the time. This is acknowledged in the restrictions in the advertising of medicines. A strong case can be made in respect of restricting the advertising of cigarettes. If fluoridation of water were more important than it is, a case might also be made for suppressing falsehoods about its effects. This is clear if one again considers the situation which could confront the Indian Government if opponents of contraception successfully preyed on the fears of the peasants, *lyingly* claiming that the pill and other contraceptives caused dangerous illnesses. Here the truth can be determined, and concern for individuality and self-development would dictate intolerance of the expression of these false views. This is so for the reason Mill so often noted in the *Principles of Political Economy*, namely, that over-population is a great enemy of individuality and self-development. The argument rests on the premise that individuality and self-development are goods and sources of other goods. Hence, when it is certain or highly probable that the free expression of a belief endangers individuality and self-development, the case for liberty of expression from this argument fails. Thus, false propaganda in favor of the taking of drugs which had this result would have no claim to freedom of expression. Similarly, moral doctrines which fostered interference with the self-development of others, e.g. various religio-medico and racialist moral doctrines, would derive no support from this argument.

In pressing these qualifications, however, it is important that two points be again stressed, namely, that intolerance is distinct from persecution, and that intolerance admits of degrees, in such a way that banning propaganda via one medium alone, e.g. TV, may achieve the desired result. A debate in medical journals over the harmfulness or otherwise of cannabis or L.S.D. is clearly unlikely to have the effects consequent upon reckless claims made over TV by irresponsible pop-group idols.

Finally, I suggest it is much more difficult to estimate the relevance of freedom of expression to self-development than liberals have suggested. Mill, in one place, claimed that genius needs an atmosphere of freedom in which to breathe. But even a cursory examination of the history of the Middle Ages and the Renaissance reveals this to be false. Mill's error suggests that the relation between freedom of expression and of discussion and self-development is much more of an empirical question, requiring research, than proponents of this argument suppose.

7. "Freedom of expression is an aid to progress." It is possible to combine the various foregoing arguments to develop an argument that freedom of expression is an aid to progress, whether or not the views expressed are true. However, it is clear that such an argument would be less plausible if it could be shown that the beliefs suppressed were all false, or that there were very telling reasons for believing them to be false. The suppression of false beliefs may well, under many conditions and in many societies, lead to progress which would be impeded by tolerance. Further, the denial of freedom of expression may be useful when, as in wartime, it is applied on a restricted, short-term basis; or even when applied for a longer term. This could be so in unstable, divided communities, and with countries threatened by outside enemies. It can be argued, for example, that if the U.S.A. is not to retrogress, but continue to progress, it will have to impose serious limitations of many freedoms, including the freedom to express racialist views.

IV. Conclusion

The arguments examined here do not establish even a prima facie case for unrestricted freedom of expression; neither do they establish a case for freedom of expression restricted by reference to the conditions set out in what was characterized earlier in this paper as a contemporary liberal principle of freedom of expression. This is so because they allow that where the probability of serious harm (which outweighs the harm involved in intolerance), or of injustices, or of lack of respect for persons, their happiness, and welfare, or of loss of progress, e.g. in respect of knowledge, is high and the probable harm and evils resulting from intolerance relatively minor, some restrictions on freedom of expression may well be justified. The restrictions may take many forms, some of a very moderate character, some extreme and covering all or most media. The circumstances of the case determine when such restrictions are necessary and desirable, and what form and degree they are to take. Among the relevant circumstances are the gravity of the likely evils, the urgency for action, the character of the people involved—their rationality, maturity, the nature and extent of their education, etc.—the seriousness of the danger, e.g. whether it be from a skilled, highly organized group which exploits all available psychological techniques to manipulate its audience, etc. Hence I suggest that no useful, summarizing principle defining the limits of freedom of expression can be stated which will take account of all the kinds and degrees of interference with freedom of expression which ought to be noted.

Liberty of Expression: Its Grounds and Limits (II)

D. H. Monro

I have no doubt that Professor McCloskey is right in saying that Mill did not wish to set the same limits to freedom of expression as to other kinds of action. Mill is sometimes interpreted as defending freedom of expression on the ground that the expression of opinion is a self-regarding action. I think this is wrong. Mill has three categories, not two: opinion, self-regarding actions and other-regarding actions. The first two, he maintains, are absolutely protected: only the third may legitimately be controlled by the State or by society.

If it is asked whether opinion is, in Mill's view, self-regarding or other-regarding, the answer may well be that it is other-regarding. Silencing an expression of opinion is, he tells us, "robbing the human race; posterity as well as the existing generation; those who dissent from the opinion, still more than those who hold it" (Everyman ed., p. 79). If opinions can affect others negatively by not being expressed, it would seem to follow that their positive expression also affects others.

Why then, McCloskey asks, should not the general principle about other-regarding actions apply to opinion as well? It would follow that the State is entitled to suppress opinion if the harm done by suppression is less than the harm done by expression, but not otherwise. On the face of it, it seems likely that there will be *some* occasions when the suppression of *some* opinions will do more good than harm. Mill is, then, hardly consistent in claiming that opinion should *never* be suppressed.

This seems a strong argument. Mill can, I think, only answer it by contending that the suppression of opinion always does more harm than good in the long run. Moreover, I think that this is the position Mill is actually arguing for. I shall contend that it is less implausible than it may seem at first sight.

But, McCloskey objects, Mill himself retreats from this position. He admits both explicit and implicit exceptions; and, once he has done this, there is really no escape from considering each case on its merits; thereby admitting that there is no general principle that would rule out suppression as such. We are left, then, with the modified, or McCloskey view that, while suppression of opinion is no doubt usually bad, it may sometimes be justified. Why shouldn't Mill accept this?

But is it true that Mill admits exceptions? McCloskey gives three instances. Let us look at these in turn.

First, there is the much discussed corn-dealer passage, in which Mill says that the opinion "that corn-dealers are starvers of the poor, or that private property is robbery . . . may justly incur punishment when delivered orally to an excited mob assembled before the house of a corn-dealer, or when handed about among the same mob in the form of a placard" (p. 114). Notice that Mill specifies that the mob must be not only excited but also actually there before the corn-dealer's house, no doubt with sticks or stones or torches in its collective hand. He would not rule out the expression of precisely the same opinions to a public meeting in a hall perhaps only a mile away.

In *Yates* v. *U.S.* the Supreme Court of the United States makes a useful if fairly obvious distinction between incitement and advocacy. "The essential distinction is that those to whom the incitement is addressed must be urged to *do* something now or in the future, rather than to merely believe in something." If an action is punished, it seems reasonable to punish incitement to that action; but, if the distinction between advocacy and incitement can be sustained, this need not imply any restriction on the expression of one's beliefs. There is a difference between saying that a law is a bad one and urging that it be broken.

I believe that Mill's corn-dealer example is meant to make the point that in some circumstances the apparent expression of a belief may, in effect, be something quite different. Just as "You may say that again" does not mean that it is permitted to repeat that remark but merely endorses the remark, so in some circumstances the shouting of slogans may simply be a way of saying "up and at him, boys!" I do not think that it is possible to infer, as McCloskey does, that Mill would extend this exception to freedom of opinion to include situations in which there is general unrest in the community at large. This is very different from there being an actual mob assembled at a specific place within yards of a possible victim to whom they intend harm. Mill is here trying to draw the line between advocacy and incitement very much in the way that the United States Supreme Court did. The corn-dealer example is already on the outer edge, as it were, of that distinction and cannot be extended further. It is a case where what, if you look simply at the verbal expression, looks like advocacy is in fact incitement. Mill would not I think want us to draw the conclusion that genuine advocacy should be suppressed in troublous times because it might, in a more indirect way, serve as incitement.

McCloskey also regards Mill's remarks about indecency as constituting an exception to his general principle on freedom of expression. It is not clear that they do. What Mill says here is very brief: unfortunately so, since one crucial question for Mill is involved: the question of what counts as harm to others. "There are many acts," Mill says, "which, being directly injurious only to the agents themselves, ought not to be legally interdicted, but which, if done publicly, are a violation of good manners, and coming thus within the category of offences against others, may rightly be prohibited. Of this kind are offences against decency; on which it is unnecessary to dwell, the rather as they are only connected indirectly with our subject, the objection to publicity being equally strong in the case of many actions not in themselves condemnable, or supposed to be so" (p. 153).

It is not entirely clear what actions Mill has in mind. Having a bath, or making love, are of course actions which, while not "condemnatory in themselves," are thought to be offensive if done in public. It is not so easy to think of examples harmful only to the agents; but probably Mill merely meant that so-called immoral behavior ought not to be thrust unnecessarily upon those likely to be offended by it. It is, as I have said, a pity that he was not more explicit, because a very difficult question does arise here. To what extent am I entitled to protection from the sight of behavior which offends me only in the sense that I find it distasteful to contemplate? I do not know how Mill would have answered this; but it is not obvious to me that he would have been forced to extend what little he does say to include speech which someone finds offensive to hear. Certainly, in the passage quoted, Mill seems to think that his remarks are relevant only to self-regarding actions.

Finally McCloskey says that, since Mill acknowledged that the State may act to protect the individual against force and fraud, he was also committed to banning the means to fraud, such as fraudulent advertising. But is this a departure from his principles? Certainly, if I sell you sand under the pretence that it is sugar, or sell you a car having first twiddled with the gadget which tells you how many miles it has covered, I am doing you an injury. If I tell you in so many words that the sand is sugar, or that the car has done only a hundred miles, it would be absurd to say that I should be immune from punishment because speech should be free. One might as well say that making perjury an offence also represents a departure from Mill's principles. To deliberately withhold or distort information which you are entitled to have (as the purchaser is clearly entitled to know what he is buying) is very different from laying before you considerations, however misguided they may be, which you may like to take into account before coming to your own conclusion.

The existence of a clear distinction does not, of course, preclude border-line cases. Baldness is clearly different from hairiness. The distinction between sincere advocacy and deliberate fraud is not vitiated by the fact that most propagandists will at least sometimes yield to the temptation to overstate their case, to cover up weaknesses in their arguments, to rely on emotional appeals. Mill touches on this in discussing the view that the free expression of all opinions should be permitted, but on condition that the manner is temperate and does not pass the bounds of fair discussion. His comment is that "to argue sophistically, to suppress facts or arguments, to misstate the elements of the case, or misrepresent the opposite opinion . . . is so continually done in perfect good faith by persons who are not considered, and in many other respects may not deserve to be considered, ignorant or incompetent, that it is rarely possible, on adequate grounds, conscientiously to stamp the misrepresentation as morally culpable" (p. 112). It seems clear from this that Mill would confine the concept of fraud to the sort of case I have mentioned. When it is so confined, there is no real reason to regard the punishment of fraud as an exception to what he says about freedom of speech.

When Mill says that "the question is doubtful only when the instigator derives a personal benefit from his advice" he is not committing himself to the view that in such cases "persuasive enticements to evil acts" should be prohibited. He means *doubtful* quite literally: he goes on to say that "the case is one of those which lie on the exact boundary line between two principles, and it is not at once apparent to which of the two it properly belongs" (p. 154). He is, actually, talking about keeping a brothel or a gambling-house, not primarily about advertising one; but it is true enough that he is expressing doubts whether the protection extended to honest advocates should be extended to those whose only interest is a financial one. He is, however, content to leave the question an open one.

There is, indeed, one exception which I think Mill might have allowed: the suppression of libel and defamation. The liberal's reason for suppressing these is that they concern private matters which are not anybody else's business. It is quite in accordance with Mill's general position that there should be a right to privacy. He is worried about the likelihood that democracy will establish a tyranny of the majority. The traditional picture of democracy (found, for example, in Montesquieu and Rousseau, not to go further back, as they did, to Sparta) was of a State in which there was no distinction at all between private and public concerns. Hence the *censor morum* was thought to be a peculiarly democratic institution. Mill was alarmed by this view. His arguments about freedom of opinion are, I believe, meant to apply to general theoretical matters of public interest, and not to the private details of someone's sex life.

Once this is realised, I do not think that McCloskey has shown that Mill, by allowing exceptions, is virtually admitting that there can be no general principle involved, and that each case must be considered on its merits. It would certainly be very odd if it just happened to be the case that the harm of suppression always outweighed the benefits. One would expect there to be some explanation for this unfailing regularity.

And so, indeed, according to Mill, there is. The suppression of opinion is, undoubtedly, an other-regarding action, but it is a special kind of action, which is bound to be self-defeating. When one is contemplating any other-regarding action, one should ask oneself whether, on balance, it will do more harm than good. To answer this, one needs access to all the relevant information, and in this case one highly relevant piece of information is whether the opinion to be suppressed is true or not. But the act of suppressing it will, by silencing its defenders, make it impossible to ascertain this with any certainty. Of course, if one is infallible, this will not matter; but for all fallible beings suppression of opinion destroys one of the conditions needed to justify any action. It is only in a society in which there is freedom of opinion that one is in a position to know whether one's actions are more likely to do harm than good. Consequently there is at least one kind of other-regarding action, the suppression of opinion, which is always to be avoided.

McCloskey is right, then, in taking the infallibility argument to be a central one, though I think he has misrepresented the argument itself. Mill's point is not that, since we are not infallible, we can never be sure that the opinion we suppress is false and that the risk that it may be true, however slight, is one we are never justified in taking. If he were to say this then he would, as McCloskey suggests, be putting a grossly inflated value on truth. I would suggest, however, that Mill's argument is rather different. It is that the only condition under which we can have a rational assurance that a belief is true is that one is free to consider contrary evidence. Hence we can confidently take the risk of our opinion being false if we are free to consider opposing arguments, but not otherwise. Once this is realized I think that McCloskey's counter-instances become much less plausible. Take what he says about the crank who believes that the earth is flat. We can feel confident that he is a crank and that we need not consider his opinions too seriously just because we believe, rightly or wrongly, that the belief that the earth is round is based on solid scientific procedures and that these procedures have built into them quite stringent falsification conditions. If we were not satisfied of that we would be much less safe in assuming that we could dismiss the flat earther. Or take McCloskey's more telling example—the one about the moral belief which all of us hold that it is wrong to torture children for our own pleasure. McCloskey says we feel confident that this is true even though most of us have not been exposed to the arguments of people who maintain that torturing children is right. I would have thought the point here is that we cannot see what kind of arguments could count against this belief. This, of course, one may remark parenthetically, would not be a good reason for suppressing such arguments if anybody else could think of them. The main point, however, is that we know that no organized attempt has been made to keep from us any considerations that might be urged against our moral belief. To the extent that we know that, we can feel confident that our belief is not mistaken. The situation would be different in circumstances where we knew that the police and the censor had been active to keep from us any contrary arguments. If Mill is right about this then it is clear that any counter arguments McCloskey may produce which rest on *our* willingness to take the risk of our opinions being false are beside the point. The question is whether justified willingness to take such a risk is not made possible by the relative absence of repression of freedom of opinion.

Although the infallibility argument is in one way central to Mill's position, I doubt if it is central in quite the way that McCloskey supposes. Mill has, of course, another argument which is at least as important: that we should not suppress even a false belief, because to do so prevents true beliefs from being rationally held. Realization of this casts doubt on much that McCloskey says in Section III of his paper under the heading "Arguments which appeal to the claim that our beliefs are fallible."

I doubt, for example, whether Mill would agree that "there would be great gains" if "the truth could be ascertained in religion, morality and politics and only the true views were accorded freedom of expression" [p. 50 of this book]. True belief in such matters, he would object, is of little value unless it is fully informed. He would certainly protest that "the genuine knowledge" McCloskey talks about, on which lives may be "wisely planned," would not be available. McCloskey is no doubt right in saying that there are some matters (the harmfulness of arsenic, for example) in which it is important that we know the truth, and not the reasons upon which it is based; but this hardly applies to politics, morality, and religion. Conscientious action on the basis of half-understood and ill-digested moral beliefs is just as dangerous as actions based on false beliefs. This is often true even of medical knowledge. McCloskey suggests that Mill's point can be met if there is authoritative presentation and explanation of the reasons for the true views and against false theories; but it is doubtful if this would be effective unless the opposing case were argued by someone who really believed in it. The opposite policy has the paradoxical result that those who do this job best, who throw themselves so conscientiously into the task of trying to make heretical beliefs seem plausible that they come to convince themselves, would thereby be disqualified from continuing to do the job. One of Mill's main points is of course that the result of any such policy is that people will no longer feel free to follow the argument whithersoever it leads. They will be continually thwarted in their attempts at thinking clearly by the fear, even if it is only an unconscious fear, that they may reach an unacceptable conclusion. Consequently there will be important indirect effects on the general temper of society: the stifling of intellectual adventurousness, and of the impulse to question even those truths which are apparently most secure. Mill would say that this impulse is of the greatest social value: McCloskey seems to suggest that it is merely time-wasting.

McCloskey objects to what Mill says about the vitality of beliefs on the ground that persecution may very often increase the intensity of emotion with which beliefs are held. This is no doubt true. The question is whether, when Mill talks about vitality and liveliness, he means the degree of emotion with which beliefs are held. There is, after all, another sense in which beliefs may be like life. Bergson, you will remember, identifies the *élan vital* with flexibility, adaptability, elasticity. It is possible that when Mill says that a belief which has not been tested by discussion lacks liveliness and vitality, he means that it will be rigid, that it will lack adaptability, that it will be held in a form which will prevent it from fitting all the facts. It will be a dogmatic and inflexible belief, however passionately held. I do not, however, want to stress this because I think that Mill was more concerned with the irrationality of such beliefs than with their lack of vitality.

McCloskey's comment here is that, while there is a danger that lack of freedom will result in beliefs being held in a superstitious or prejudiced way, this is merely a danger, and may be guarded against [pp. 52–53 of this book]. He adds that there are many truths which may be accepted rationally even though the objections to them are not understood. I am not quite sure what *rational* and *rationally* mean here. Certainly it is not irrational to believe some things on authority. The question is, however, whether such beliefs have much value. To take one of McCloskey's examples, it seems to me that any competent teacher of arithmetic would be delighted if a pupil came along with one of those ingenious proofs that $2+2=5$. The reason he would be delighted is of course that examining such proofs and discovering what is wrong with them is of far more value than simply accepting the multiplication table learned off by heart as a matter of faith. Perhaps this is not true if one's only concern with arithmetic is to be able to count one's change; though even then I should have thought it necessary to understand, not only that $2+2$ does as a matter of fact equal 4, but that it must equal 4. McCloskey says that it is unnecessary to know "the arguments, if any" in support of such propositions as that lemons are sweet [p. 52 of this book]. But this example seems persuasive just because there do not seem to be any arguments. If there are no arguments, however, there is no point in forbidding their expression. On the other hand, if there were any arguments, it would follow not so much that there would be a slight chance of lemons turning out to be sweet after all (that might well be negligible) but that there was something more than meets the taste-buds to be known and understood about sweetness. Of course we do not have the time, or the inclination, to try to know and understand everything: we are content to take many things on trust. But that is no reason why those who do have the time and inclination should be deterred by official prohibitions. It seems to me that it is McCloskey rather than Mill who puts an inflated value on truth: at any rate on the value of information as such and the importance of its being correct. Mill, I think, would be much more inclined to agree with Socrates that the unexamined life is not worth living.

This dictum, of course, applies particularly to those "basic moral, political and aesthetic beliefs" [p. 53 of this book] with which, McCloskey points out, Mill was most concerned. Here McCloskey has a further point to make: that "such beliefs are not open to rational *testing*." Earlier McCloskey suggests that Mill's position depends on a cognitivist meta-ethic. It is arguable, however, that all that one needs in order to have a case against suppressing moral beliefs, whether these are taken to be beliefs about objective truths or merely expressions of attitudes, is to hold that they are of value and that suppressing them may prevent them from being held. McCloskey, of course, would raise the question of what kind of value they could be supposed to have if they do not have the peculiar value which attaches to true propositions. One possible answer is that their value resides in their consequences, that having certain attitudes will lead people to behave in ways which will be useful to society, or something of that sort. This, of course, at once leaves it open to McCloskey to say that in that case there could be no objection to the suppression of those attitudes which are likely to lead to behavior that is harmful to society. What may be said, however, is that in deciding what one's moral attitudes are, one is engaged in a process of self-exploration and is finding out what kind of ultimate desire one really has; what kind of world one really wants oneself and others to live in. If one is prevented from discovering this and is led into pursuing aims which are, in a sense, not really one's own, then one is likely to feel frustrated and discontented without fully understanding why. This is one of the points that Mill makes in his chapter on individuality. What this brings out, I suggest, is that the rational man for Mill is not the man who intuits those moral truths which would be self-evident to an ideally good man but is someone who understands himself and his own aspirations fully and is clear-sighted about whatever goals he does pursue, even though these may not be goals that an ideally good or even ideally rational man would pursue. It is hardly possible to attain this clear-sightedness without examining all that can be said against one's beliefs.

On the evil of forcing conscience McCloskey says that we have no qualms about preventing people from doing things which are beyond doubt evil. Consequently he says we should not have no, but few, qualms about preventing people propagating as a matter of conscience views which are, in fact, false. I want to dispute this. I think that we do have qualms about preventing a person from doing what he genuinely believes to be right even if we are quite sure that he is mistaken. There is a general principle which I would suggest most liberals would hold about this. The general principle is that the State has a right to force a morality on those who do not share it only when it would be impossible in practice for different members of the community to *act* upon different moralities. Otherwise each individual citizen should be allowed to practise his own morality. The State should not force an alien morality on him, but he, in his turn, must not force his morality upon others. The Christian Fundamentalist, for example, who, for queer reasons of his own, thinks blood transfusions immoral, may be permitted to refuse this operation on his own behalf, but not to sacrifice his child's life to his scruples. The disciple of Robin Hood is not prevented from giving his own goods to the poor if he wants to. He is merely prevented from forcing others to do the same. If this principle is applied, then it would follow that a man is allowed, if he thinks it is his duty to do so, to propagate false beliefs. He is not allowed, however, to force others to do the same. I suggest that any other practice would give us qualms and very serious ones. It is not adequate to say that merely forcing a man to keep silent is not to force his conscience: most people would feel bound in conscience to protest against a law they thought evil, even if they also felt bound in conscience, as law-abiding citizens, to obey it.

McCloskey says about the argument from lack of respect for persons that it, too, loses much of its force if the view to be suppressed is a false one. I should have thought that to dismiss a view out of hand because we are quite sure that it is false, even though its proponent puts it forward in good faith believing it to be true, is to show a great lack of respect for him. Even at the ordinary level of good manners, to go no deeper, it is intolerably rude. The distinction that is involved here is the hackneyed, but I believe useful, one between indoctrination and education. To indoctrinate is to take whatever steps may be necessary to impress beliefs believed to be true (let us suppose for the sake of argument that they actually *are* true) on the pupil. To educate is to teach the pupil those techniques by which he will become capable of judging for himself whether beliefs are true or false, and will also, of course, be put in the way of discovering new truths unknown to his instructors. I should have thought it quite obvious that education does suggest a respect for the pupil whereas indoctrination suggests a lack of respect for him. To restrict expression of some views is certainly to indoctrinate rather than to educate, at least with regard to those views.

McCloskey would reply that to allow someone to advocate the use of harmful drugs may show lack of respect for those persons he is likely to influence. The lack of respect presumably consists in not caring enough about the harm done to them if they take drugs. But the harm comes from taking drugs, not from talking about it. There is nothing in the argument about freedom of expression to prevent prohibiting the actual taking of drugs. Mill does, of course, have another argument that might prevent this, the one about self-regarding actions; but that is not relevant to the present discussion. The point is that, whether or not it shows lack of respect for a person to prevent him from doing something, it certainly does show lack of respect to prevent him from discussing the reasons both for and against allowing him to do it. In reading McCloskey one suspects that his concept of self-development and of a person is not quite the same as Mill's. The basic question is whether we regard the self or the person as the individual who has the desires which he is actually conscious of here and now or whether we rather think of him as an imperfect approximation to a purely good or ideally rational being. If you respect only the true self which he is more or less confusedly trying to realize and not the actual man with his false beliefs and unfortunate aspirations, then, no doubt, you will not mind molding him and coercing him. I don't suppose that McCloskey would accept the self-realization view in its entirety, but I have a feeling that some of his remarks show this kind of influence.

This is relevant to what McCloskey says about individuality and self-development. Here again his case is that, while free discussion is important to the development of man as a rational being, no man is just that, and some men are really very little interested in their intellectual development. One needs, then, to balance the harm that intolerance may do to their intellectual development against the harm that tolerance may do to their development in other ways. If Indian women were prevented from exposure to lying propaganda about the evils of birth control, very little harm would be done to their intellectual development: certainly nothing like as much harm as would be done to their development in other ways by ceaseless child-bearing and the consequent poverty.

It is a persuasive example; and, moreover, one which may serve to illustrate an argument which, if not quite McCloskey's, is at least suggested by his remarks, and which I think he would endorse. Let us, it might be said, grant the general point that it is possible to have rationally grounded opinions only if we live in a society in which free enquiry is encouraged. Given this generally tolerant atmosphere, there may still be some relatively minor matters about which the received opinion is not likely to be mistaken, and in which it is of great practical importance that people should hold that opinion. In such a case it seems clear that more good than harm will be done by suppression. As a utilitarian, then, Mill is not entitled to say that the infallibility argument (i.e. my interpretation of it rather than McCloskey's) justifies complete tolerance.

What is involved here is a general question which affects what is perhaps the central objection to utilitarianism. It is often claimed that utilitarianism necessarily condones committing the occasional murder or executing the occasional innocent man for the general good. This argument is, of course, usually advanced as a *reductio ad absurdum* of utilitarianism. But McCloskey, who is no utilitarian, is suggesting quite seriously that the occasional suppression of opinion may be permissible in the general good. The challenge to the utilitarian is, however, the same: either abandon the view that only consequences count (and so admit that punishing the innocent, or suppressing opinion, is bad in itself) or condone the occasional injustice or the occasional suppression. It follows that if there is a satisfactory utilitarian reply to the charge about injustice, it may also serve Mill against McCloskey.

The classical utilitarian reply invokes Bentham's distinction between first-order evil and second-order evil, between the direct consequences of an action in doing harm to specifiable individuals and the indirect consequences of shattering public trust and confidence and so on. The stock objections are: first, that the blow to the public confidence by any individual breach of the general rule is not very great, whereas the good to be achieved may be considerable; and secondly, that the indirect consequences may be avoided altogether by secrecy.

Let us take the second of these, and consider one of the stock illustrations. Two men are alone on a desert island. One dies, having first induced the other to promise to bury him on the hill-top, in the center of the island. Since this involves some arduous porterage, followed by some difficult digging, utilitarianism would decree that it is permissible (perhaps even obligatory) for the survivor to disregard his promise and consign the body to the ocean, to be tidily disposed of by sharks.

Much can be (and has been) said about this case, which I do not intend to repeat. But there is one point which has not, I believe, been given much attention. If two men live together on a desert island they get to know each other pretty well. If the survivor is indeed the kind of man who would feel free to disregard a promise made in these circumstances, his companion would come to realize this. It is not, of course, necessary to suppose that he could not know it unless there had been another case exactly like this one: another dying man to whom a promise was made. We all form expectations about the way our friends and acquaintances will behave: and these are based, not on induction from precisely similar cases, but on a general assessment of character. But, of course, just to the extent that the dying man knew, or suspected, that his companion was the kind of man who would act on what are alleged to be utilitarian principles, it would be impossible for that companion to comfort him by making a promise.

This observation is of general importance. One may add to it a different but related point: that if utiliarianism did lead to professing one principle and acting on another, a utilarian would have to conceal the fact that he was a utilitarian, or alternatively misrepresent the true nature of utilitarianism. Since it is presumably for the general good that utilitarianism should be known and understood, this would be an indirect consequence that would far outweigh the good done by occasional secret breaches of general rules. But if the total consequences of such secret breaches are harmful, it would follow that utilitarians are not after all committed to them.

This is a related point, because it brings out that we are concerned with the total behavior of an individual and not merely with the cumulative effect of the isolated acts of a number of individuals. The point is really one that Hobbes made: if society is to work, one needs to feel confidence that one's fellows are the kind of people who do not do one thing when people are looking and another when their backs are turned. But the only effective way of convincing others that you are that sort of person is to be that sort of person.

To convince others of this is the more difficult, Hobbes might add, because in a sense no one is this sort of person. Man is not a social animal by nature, and becomes fit for society only by rigid self-discipline, which is none the less self-discipline because its ultimate motivation is self-interest. Consequently, if the enterprise is to succeed, one must be especially careful not to rouse suspicions of back-sliding, which will be only too readily aroused.

What is the bearing of all this on McCloskey's example about the Indian women? Mill, I would suggest, might be saying something like this: Just as an individual, if he is to make an effective contribution to the general happiness, needs to turn himself into the sort of person who can be trusted even out of sight, so a government, if it is to make an effective contribution to the same end, needs to be the kind of authority that can be trusted not to repress opinion, even when strongly tempted to. Just as the atmosphere of mutual trust on which satisfactory relations between individuals depend is difficult to attain and easily shattered, so too is the atmosphere of intellectual adventurousness, of free and fearless enquiry on which social advancement depends. The straightforward way to deal with false and dangerous beliefs is to expose their falsity. To take the apparent short cut of suppression is, of course, to generate the suspicion that the view suppressed cannot in fact be shown to be false. What is more important, it is, in a sense, to change the rules of the game: to appeal to force and not to argument, and in so doing to begin to create an entirely different social atmosphere, the atmosphere of the benevolent dictator.

If one does genuinely despair of making men rational, then benevolent dictatorship would seem to be the sensible solution. But the qualities one requires of the citizen of a benevolent dictatorship are very different from those one requires of the citizen of a free and open society. In place of intellectual adventurousness, one asks for docility and the conviction that one's betters know best. If the aim is the open society, and it is realized that men are not as rational as one would like them to be, the obvious expedient is to try to make them more rational, which means exposing them to discussion rather than shielding them from it. If the aim is benevolent dictatorship, then one tries to make them less rational, so far as a willingness to stifle one's critical faculties and accept opinions on trust is less rational. The point is that the two do not mix: to the extent that one creates the conditions necessary for the one, so one destroys the conditions necessary for the other. If this is true, then the indirect consequences of resorting to repression, even occasionally and in exceptional cases, may be greater than appears at first sight.

All this is vague and rather rhetorical. Why not, McCloskey asks, have tolerance as a general rule but keep suppression in reserve for those situations in which it seems clear that much good and comparatively little harm will result? Mill's answer (or the answer I have put into his mouth) is that the indirect consequences may be disastrous: the atmosphere in which tolerance thrives is hard to build up and easy to destroy. But how convincing is this?

There is one consideration which may serve to reinforce the general argument. The open society, McCloskey argues, demands a degree of rationality from its citizens of which most men are incapable. It may be replied that the ideal of benevolent dictatorship is equally unrealistic. It is not merely that dictators are rarely benevolent, though that is true enough: McCloskey is asking not just for a benevolent dictator but for one who is something of a philosopher-king. He suppresses only those opinions which are clearly false and which a wise and dispassionate observer can see to cause more harm than good, even when the fullest value is given to the indirect harm which results, to at least some extent, from all suppression. The sad truth is that those who gain power, in all societies, are not the people whose opinions on these matters one would readily trust. If Mill is too optimistic about the rationality of the ordinary man, McCloskey is too optimistic about the dangers of encouraging rulers to exercise their power unwisely. This is another reason for believing that the two kinds of society militate against each other, and that consequently the mixture McCloskey proposes will be an unstable one.

Again, consider another of McCloskey's examples: the temporary suppression or restriction of the statistics of Negro murders and rapes in the U.S.A. Suppressing the publication of such facts, especially if they have been published regularly in the past, would lead people to suspect the truth (indeed to suspect rather more than the truth) and so would defeat its own purpose. If the suppression were merely temporary, there would certainly be such suspicions the next time publication was delayed. This illustrates the difficulties of taking repressive action half-heartedly: the only really effective measure would be to see to it that such information was never published in the first place.

Incidentally, McCloskey uses this example to make the point that it may be thought desirable to suppress an opinion which is not thought to be false. He thinks that this fact points to a confusion in Mill. "Mill, and any reasonable political theorist, must acknowledge that we can make well-founded judgments about the harmful effects of actions, speeches, articles, and books" [p. 48 of this book]. But Mill would say that we cannot make this or any other well-founded judgment without considering carefully all that can be said against it, which in his view involves public discussion. He also says that any public discussion of the harmfulness of an opinion will involve some discussion of its truth, since the effects of suppressing a true opinion will be different from the effects of suppressing a false one. If there were any doubt about the accuracy of the statistics McCloskey mentions, the case for suppressing them would be stronger.

The main point is that one cannot trust the authorities (or oneself) to take repressive (or any other) action wisely unless there is a general atmosphere of free discussion, which will force one to consider all the objections to the proposed course of action. But to suppress opinion is to destroy that atmosphere, at least to some extent. There will always be a temptation to suppose, once this atmosphere has been built up, that it is now safe to suppress at least some inconvenient opinions. But to do so is to kick away the ladder by which one has climbed, or at least to make it less secure. It is largely on this ground that Mill argues that, in the long run and taking account of all the indirect effects, suppression will always do more harm than good. In the nature of the case, the point cannot be proved conclusively; but there does seem to be a good deal to support it.

What Rights Do We Have?
Ronald Dworkin

I. No Right To Liberty

Do we have a right to liberty?[1] Thomas Jefferson thought so, and since his day the right to liberty has received more play than the competing rights he mentioned to life and the pursuit of happiness. Liberty gave its name to the most influential political movement of the last century, and many of those who now despise liberals do so on the ground that they are not sufficiently libertarian. Of course, almost everyone concedes that the right to liberty is not the only political right, and that therefore claims to freedom must be limited, for example, by restraints that protect the security or property of others. Nevertheless the consensus in favor of some right to liberty is a vast one, though it is, as I shall argue in this chapter, misguided.

The right to liberty is popular all over this political spectrum. The rhetoric of liberty fuels every radical movement from international wars of liberation to campaigns for sexual freedom and women's liberation. But liberty has been even more prominent in conservative service. Even the mild social reorganizations of the anti-trust and unionization movements, and of the early New Deal, were opposed

Reprinted by permission of the author and publisher from *Taking Rights Seriously* by Ronald Dworkin. Cambridge, Mass.: Harvard University Press, copyright © 1977, 1978 by Ronald Dworkin. Footnotes have been renumbered.

[1] I use *liberty* in this essay in the sense Isaiah Berlin called "negative".

on the grounds that they infringed the right to liberty, and just now efforts to achieve some racial justice in America through techniques like the busing of black and white schoolchildren, and social justice in Britain through constraints in private education are bitterly opposed on that ground.

It has become common, indeed, to describe the great social issues of domestic politics, and in particular the racial issue, as presenting a conflict between the demands of liberty and equality. It may be, it is said, that the poor and the black and the uneducated and the unskilled have an abstract right to equality, but the prosperous and the whites and the educated and the able have a right to liberty as well and any efforts at social reorganization in aid of the first set of rights must reckon with and respect the second. Everyone except extremists recognizes, therefore, the need to compromise between equality and liberty. Every piece of important social legislation, from tax policy to integration plans, is shaped by the supposed tension between these two goals.

I have this supposed conflict between equality and liberty in mind when I ask whether we have a *right* to liberty, as Jefferson and everyone else has supposed. That is a crucial question. If freedom to choose one's schools, or employees, or neighborhood is simply something that we all want, like air conditioning or lobsters, then we are not entitled to hang on to these freedoms in the face of what we concede to be the rights of others to an equal share of respect and resources. But if we can say, not simply that we want these freedoms, but that we are ourselves entitled to them, then we have established at least a basis for demanding a compromise.

There is now a movement, for example, in favor of a proposed amendment to the constitution of the United States that would guarantee every school child the legal right to attend a "neighborhood school" and thus outlaw busing. The suggestion, that neighborhood schools somehow rank with jury trials as constitutional values, would seem silly but for the sense many Americans have that forcing school children into buses is somehow as much an interference with the fundamental right to liberty as segregated schooling was an insult to equality. But that seems to me absurd; indeed it seems to me absurd to suppose that men and women have any general right to liberty at all, at least as liberty has traditionally been conceived by its champions.

I have in mind the traditional definition of liberty as the absence of constraints placed by a government upon what a man might do if he wants to. Isaiah Berlin, in the most famous modern essay on liberty, put the matter this way: "The sense of freedom, in which I use this term, entails not simply the absence of frustration but the absence of obstacles to possible choices and activities—absence of obstructions on roads along which a man can decide to walk." This conception of liberty as license is neutral amongst the various activities a man might pursue, the various roads he might wish to walk. It diminishes a man's liberty when we prevent him from talking or making love as he wishes, but it also diminishes his liberty when we prevent him from murdering or defaming others. These latter constraints may be justifiable, but only because they are compromises necessary to protect the liberty or security of others, and not because they do not, in themselves, infringe the independent value of liberty. Bentham said that any law whatsoever is an "infraction" of liberty, and though some such infractions might be necessary, it is obscurantist to pretend that they are not infractions after all. In this neutral, all embracing sense of liberty as license, liberty and equality are plainly in competition. Laws are needed to protect equality, and laws are inevitably compromises of liberty.

Liberals like Berlin are content with this neutral sense of liberty, because it seems to encourage clear thinking. It allows us to identify just what is lost, though perhaps unavoidably, when men accept constraints on their actions for some other goal or value. It would be an intolerable muddle, in this view, to use the concept of liberty or freedom in such a way that we counted a loss of freedom only when men were prevented from doing something that we thought they ought to do. It would allow totalitarian governments to masquerade as liberal, simply by arguing that they prevent men from doing only what is wrong. Worse, it would obscure the most distinctive point of the liberal tradition, which is that interfering with a man's free choice to do what he might want to do is in and of itself an insult to humanity, a wrong that may be justified but can never be wiped away by competing considerations. For a true liberal, any constraint upon freedom is something that a decent government must regret, and keep to the minimum necessary to accommodate the other rights of its constituents.

In spite of this tradition, however, the neutral sense of liberty seems to me to have caused more confusion than it has cured, particularly when it is joined to the popular and inspiring idea that men and women have a right to liberty. For we can maintain that idea only by so watering down the idea of a right that the right to liberty is something hardly worth having at all.

The term *right* is used in politics and philosophy in many different senses, some of which I have tried to disentangle elsewhere.[2] In order sensibly to ask whether we have a right to liberty in the neutral sense, we must fix on some one meaning of *right*. It would not be difficult to find a sense of that term in which we could say with some confidence that men have a right to liberty. We might say, for example, that someone has a right to liberty if it is in his interest to have liberty, that is, if he either wants it or if it would be good for him to have it. In this sense, I would be prepared to concede that citizens have a right to liberty. But in this sense I would also have to concede that they have a right, at least generally, to vanilla ice cream. My concession about liberty, moreover, would have very little value in political debate. I should want to claim, for example, that people have a right to equality in a much stronger sense, that they do not simply want equality but that they are entitled to it, and I would therefore not recognize the claim that some men and women want liberty as requiring any compromise in the efforts that I believe are necessary to give other men and women the equality to which they are entitled.

If the right to liberty is to play the role cut out for it in political debate, therefore, it must be a right in a much stronger sense. In Chapter 7 [of *Taking Rights Seriously*] I defined a strong sense of right that seems to me to capture the claims

[2]See *Taking Rights Seriously*, Chapter 7.

men mean to make when they appeal to political and moral rights. I do not propose to repeat my analysis here, but only to summarize it in this way. A successful claim of right, in the strong sense I described, has this consequence. If someone has a right to something, then it is wrong for the government to deny it to him even though it would be in the general interest to do so. This sense of a right (which might be called the anti-utilitarian concept of a right) seems to me very close to the sense of right principally used in political and legal writing and argument in recent years. It marks the distinctive concept of an individual right against the State which is the heart, for example, of constitutional theory in the United States.

I do not think that the right to liberty would come to very much, or have much power in political argument, if it relied on any sense of the right any weaker than that. If we settle on this concept of a right, however, then it seems plain that there exists no general right to liberty as such. I have no political right to drive up Lexington Avenue. If the government chooses to make Lexington Avenue one-way down town, it is a sufficient justification that this would be in the general interest, and it would be ridiculous for me to argue that for some reason it would nevertheless be wrong. The vast bulk of the laws which diminish my liberty are justified on utilitarian grounds, as being in the general interest or for the general welfare; if, as Bentham supposes, each of these laws diminishes my liberty, they nevertheless do not take away from me any thing that I have a right to have. It will not do, in the one-way street case, to say that although I have a right to drive up Lexington Avenue, nevertheless the government for special reasons is justified in overriding that right. That seems silly because the government needs no special justification—but only *a* justification—for this sort of legislation. So I can have a political right to liberty, such that every act of constraint diminishes or infringes that right, only in such a weak sense of right that the so-called right to liberty is not competitive with strong rights, like the right to equality, at all. In any strong sense of right, which would be competitive with the right to equality, there exists no general right to liberty at all.

It may now be said that I have misunderstood the claim that there is a right to liberty. It does not mean to argue, it will be said, that there is a right to all liberty, but simply to important or basic liberties. Every law is, as Bentham said, an infraction of liberty, but we have a right to be protected against only fundamental or serious infractions. If the constraint on liberty is serious or severe enough, then it is indeed true that the government is not entitled to impose that constraint simply because that would be in the general interest; the government is not entitled to constrain liberty of speech, for example, whenever it thinks that would improve the general welfare. So there is, after all, a general right to liberty as such, provided that that right is restricted to important liberties or serious deprivations. This qualification does not affect the political arguments I described earlier, it will be said, because the rights to liberty that stand in the way of full equality are rights to basic liberties like, for example, the right to attend a school of one's choice.

But this qualification raises an issue of great importance for liberal theory, which those who argue for a right to liberty do not face. What does it mean to say that the right to liberty is limited to basic liberties, or that it offers protection only against serious infractions of liberty? That claim might be spelled out in two different ways, with very different theoretical and practical consequences. Let us suppose two cases in which government constrains a citizen from doing what he might want to do: the government prevents him from speaking his mind on political issues; from driving his car uptown on Lexington Avenue. What is the connection between these two cases, and the difference between them, such that though they are both cases in which a citizen is constrained and deprived of liberty, his right to liberty is infringed only in the first, and not in the second?

On the first of the two theories we might consider, the citizen is deprived of the same commodity, namely liberty, in both cases, but the difference is that in the first case the amount of that commodity taken away from him is, for some reason, either greater in amount or greater in its impact than in the second. But that seems bizarre. It is very difficult to think of liberty as a commodity. If we do try to give liberty some operational sense, such that we can measure the relative diminution of liberty occasioned by different sorts of laws or constraints, then the result is unlikely to match our intuitive sense of what are basic liberties and what are not. Suppose, for example, we measure a diminution in liberty by calculating the extent of frustration that it induces. We shall then have to face the fact that laws against theft, and even traffic laws, impose constraints that are felt more keenly by most men than constraints on political speech would be. We might take a different tack, and measure the degree of loss of liberty by the impact that a particular constraint has on future choices. But we should then have to admit that the ordinary criminal code reduces choice for most men more than laws which forbid fringe political activity. So the first theory—that the difference between cases covered and those not covered by our supposed right to liberty is a matter of degree—must fail.

The second theory argues that the difference between the two cases has to do, not with the degree of liberty involved, but with the special character of the liberty involved in the case covered by the right. On this theory, the offense involved in a law that limits free speech is of a different character, and not just different in degree, from a law that prevents a man from driving up Lexington Avenue. That sounds plausible, though as we shall see it is not easy to state what this difference in character comes to, or why it argues for a right in some cases though not in others. My present point, however, is that if the distinction between basic liberties and other liberties is defended in this way, then the notion of a general right to liberty as such has been entirely abandoned. If we have a right to basic liberties not because they are cases in which the commodity of liberty is somehow especially at stake, but because an assault on basic liberties injures us or demeans us in some way that goes beyond its impact on liberty, then what we have a right to is not liberty at all, but to the values or interests or standing that this particular constraint defeats.

This is not simply a question of terminology. The idea of a right to liberty is a misconceived concept that does a disservice to political thought in at least two ways. First, the idea creates a false sense of a necessary conflict between liberty and other values when social regulation, like the busing program, is proposed. Second, the idea provides too easy an answer to the question of why we regard certain kinds of restraints, like the restraint on free speech or the exercise of religion, as especially unjust. The idea of a right to liberty allows us to say that these constraints are unjust because they have a special impact on liberty as such. Once we recognize that this answer is spurious, then we shall have to face the difficult question of what is indeed at stake in these cases.

I should like to turn at once to that question. If there is no general right to liberty, then why do citizens in a democracy have rights to any specific kind of liberty, like freedom of speech or religion or political activity? It is no answer to say that if individuals have these rights, then the community will be better off in the long run as a whole. This idea—that individual rights may lead to overall utility—may or may not be true, but it is irrelevant to the defence of rights as such, because when we say that someone has a right to speak his mind freely, in the relevant political sense, we mean that he is entitled to do so even if this would not be in the general interest. If we want to defend individual rights in the sense in which we claim them, then we must try to discover something beyond utility that argues for these rights.

I mentioned one possibility earlier. We might be able to make out a case that individuals suffer some special damage when the traditional rights are invaded. On this argument, there is something about the liberty to speak out on political issues such that if that liberty is denied the individual suffers a special kind of damage which makes it wrong to inflict that damage upon him even though the community as a whole would benefit. This line of argument will appeal to those who themselves would feel special deprivation at the loss of their political and civil liberties, but it is nevertheless a difficult argument to pursue for two reasons.

First, there are a great many men and women and they undoubtedly form the majority even in democracies like Britain and the United States, who do not exercise political liberties that they have, and who would not count the loss of these liberties as especially grievous. Second, we lack a psychological theory which would justify and explain the idea that the loss of civil liberties, or any particular liberties, involves inevitable or even likely psychological damage. On the contrary, there is now a lively tradition in psychology, led by psychologists like Ronald Laing, who argue that a good deal of mental instability in modern societies may be traced to the demand for too much liberty rather than too little. In their account, the need to choose, which follows from liberty, is an unnecessary source of destructive tension. These theories are not necessarily persuasive, but until we can be confident that they are wrong, we cannot assume that psychology demonstrates the opposite, however appealing that might be on political grounds.

If we want to argue for a right to certain liberties, therefore, we must find another ground. We must argue on grounds of political morality that it is wrong to deprive individuals of these liberties, for some reason, apart from direct psychological damage, in spite of the fact that the common interest would be served by doing so. I put the matter this vaguely because there is no reason to assume, in advance, that only one kind of reason would support that moral position. It might be that a just society would recognize a variety of individual rights, some grounded on very different sorts of moral considerations from others. In what remains of this chapter I shall try to describe only one possible ground for rights. It does not follow that men and women in civil society have only the rights that the argument I shall make would support; but it does follow that they have at least these rights, and that is important enough.

II. The Right To Liberties

The central concept of my argument will be the concept not of liberty but of equality. I presume that we all accept the following postulates of political morality. Government must treat those whom it governs with concern, that is, as human beings who are capable of suffering and frustration, and with respect, that is, as human beings who are capable of forming and acting on intelligent conceptions of how their lives should be lived. Government must not only treat people with concern and respect, but with equal concern and respect. It must not distribute goods or opportunities unequally on the ground that some citizens are entitled to more because they are worthy of more concern. It must not constrain liberty on the ground that one citizen's conception of the good life of one group is nobler or superior to another's. These postulates, taken together, state what might be called the liberal conception of equality; but it is a conception of equality, not of liberty as license, that they state.

The sovereign question of political theory, within a state supposed to be governed by the liberal conception of equality, is the question of what inequalities in goods, opportunities and liberties are permitted in such a state, and why. The beginning of an answer lies in the following distinction. Citizens governed by the liberal conception of equality each have a right to equal concern and respect. But there are two different rights that might be comprehended by that abstract right. The first is the right to equal treatment, that is, to the same distribution of goods or opportunities as anyone else has or is given. The Supreme Court, in the Reapportionment Cases, held that citizens have a right to equal treatment in the distribution of voting power; it held that one man must be given one vote in spite of the fact that a different distribution of votes might in fact work for the general benefit. The second is the right to treatment as an equal. This is the right, not to an equal distribution of some good or opportunity, but the right to equal concern and respect in the political decision about how these goods and opportunities are to be distributed. Suppose the question is raised whether an economic policy that injures long-term bondholders is in the general interest. Those who will be injured have a right that their prospective loss be taken into account in deciding whether the general interest is served by the policy. They may not simply be ignored in that calculation. But when their interest is taken into account it may nevertheless be outweighed by the interests of others who will gain from the policy, and in that case their right to equal concern and respect, so defined, would provide no objection. In the case of economic policy, therefore, we might wish to say that those who will be injured if inflation is permitted have a right to treatment as equals in the decision whether that policy would serve the general interest, but no right to equal treatment that would outlaw the policy even if it passed that test.

I propose that the right to treatment as an equal must be taken to be fundamental under the liberal conception of equality, and that the more restrictive right to equal treatment holds only in those special circumstances in which, for some special reason, it follows from the more fundamental right, as perhaps it does in the special circumstance of the Reapportionment Cases. I also propose that individual rights to distinct liberties must be recognized only when the fundamental right to treatment as an equal can be shown to require these rights. If this is correct, then the right to distinct liberties does not conflict with any supposed competing right to equality, but on the contrary follows from a conception of equality conceded to be more fundamental.

I must now show, however, how the familiar rights to distinct liberties—those established, for example, in the United States constitution—might be thought to be required by that fundamental conception of equality. I shall try to do this, for present purposes, only by providing a skeleton of the more elaborate argument that would have to be made to defend any particular liberty on this basis, and then show why it would be plausible to expect that the more familiar political and civil liberties would be supported by such an argument if it were in fact made.

A government that respects the liberal conception of equality may properly constrain liberty only on certain very limited types of justification. I shall adopt, for purposes of making this point, the following crude typology of political justifications. There are, first, arguments of principle, which support a particular constraint on liberty on the argument that the constraint is required to protect the distinct right of some individual who will be injured by the exercise of the liberty. There are, second, arguments of policy, which support constraints on the different ground that such constraints are required to reach some overall political goal, that is, to realize some state of affairs in which the community as a whole, and not just certain individuals, are better off by virtue of the constraint. Arguments of policy might be further subdivided in this way. Utilitarian arguments of policy argue that the community as a whole will be better off because (to put the point roughly) more of its citizens will have more of what they want overall, even though some of them will have less. Ideal arguments of policy, on the other hand, argue that the community will be better off, not because more of its members will have more of what they want, but because the community will be in some way closer to an ideal community, whether its members desire the improvement in question or not.

The liberal conception of equality sharply limits the extent to which ideal arguments of policy may be used to justify any constraint on liberty. Such arguments cannot be used if the idea in question is itself controversial within the community. Constraints cannot be defended, for example, directly on the ground that they contribute to a culturally sophisticated community, whether the community wants the sophistication or not, because that argument would violate the canon of the liberal conception of equality that prohibits a government from relying on the claim that certain forms of life are inherently more valuable than others.

Utilitarian arguments of policy, however, would seem secure from that objection. They do not suppose that any form of life is inherently more valuable than any other, but instead base their claim, that constraints on liberty are necessary to advance some collective goal of the community, just on the fact that that goal happens to be desired more widely or more deeply than any other. Utilitarian arguments of policy, therefore, seem not to oppose but on the contrary to embody the fundamental right of equal concern and respect, because they treat the wishes of each member of the community on a par with the wishes of any other, with no bonus or discount reflecting the view that that member is more or less worthy of concern, or his views more or less worthy of respect, than any other.

This appearance of egalitarianism has, I think, been the principal source of the great appeal that utilitarianism has had, as a general political philosophy, over the last century. In Chapter 9 [of *Taking Rights Seriously*], however, I pointed out that the egalitarian character of a utiliarian argument is often an illusion. I will not repeat, but only summarize, my argument here.

Utilitarian arguments fix on the fact that a particular constraint on liberty will make more people happier, or satisfy more of their preferences, depending upon whether psychological or preference utilitarianism is in play. But people's overall preference for one policy rather than another may be seen to include, on further analysis, both preferences that are *personal*, because they state a preference for the assignment of one set of goods or opportunities to him and preferences that are *external*, because they state a preference for one assignment of goods or opportunities to others. But a utilitarian argument that assigns critical weight to the external preferences of members of the community will not be egalitarian in the sense under consideration. It will not respect the right of everyone to be treated with equal concern and respect.

Suppose, for example, that a number of individuals in the community holds racist rather than utilitarian political theories. They believe, not that each man is to count for one and no one for more than one in the distribution of goods, but rather that a black man is to count for less and a white man therefore to count for more than one. That is an external preference, but it is nevertheless a genuine preference for one policy rather than another, the satisfaction of which will bring pleasure. Nevertheless if this preference or pleasure is given the normal weight in a utilitarian calculation, and blacks suffer accordingly, then their own assignment of goods and opportunities will depend, not simply on the competition among personal preferences that abstract statements of utilitarianism suggest, but precisely on the fact that they are thought less worthy of concern and respect than others are.

Suppose, to take a different case, that many members of the community disapprove on moral grounds of homosexuality, or contraception, or pornography, or expressions of adherence to the Communist party. They prefer not only that they themselves do not indulge in these activities, but that no one else does so either, and they believe that a community that permits rather than prohibits these acts is inherently a worse community. These are external preferences, but, once again, they are no less genuine, nor less a source of pleasure when satisfied and displeasure when ignored, than purely personal preferences. Once again, however, if these external preferences are counted, so as to justify a constraint on liberty, then those constrained suffer, not simply because their personal preferences have lost in a competition for scarce resources with the personal preferences of others, but precisely because their conception of a proper or desirable form of life is despised by others.

These arguments justify the following important conclusion. If utilitarian arguments of policy are to be used to justify constraints on liberty, then care must be taken to insure that the utilitarian calculations on which the argument is based fix only on personal and ignore external preferences. That is an important conclusion for political theory because it shows, for example, why the arguments of John Stuart Mill in *On Liberty* are not counter-utilitarian but, on the contrary, arguments in service of the only defensible form of utilitarianism.

Important as that conclusion is at the level of political philosophy, however, it is in itself of limited practical significance, because it will be impossible to devise political procedures that will accurately discriminate between personal and external preferences. Representative democracy is widely thought to be the institutional structure most suited, in a complex and diverse society, to the identification and achievement of utilitarian policies. It works imperfectly at this, for the familiar reason that majoritarianism cannot sufficiently take account of the intensity, as distinct from the number, of particular preferences, and because techniques of political persuasion, backed by money, may corrupt the accuracy with which votes represent the genuine preferences of those who have voted. Nevertheless democracy seems to enforce utilitarianism more satisfactorily, in spite of these imperfections, than any alternative general political scheme would.

But democracy cannot discriminate, within the overall preferences imperfectly revealed by voting, distinct personal and external components, so as to provide a method for enforcing the former while ignoring the latter. An actual vote in an election or referendum must be taken to represent an overall preference rather than some component of the preference that a skillful cross-examination of the individual voter, if time and expense permitted, would reveal. Personal and external preferences are sometimes so inextricably combined, moreover, that the discrimination is psychologically as well as institutionally impossible. That will be true, for example, in the case of the associational preferences that many people have for members of one race, or people of one talent or quality, rather than another, for this is a personal preference so parasitic upon external preferences that it is impossible to say, even as a matter of introspection, what personal preferences would remain if the underlying external preference were removed. It is also true of certain self-denying preferences that many individuals have; that is preferences for less of a certain good on the assumption, or rather proviso, that other people will have more. That is also a preference, however noble, that is parasitic upon external preferences, in the shape of political and moral theories, and they may no more be counted in a defensible utilitarian argument than less attractive preferences rooted in prejudice rather than altruism.

I wish now to propose the following general theory of rights. The concept of an individual political right, in the strong anti-utilitarian sense I distinguished earlier, is a response to the philosophical defects of a utilitarianism that counts external preferences and the practical impossibility of a utilitarianism that does not. It allows us to enjoy the institutions of political democracy, which enforce overall or unrefined utilitarianism, and yet protect the fundamental right of citizens to equal concern and respect by prohibiting decisions that seem, antecedently, likely to have been reached by virtue of the external components of the preferences democracy reveals.

It should be plain how this theory of rights might be used to support the idea, which is the subject of this chapter, that we have distinct rights to certain liberties like the liberty of free expression and of free choice in personal and sexual relations. It might be shown that any utilitarian constraint on these liberties must be based on overall preferences in the community that we know, from our general knowledge of society, are likely to contain large components of external preferences, in the shape of political or moral theories, which the political process cannot discriminate and eliminate. It is not, as I said, my present purpose to frame the arguments that would have to be made to defend particular rights to liberty in this way, but only to show the general character such arguments might have.

I do wish, however, to mention one alleged right that might be called into question by my general argument, which is the supposed individual right to the free use of property. In chapter 11 [of *Taking Rights Seriously*] I complained about the argument, popular in certain quarters, that it is inconsistent for liberals to defend a liberty of speech, for example, and not also concede a parallel right of some sort of property and its use. There might be force in that argument if the claim, that we have a right of free speech, depended on the more general proposition that we have a right to something called liberty as such. But that general idea is untenable and incoherent; there is no such thing as any general right to liberty. The argument for any given specific liberty may therefore be entirely independent of the argument for any other, and there is no antecedent inconsistency or even implausibility in contending for one while disputing the other.

What can be said, on the general theory of rights I offer, for any particular right of property? What can be said, for example, in favor of the right to liberty of contract sustained by the Supreme Court in the famous *Lochner* case, and later regretted, not only by the court, but by liberals generally? I cannot think of any argument that a political decision to limit such a right, in the way in which minimum wage laws limited it, is antecedently likely to give effect to external preferences, and in that way offend the right of those whose liberty is curtailed to equal concern and respect. If, as I think, no such argument can be made out, then the alleged right might not exist; in any case there can be no inconsistency in denying that it exists while warmly defending a right to other liberties.

The Concept of an Absolute Constitutional Right

Joel Feinberg

A controversy has raged in recent years over whether constitutional rights, especially those guaranteed by the First Amendment, should be interpreted by the courts as "absolute." Many First Amendment cases were decided by the U.S. Supreme Court in the period from 1959–1962 over the eloquent dissents of Justice Hugo Black, the leading spokesman for the "absolutist" position. Justice Black in one case insisted that "the First Amendment means what it says."[1] What the First Amendment *says* is:

> Congress shall make no law respecting an establishment of religion, or prohibiting the free exercise thereof; or abridging the freedom of speech, or of the press; or the right of the people peaceably to assemble, and to petition the Government for a redress of grievances.

"I read 'no law . . . abridging,'" said Justice Black, "to mean *no law abridging*,"[2] which is to say (he makes clear) that the First Amendment prohibition is complete, exceptionless, and unconditional: ". . . the principles of the First Amendment are stated in precise and mandatory terms and unless they are applied in those

From *Social Philosophy*, copyright © 1973 by Prentice-Hall, Inc. Reprinted by permission. Footnotes have been renumbered.

[1]Barenblatt v. United States, 360 U.S. 109, 143–44 (1959). Dissenting opinion.
[2]Smith v. California, 361 U.S. 147, 157 (1959). Concurring opinion.

terms, the freedoms of religion, speech, press, assembly, and petition will have no effective protection."[3]

The opposing position, and the one that actually prevailed in the early 1960s, is most frequently associated with the late Justice Felix Frankfurter. In this view, there are no absolute rights, even in the First Amendment, and when the interest protected by a constitutional right conflicts with a weightier interest in public safety or public order, the courts must permit infringement of the right. In one free speech case, Frankfurter declared that "The demands of free speech in a democratic society as well as the interest in national security are better served by candid and informed weighing of the competing interests, within the confines of the judicial process, than by announcing dogmas too inflexible for the . . . problems to be solved."[4] The alternative to inflexible dogmas is the method of ad hoc "interest-balancing." Even when a judicially recognized constitutional right is on one side of the balance, it might be invaded or even "infringed" when the interest on the other side more than balances it:

> *We agree that compulsory disclosure of the names of an organization's members may in certain instances infringe constitutionally protected rights of association. . . . But to say this much is only to recognize one of the points of reference from which analysis must begin. . . . Against the impediments which particular governmental regulation causes to entire freedom of individual action, there must be weighed the value to the public of the end which the regulation may achieve.*[5]

It is of course beyond the scope of this work to decide whether any American constitutional rights *are* absolute. The philosophically prior question is: How *could* a right be "absolute"? What can it *mean* to say of a right that it is absolute? One source of confusion can be eliminated by a distinction between a right's *scope* and its degree of *incumbency* within that scope. It is plain that such First Amendment rights as free speech cannot be unlimited in scope; no one can expect the courts to guarantee his "right" to say anything, any time, any place. If there were such a right there could be no law of defamation, no protection against fraud, no penalty for solicitation to crime, and, in short, no protection of other rights as vital to private and public interests as free speech itself. Consequently, various implicit exceptive clauses must be understood as part of the rule that spells out the right to free speech. Some of these clauses presumably were understood at the time the First Amendment was adopted, for there was even then a well-developed body of law on defamation, fraud, incitement, and solicitation. Other exceptions have no doubt developed slowly through the piecemeal evolution of the common law and forced judicial clarifications of borderline cases. As a result, the boundaries of the right's domain have become reasonably clear and stable, though there may still

[3]Wilkinson v. United States, 365 U.S. 399, 422–23 (1961). Dissenting opinion.
[4]Dennis v. United States, 341 U.S. 524–25 (1951).
[5]Communist Party v. Subversive Activities Control Board, 367 U.S. 190–91 (1961).

be occasional waverings, and controversial marginal cases on both sides of the boundaries may always exist.

First Amendment rights, then, are not "absolute" in the sense of "unlimited in scope": the scope of free speech must necessarily be narrower than the range of all possible speech. But that is no reason why these rights, as qualified by exceptive clauses, cannot be absolute in the sense of laying *unconditionally incumbent* duties of respect and enforcement upon the courts. A rule with exceptive clauses may itself have no exceptions. A First Amendment right, in short, may be limited in extent by the definitions of established judicial rules, yet be unconditionally obligatory within its proper domain. The courts would decide whether a given exercise of free speech, for example, falls *clearly* within the boundaries of First Amendment protection; if it does, then any statute that prohibits it, or any governmental action that restricts it, must be declared unconstitutional. If the speech in question falls in the vague no man's land near the right's wavering boundaries, the court must further clarify the law and fix its boundaries by whatever procedures of constitutional interpretation (perhaps including "interest-balancing") are open to it. But once having pronounced the act in question to be within the area of constitutional protection, on the intelligible "absolutistic" view we are considering, it is no longer open to the court to "weigh" that protection against other considerations, for the constitution says that its guaranteed rights, once correctly determined, always have more weight than any possible combination of opposing interests, private or public.

The "defining of absolutes" method is possible only in a legal system of sufficient maturity to have reasonably settled boundary lines, established after much conflict and redefinition through explicit and implicitly understood exceptive clauses, between the various rights it confers. The method presupposes that each right, no matter how vague its boundaries at the periphery, has a central core of clear and certain cases that are (unless resort is made to constitutional amendment) permanently and unconditionally established. Thus, it is always open to an American citizen, without any question, to express in speech or writing his opinion that a policy of his government is unwise, unjust, or otherwise mistaken, or his opinion as to "what the public welfare requires."[6] It is unconditionally open to an American to receive without interference the sacraments of his church, or to have some time and place to engage in prayer or worship, or simply to be a member of a church. These activities are at the "hard core" of the free exercise of religion right, well away from the boundaries with other rights, unrestricted by legislated exceptive clauses, and unencumbranced.

Laurent Frantz has pointed out that some constitutional rights other than those in the First Amendment are universally accepted as absolutely unconditional in their central core cases. If an accused person is to be denied the right to counsel, the Constitution will have to be amended first, for its guarantee is not subject to judicial overruling as a result of "interest-balancing" in a given case. It is simply not

---

[6]Laurent B. Frantz, "The First Amendment in the Balance," *Yale Law Journal*, LXXI (1962), 1438.

open to courts to balance a clearly defined and acknowledged right against *any* interests, even those in public safety and public welfare. If, on the other hand, a court could weigh interests against acknowledged core cases of constitutional rights, case by case, then the results might be contrary to everyone's present understanding:

> *Defendants in criminal cases can be tried in secret, or held incommunicado without trial, can be denied knowledge of the accusation against them, and the right to counsel, and the right to call witnesses in their own defense, and the right to trial by jury. Ex post facto laws and bills of attainder can be passed. Habeas corpus can be suspended, though there is neither rebellion nor invasion. Private property can be taken for public use without just, or any, compensation. Suffrage qualifications based on sex or race can be reinstituted. Anything which the Constitution says cannot be done can be done, if Congress thinks and the Court agrees (or is unwilling to set aside the congressional judgment) that the interests thereby served outweighed those which were sacrificed. Thus the whole idea of a government of limited powers, and of a written constitution as a device for attaining that end, is at least potentially at stake.[7]*

Are these hard core rights *never*, under any conceivable circumstances, abridgeable? (They are of course subject to change by constitutional amendment, but that is another matter.) Is an individual to be given his rights even if the whole public safety or welfare must be sacrificed in the process, or national independence lost as a consequence? Would it not be better in extreme emergencies, where all that is precious rides on what we do, to deny a given individual his opinion, his sacrament, his trial by jury? *Better*, perhaps, or wiser, or more prudent, or even more justifiable on the whole, but still a desperate emergency measure, like the amputation of a limb. It would be the sacrifice of legality itself, of justice, of an undenied right, for the sake of something held even more important. Perhaps courts *ought* to infringe rights in desperate circumstances, but that can never be their understood legal function. If or when judges take such desperate extralegal steps, their actions are special, ad hoc, and presumably sorrowful infringements or suspensions of rights, not the authoritative redefining of right-boundaries, or the official denial that a right existed in the first place. "One's need for a new car," wrote Frantz, "may be balanced against the other uses to which the same money might be put but not against 'Thou shalt not steal.'"[8] In truly extraordinary circumstances, one might conceivably be justified, in one's own conscience, in stealing another's car, but that justification doesn't affect the shape of the other's property rights. A justified violation of another's legal rights is still a violation of his rights, which one can never have a legal right to do. The point applies even to violations by courts of law.

[7]Frantz, "The First Amendment in the Balance," 1445.
[8]Frantz, "The First Amendment in the Balance," 1440.

A guaranteed *right*, "absolute" within its established sphere, adds something of great importance to a liberty, or a "mere privilege," or a "right" that is vulnerable to overturning by interest-balancing procedures. When the government leaves me at liberty (merely) to do X, it tells me in effect that I may do X if I can, but it will not protect me by imposing a duty of noninterference upon others. A liberty is a permission without a protection. A "mere privilege" may or may not add protection to the permission. When it does, the privilege looks more like a right than like a liberty. Unlike rights, however, neither the permission nor the continued protection are assured; either can be withdrawn at any time at the state's pleasure, although the holder of a privilege will be warned in advance that withdrawal is coming. It would be otherwise with a so-called nonabsolute right. When the government grants me a "right" that is vulnerable to interest-balancing tests even at its core, it tells me, in effect, that I may do X and others may not interfere, *but* that this permission cum protection does not apply whenever the state finds it useful to withdraw it, without prior warning, in a given case. "When you speak quietly at a private gathering," says the state, "you may say anything you please about the wisdom of a government policy *unless* a court later determines that interfering with your right at the time was more conducive to the public interest than protecting it." Such a right begins to resemble a so-called prima-facie right in that its exceptive clause is virtually unspecified and unlimited. It is only a small parody to interpret the prima-facie right as permission to do anything except what one shouldn't, and to interpret the nonabsolute "right" as permission to do anything for which permission is not subsequently withdrawn. These are hardly "rights" that one can stand upon, demand, fight for, or treasure. They are "rights" that make men humble, not claims that make men bold.

Paris Adult Theatre I v. *Slaton*, 413 U.S. 49 (1973)

[This case involved the showing of two films in a theater in Atlanta, Georgia. The state of Georgia sought to enjoin the showing of the films, claiming they were obscene under Georgia law. The injunction was initially denied, but the Georgia Supreme Court reversed the trial court decision. On appeal, the U.S. Supreme Court held that the Georgia law did not violate the protections of the First Amendment. Included here is Part II of the majority opinion, written by Chief Justice Burger, and excerpted portions of the dissenting opinion of Mr. Justice Brennan. Case citations have been edited, and footnotes renumbered.]

Opinion of the Court

We categorically disapprove the theory, apparently adopted by the trial judge, that obscene, pornographic films acquire constitutional immunity from state regulation simply because they are exhibited for consenting adults only. This holding was properly rejected by the Georgia Supreme Court. Although we have often pointedly recognized the high importance of the state interest in regulating the exposure of obscene materials to juveniles and unconsenting adults, . . . this Court has never declared these to be the only legitimate state interests permitting regulation of obscene material. The States have a long-recognized legitimate interest in regulating the use of obscene material in local commerce and in all places of public accommodation, as long as these regulations do not run afoul of specific constitutional prohibitions. . . . "In an unbroken series of cases extending over a long stretch of this Court's history, it has been accepted as a postulate that 'the primary requirements of decency may be enforced against obscene publications.' (*Near* v. *Minnesota*, 283 U. S. 697, 716 [1931])." *Kingsley Books, Inc.* v. *Brown*, 354 U.S. 436 (1957).

In particular, we hold that there are legitimate state interests at stake in stemming the tide of commercialized obscenity, even assuming it is feasible to enforce effective safeguards against exposure to juveniles and to passersby.[1] Rights and interests "other than those of the advocates are involved." *Breard* v. *Alexandria*, 341 U. S. 622, 642 (1951). These include the interest of the public in the quality of life and the total community environment, the tone of commerce in the great city centers, and, possibly, the public safety itself. The Hill-Link Minority Report of the Commission on Obscenity and Pornography indicates that there is at least an arguable correlation between obscene material and crime.[2] Quite apart from sex crimes, however, there remains one problem of large proportions aptly described by Professor Bickel:

> It concerns the tone of the society, the mode, or to use terms that have perhaps greater currency, the style and quality of life, now and in the

---

[1] It is conceivable that an "adult" theater can—if it really insists—prevent the exposure of its obscene wares to juveniles. An "adult" bookstore, dealing in obscene books, magazines, and pictures, cannot realistically make this claim. The Hill-Link Minority Report of the Commission on Obscenity and Pornography emphasizes evidence (the Abelson National Survey of Youth and Adults) that, although most pornography may be bought by elders, "the heavy users and most highly exposed people to pornography are adolescent females (among women) and adolescent and young adult males (among men)." *The Report of the Commission on Obscenity and Pornography* 401 (1970). The legitimate interest in preventing exposure of juveniles to obscene material cannot be fully served by simply barring juveniles from the immediate physical premises of "adult" bookstores, when there is a flourishing "outside business" in these materials.

[2] *The Report of the Commission on Obscenity and Pornography* 390–412 (1970). For a discussion of earlier studies indicating "a division of thought [among behavioral scientists] on the correlation between obscenity and socially deleterious behavior," *Memoirs* v. *Massachusetts*, 383 U. S. 413, 451 (1966), and references to expert opinions that obscene material may induce crime and antisocial conduct, see *id.*, at 451–453 (Clark, J., dissenting). Mr. Justice Clark emphasized:
"While erotic stimulation caused by pornography may be legally insignificant in itself, there are medical experts who believe that such stimulation frequently manifests itself in criminal sexual behavior or other antisocial conduct. For example, Dr. George W. Henry of Cornell University has expressed the opinion that obscenity, with its exaggerated and morbid emphasis on sex, particularly abnormal and perverted practices, and its unrealistic presentation of sexual behavior and attitudes, may induce antisocial conduct by the average person. A number of sociologists think that this material may have adverse effects upon individual mental health, with potentially disruptive consequences for the community. . . .
"Congress and the legislatures of every State have enacted measures to restrict the distribution of erotic and pornographic material, justifying these controls by reference to evidence that antisocial behavior may result in part from reading obscenity." *Id.*, at 452–453 (footnotes omitted).

future. A man may be entitled to read an obscene book in his room, or expose himself indecently there. . . . We should protect his privacy. But if he demands a right to obtain the books and pictures he wants in the market, and to foregather in public places—discreet, if you will, but accessible to all—with others who share his tastes, then to grant him his right is to affect the world about the rest of us, and to impinge on other privacies. *Even supposing that each of us can, if he wishes, effectively avert the eye and stop the ear (which, in truth, we cannot), what is commonly read and seen and heard and done intrudes upon us all, want it or not.* 22 The Public Interest 25–26 (Winter, 1971).[3] (Emphasis added.)

As Mr. Chief Justice Warren stated, there is a "right of the Nation and of the States to maintain a decent society . . . ," *Jacobellis* v. *Ohio*, 378 U. S. 184, 199 (1964) (dissenting opinion).[4] . . .

But, it is argued, there are no scientific data which conclusively demonstrate that exposure to obscene material adversely affects men and women or their society. It is urged on behalf of the petitioners that, absent such a demonstration, any kind of state regulation is "impermissible." We reject this argument. It is not for us to resolve empirical uncertainties underlying state legislation, save in the exceptional case where that legislation plainly impinges upon rights protected by the Constitution itself. Mr. Justice Brennan, speaking for the Court in *Ginsberg* v. *New York*, 390 U. S. 629, 642–643 (1968), said: "We do not demand of legislatures 'scientifically certain criteria of legislation.' *Noble State Bank* v. *Haskell*, 219 U. S. 104, 110." Although there is no conclusive proof of a connection between antisocial behavior and obscene material, the legislature of Georgia could quite reasonably determine that such a connection does or might exist. In deciding *Roth*, this Court implicitly accepted that a legislature could legitimately act on such a conclusion to protect *"the social interest in order and morality." Roth* v. *United States*, 354 U. S. at 485, quoting *Chaplinsky* v. *New Hampshire*, 315 U. S. 568, 572 (1942) (emphasis added in *Roth*).[5]

From the beginning of civilized societies, legislators and judges have acted on various unprovable assumptions. Such assumptions underlie much lawful state

[3]See also Berns, "Pornography vs. Democracy: The Case for Censorship," in 22 *The Public Interest* 3 (Winter 1971); van den Haag, in *Censorship: For & Against* 156–157 (H. Hart ed. 1971).

[4]"In this and other cases in this area of the law, which are coming to us in ever-increasing numbers, we are faced with the resolution of rights basic both to individuals and to society as a whole. Specifically, we are called upon to reconcile the right of the Nation and of the States to maintain a decent society and, on the other hand, the right of individuals to express themselves freely in accordance with the guarantees of the First and Fourteenth Amendments." Jacobellis v. Ohio, supra, at 199 (Warren, C. J., dissenting).

[5]"It has been well observed that such [lewd and obscene] *utterances are no essential part of any exposition of ideas, and are of such slight social value as a step to truth that any benefit that may be derived from them is clearly outweighed by the social interest in order and morality."* Roth v. United States, 354 U. S. 476, 485 (1957), quoting Chaplinsky v. New Hampshire, 315 U. S. 568, 572 (1942) (emphasis added in Roth).

regulation of commercial and business affairs. . . . The same is true of the federal securities and antitrust laws and a host of federal regulations. . . . On the basis of these assumptions both Congress and state legislatures have, for example, drastically restricted associational rights by adopting antitrust laws, and have strictly regulated public expression by issuers of and dealers in securities, profit sharing "coupons," and "trading stamps," commanding what they must and must not publish and announce. . . . Understandably those who entertain an absolutist view of the First Amendment find it uncomfortable to explain why rights of association, speech, and press should be severely restrained in the marketplace of goods and money, but not in the marketplace of pornography.

Likewise, when legislatures and administrators act to protect the physical environment from pollution and to preserve our resources of forests, streams, and parks, they must act on such imponderables as the impact of a new highway near or through an existing park or wilderness area. . . . Thus, §18 (a) of the Federal-Aid Highway Act of 1968, 23 U. S. C. §138, and the Department of Transportation Act of 1966, as amended, 82 Stat. 824, 49 U. S. C. §1653 (f), have been described by Mr. Justice Black as "a solemn determination of the highest lawmaking body of this Nation that the beauty and health-giving facilities of our parks are not to be taken away for public roads without hearings, fact-findings, and policy determinations under the supervision of a Cabinet officer. . . ." *Citizens to Preserve Overton Park* v. *Volpe*, 401 U. S. 402, 421 (1971) (separate opinion joined by Brennan, J.). The fact that a congressional directive reflects unprovable assumptions about what is good for the people, including imponderable aesthetic assumptions, is not a sufficient reason to find that statute unconstitutional.

If we accept the unprovable assumption that a complete education requires the reading of certain books, . . . and the well nigh universal belief that good books, plays, and art lift the spirit, improve the mind, enrich the human personality, and develop character, can we then say that a state legislature may not act on the corollary assumption that commerce in obscene books, or public exhibitions focused on obscene conduct, have a tendency to exert a corrupting and debasing impact leading to antisocial behavior? "Many of these effects may be intangible and indistinct, but they are nonetheless real." *American Power & Light Co.* v. *SEC*, 329 U. S. 90, 103 (1946). Mr. Justice Cardozo said that all laws in Western civilization are "guided by a robust common sense. . . ." *Steward Machine Co.* v. *Davis*, 301 U.S. 548, 590 (1937). The sum of experience, including that of the past two decades, affords an ample basis for legislatures to conclude that a sensitive, key relationship of human existence, central to family life, community welfare, and the development of human personality, can be debased and distorted by crass commercial exploitation of sex. Nothing in the Constitution prohibits a State from reaching such a conclusion and acting on it legislatively simply because there is no conclusive evidence or empirical data.

It is argued that individual "free will" must govern, even in activities beyond the protection of the First Amendment and other constitutional guarantees of privacy, and that government cannot legitimately impede an individual's desire to see or acquire obscene plays, movies, and books. We do indeed base our society on certain assumptions that people have the capacity for free choice. Most exercises of individual free choice—those in politics, religion, and expression of ideas—are explicitly protected by the Constitution. Totally unlimited play for free will, however, is not allowed in our or any other society. We have just noted, for example, that neither the First Amendment nor "free will" precludes States from having "blue sky" laws to regulate what sellers of securities may write or publish about their wares. See *supra,* at 90. Such laws are to protect the weak, the uninformed, the unsuspecting, and the gullible from the exercise of their own volition. Nor do modern societies leave disposal of garbage and sewage up to the individual "free will," but impose regulation to protect both public health and the appearance of public places. States are told by some that they must await a "laissez-faire" market solution to the obscenity-pornography problem, paradoxically "by people who have never otherwise had a kind word to say for laissez-faire," particularly in solving urban, commercial, and environmental pollution problems. See I. Kristol, *On the Democratic Idea in America* 37 (1972).

The States, of course, may follow such a "laissez-faire" policy and drop all controls on commercialized obscenity, if that is what they prefer, just as they can ignore consumer protection in the marketplace, but nothing in the Constitution *compels* the States to do so with regard to matters falling within state jurisdiction. . . . "We do not sit as a super-legislature to determine the wisdom, need, and propriety of laws that touch economic problems, business affairs, or social conditions." *Griswold* v. *Connecticut,* 381 U. S. 479, 482 (1965). . . .

It is asserted, however, that standards for evaluating state commercial regulations are inapposite in the present context, as state regulation of access by consenting adults to obscene material violates the constitutionally protected right to privacy enjoyed by petitioners' customers. Even assuming that petitioners have vicarious standing to assert potential customers' rights, it is unavailing to compare a theater open to the public for a fee, with the private home of *Stanley* v. *Georgia,* 394 U. S. 557, 568 (1969), at 568, and the marital bedroom of *Griswold* v. *Connecticut, supra,* at 485–486. This Court, has, on numerous occasions, refused to hold that commercial ventures such as a motion-picture house are "private" for the purpose of civil rights litigation and civil rights statutes. . . . The Civil Rights Act of 1964 specifically defines motion-picture houses and theaters as places of "public accommodation" covered by the Act as operations affecting commerce. . . .

Our prior decisions recognizing a right to privacy guaranteed by the Fourteenth Amendment included "only personal rights that can be deemed 'fundamental' or 'implicit in the concept of ordered liberty.' *Palko* v. *Connecticut,* 302 U. S. 319, 325 (1937)." *Roe* v. *Wade,* 410 U. S. 113, 152 (1973). This privacy right encompasses and protects the personal intimacies of the home, the family, marriage, motherhood, procreation, and child rearing. . . . Nothing, however, in this Court's decisions intimates that there is any "fundamental" privacy right "implicit in the concept of ordered liberty" to watch obscene movies in places of public accommodation.

If obscene material unprotected by the First Amendment in itself carried with it a "penumbra" of constitutionally protected privacy, this Court would not have found it necessary to decide *Stanley* on the narrow basis of the "privacy of the home," which was hardly more than a reaffirmation that "a man's home is his castle." Cf. *Stanley* v. *Georgia, supra,* at 564.⁶ Moreover, we have declined to equate the privacy of the home relied on in *Stanley* with a "zone" of "privacy" that follows a distributor or a consumer of obscene materials wherever he goes. . . . The idea of a "privacy" right and a place of public accommodation are, in this context, mutually exclusive. Conduct or depictions of conduct that the state police power can prohibit on a public street do not become automatically protected by the Constitution merely because the conduct is moved to a bar or a "live" theater stage, any more than a "live" performance of a man and woman locked in a sexual embrace at high noon in Times Square is protected by the Constitution because they simultaneously engage in a valid political dialogue.

It is also argued that the State has no legitimate interest in "control [of] the moral content of a person's thoughts," *Stanley* v. *Georgia, supra,* at 565, and we need not quarrel with this. But we reject the claim that the State of Georgia is here attempting to control the minds or thoughts of those who patronize theaters. Preventing unlimited display or distribution of obscene material, which by definition lacks any serious literary, artistic, political, or scientific value as communication, *Miller* v. *California,* 413 U. S. 15, 24, 34 (1973), is distinct from a control of reason and the intellect. . . . Where communication of ideas, protected by the First Amendment, is not involved, or the particular privacy of the home protected by *Stanley,* or any of the other "areas or zones" of constitutionally protected privacy, the mere fact that, as a consequence, some human "utterances" or "thoughts" may be incidentally affected does not bar the State from acting to protect legitimate state interests. . . . The fantasies of a drug addict are his own and beyond the reach of government, but government regulation of drug sales is not prohibited by the Constitution. . . .

Finally, petitioners argue that conduct which directly involves "consenting adults" only has, for that sole reason, a special claim to constitutional protection. Our Constitution establishes a broad range of conditions on the exercise of power by the States, but for us to say that our Constitution incorporates the proposition that conduct involving consenting adults only is always beyond state regulation,⁷ is a step we are unable to take.⁸ Commercial exploitation of depictions, descriptions, or exhibitions of obscene conduct on commercial premises open to the adult public falls within a State's broad power to regulate commerce and protect the public

---

⁶The protection afforded by Stanley v. Georgia, 394 U. S. 557 (1969), is restricted to a place, the home. In contrast, the constitutionally protected privacy of family, marriage, motherhood, procreation, and child rearing is not just concerned with a particular place, but with a protected intimate relationship. Such protected privacy extends to the doctor's office, the hospital, the hotel room, or as otherwise required to safeguard the right to intimacy involved. Cf. Roe v. Wade, 410 U. S. 113, 152–154 (1973); Griswold v. Connecticut, 381 U. S. 479, 485–486 (1965). Obviously, there is no necessary or legitimate expectation of privacy which would extend to marital intercourse on a street corner or a theater stage.

⁷Cf. J. Mill, *On Liberty* 13 (1955 ed.).

⁸The state statute books are replete with constitutionally unchallenged laws against prostitution, suicide, voluntary self-mutilation, brutalizing "bare fist" prize fights, and duels, although these crimes may only directly involve "consenting adults." Statutes making bigamy

environment. The issue in this context goes beyond whether someone, or even the majority, considers the conduct depicted as "wrong" or "sinful." The States have the power to make a morally neutral judgment that public exhibition of obscene material, or commerce in such material, has a tendency to injure the community as a whole, to endanger the public safety, or to jeopardize, in Mr. Chief Justice Warren's words, the States '"right . . . to maintain a decent society." *Jacobellis* v. *Ohio, supra,* at 199 (dissenting opinion).

To summarize, we have today reaffirmed the basic holding of *Roth* v. *United States, supra,* that obscene material has no protection under the First Amendment. . . . We have directed our holdings, not at thoughts or speech, but at depiction and description of specifically defined sexual conduct that States may regulate within limits designed to prevent infringement of First Amendment rights. We have also reaffirmed the holdings of *United States* v. *Reidel,* 402 U. S. 351 (1971), and *United States* v. *Thirty-seven Photographs,* 402 U. S. 363 (1971), that commerce in obscene material is unprotected by any constitutional doctrine of privacy. . . . In this case we hold that the States have a legitimate interest in regulating commerce in obscene material and in regulating exhibition of obscene material in places of public accommodation, including so-called adult theaters from which minors are excluded. In light of these holdings, nothing precludes the State of Georgia from the regulation of the allegedly obscene material exhibited in Paris Adult Theatre I or II, provided that the applicable Georgia law, as written or authoritatively interpreted by the Georgia courts, meets the First Amendment standards set forth in *Miller* v. *California, supra,* at 23–25.

Mr. Justice Brennan, Dissenting

Our experience with the *Roth* approach has certainly taught us that the outright suppression of obscenity cannot be reconciled with the fundamental principles of the First and Fourteenth Amendments. For we have failed to formulate a standard that sharply distinguishes protected from unprotected speech, and out of necessity, we have resorted to the *Redrup* approach, which resolves cases as between the parties, but offers only the most obscure guidance to legislation, adjudication by other courts, and primary conduct. By disposing of cases through summary reversal or denial of certiorari we have deliberately and effectively obscured the rationale underlying the decisions. It comes as no surprise that judicial attempts to follow our lead conscientiously have often ended in hopeless confusion.

a crime surely cut into an individual's freedom to associate, but few today seriously claim such statutes violate the First Amendment or any other constitutional provision. . . . See also the summary of state statutes prohibiting bearbaiting, cockfighting, and other brutalizing animal "sports," in Stevens, "Fighting and Baiting," in *Animals and Their Legal Rights* 112–127 (Leavitt ed. 1970). As Professor Irving Kristol has observed: "Bearbaiting and cockfighting are prohibited only in part out of compassion for the suffering animals; the main reason they were abolished was because it was felt that they debased and brutalized the citizenry who flocked to witness such spectacles." *On the Democratic Idea in America* 33.

Of course, the vagueness problem would be largely of our own creation if it stemmed primarily from our failure to reach a consensus on any one standard. But after 16 years of experimentation and debate I am reluctantly forced to the conclusion that none of the available formulas, including the one announced today, can reduce the vagueness to a tolerable level while at the same time striking an acceptable balance between the protections of the First and Fourteenth Amendments, on the one hand, and on the other the asserted state interest in regulating the dissemination of certain sexually oriented materials. Any effort to draw a constitutionally acceptable boundary on state power must resort to such indefinite concepts as "prurient interest," "patent offensiveness," "serious literary value," and the like. The meaning of these concepts necessarily varies with the experience, outlook, and even idiosyncrasies of the person defining them. Although we have assumed that obscenity does exist and that we "know it when [we] see it," *Jacobellis* v. *Ohio, supra,* at 197 (Stewart, J., concurring), we are manifestly unable to describe it in advance except by reference to concepts so elusive that they fail to distinguish clearly between protected and unprotected speech. . . .

The vagueness of the standards in the obscenity area produces a number of separate problems, and any improvement must rest on an understanding that the problems are to some extent distinct. First, a vague statute fails to provide adequate notice to persons who are engaged in the type of conduct that the statute could be thought to proscribe. The Due Process Clause of the Fourteenth Amendment requires that all criminal laws provide fair notice of "what the State commands or forbids." *Lanzetta* v. *New Jersey,* 306 U. S. 451, 453 (1939); *Connally* v. *General Construction Co.,* 269 U. S. 385 (1926). In the service of this general principle we have repeatedly held that the definition of obscenity must provide adequate notice of exactly what is prohibited from dissemination. . . . While various tests have been upheld under the Due Process Clause, . . . I have grave doubts that any of those tests could be sustained today. . . . In this context, even the most painstaking efforts to determine in advance whether certain sexually oriented expression is obscene must inevitably prove unavailing. For the insufficiency of the notice compels persons to guess not only whether their conduct is covered by a criminal statute, but also whether their conduct falls within the constitutionally permissible reach of the statute. The resulting level of uncertainty is utterly intolerable, not alone because it makes "bookselling . . . a hazardous profession," *Ginsberg* v. *New York, supra,* at 674 (Fortas, J., dissenting), but as well because it invites arbitrary and erratic enforcement of the law. . . .

In addition to problems that arise when any criminal statute fails to afford fair notice of what it forbids, a vague statute in the areas of speech and press creates a second level of difficulty. We have indicated that "stricter standards of permissible statutory vagueness may be applied to a statute having a potentially inhibiting effect on speech; a man may the less be required to act at his peril here, because the free dissemination of ideas may be the loser."[9] *Smith* v. *California,* 361 U. S. 147, 151 (1959). That proposition draws its strength from our recognition that

---

[9]In this regard, the problems of vagueness and overbreadth are, plainly, closely intertwined. See NAACP v. Button, 371 U. S. 415, 432–433 (1963); Note, "The First Amendment Overbreadth Doctrine," 83 *Harv. L. Rev.* 844, 845 (1970).

the fundamental freedoms of speech and press have contributed greatly to the development and well-being of our free society and are indispensable to its continued growth. Ceaseless vigilance is the watchword to prevent their erosion by Congress or by the States. The door barring federal and state intrusion into this area cannot be left ajar. . . . Roth, supra, at 488.[10]

The problems of fair notice and chilling protected speech are very grave standing alone. But it does not detract from their importance to recognize that a vague statute in this area creates a third, although admittedly more subtle, set of problems. These problems concern the institutional stress that inevitably results where the line separating protected from unprotected speech is excessively vague. In *Roth* we conceded that "there may be marginal cases in which it is difficult to determine the side of the line on which a particular fact situation falls. . . ." *supra* at 491–492. Our subsequent experience demonstrates that almost every case is "marginal." And since the "margin" marks the point of separation between protected and unprotected speech, we are left with a system in which almost every obscenity case presents a constitutional question of exceptional difficulty. "The suppression of a particular writing or other tangible form of expression is . . . an *individual* matter, and in the nature of things every such suppression raises an individual constitutional problem, in which a reviewing court must determine for *itself* whether the attacked expression is suppressable within constitutional standards." *Roth, supra,* at 497 (separate opinion of Harlan, J.). . . .

As a result of our failure to define standards with predictable application to any given piece of material, there is no probability of regularity in obscenity decisions by state and lower federal courts. That is not to say that these courts have performed badly in this area or paid insufficient attention to the principles we have established. The problem is, rather, that one cannot say with certainty that material is obscene until at least five members of this Court, applying inevitably obscure standards, have pronounced it so. The number of obscenity cases on our docket gives ample testimony to the burden that has been placed upon this Court. . . .

Moreover, we have managed the burden of deciding scores of obscenity cases by relying on *per curiam* reversals or denials of certiorari—a practice which

---

[10]See also Speiser v. Randall, 357 U.S. 513 (1958); cf. Barenblatt v. United States, 360 U.S. 109, 137–138 (1959) (Black, J., dissenting):
"This Court . . . has emphasized that the 'vice of vagueness' is especially pernicious where legislative power over an area involving speech, press, petition and assembly is involved. . . . For a statute broad enough to support infringement of speech, writings, thoughts and public assemblies, against the unequivocal command of the First Amendment necessarily leaves all persons to guess just what the law really means to cover, and fear of a wrong guess inevitably leads people to forego the very rights the Constitution sought to protect above all others. Vagueness becomes even more intolerable in this area if one accepts, as the Court today does, a balancing test to decide if First Amendment rights shall be protected. It is difficult at best to make a man guess—at the penalty of imprisonment—whether a court will consider the State's need for certain information superior to society's interest in unfettered freedom. It is unconscionable to make him choose between the right to keep silent and the need to speak when the statute supposedly establishing the 'state's interest' is too vague to give him guidance." (Citations omitted.)

conceals the rationale of decision and gives at least the appearance of arbitrary action by this Court. See *Bloss* v. *Dykema,* 398 U. S. 278 (1970) (Harlan, J., dissenting.) More important, no less than the procedural schemes struck down in such cases as *Blount* v. *Rizzi,* 400 U.S. 410 (1971), and *Freedman* v. *Maryland,* 380 U. S. 51 (1965), the practice effectively censors protected expression by leaving lower court determinations of obscenity intact even though the status of the allegedly obscene material is entirely unsettled until final review here. In addition, the uncertainty of the standards creates a continuing source of tension between state and federal courts, since the need for an independent determination by this Court seems to render superfluous even the most conscientious analysis by state tribunals. And our inability to justify our decisions with a persuasive rationale—or indeed, any rationale at all—necessarily creates the impression that we are merely second-guessing state court judges.

The severe problems arising from the lack of fair notice, from the chill on protected expression, and from the stress imposed on the state and federal judicial machinery persuade me that a significant change in direction is urgently required. . . .

But, whatever the strength of the state interests in protecting juveniles and unconsenting adults from exposure to sexually oriented materials, those interests cannot be asserted in defense of the holding of the Georgia Supreme Court in this case. That court assumed for the purposes of its decision that the films in issue were exhibited only to persons over the age of 21 who viewed them willingly and with prior knowledge of the nature of their contents. And on that assumption the state court held that the films could still be suppressed. The justification for the suppression must be found, therefore, in some independent interest in regulating the reading and viewing habits of consenting adults.

At the outset it should be noted that virtually all of the interests that might be asserted in defense of suppression, laying aside the special interests associated with distribution to juveniles and unconsenting adults, were also posited in *Stanley* v. *Georgia, supra,* where we held that the State could not make the "mere private possession of obscene material a crime." *Id.,* at 568. That decision presages the conclusions I reach here today.

In *Stanley* we pointed out that "there appears to be little empirical basis for" the assertion that "exposure to obscene materials may lead to deviant sexual behavior or crimes of sexual violence." *Id.,* at 566 and n. 9.[11] In any event, we

---

[11]Indeed, since Stanley was decided, the President's Commission on Obscenity and Pornography has concluded:

"In sum, empirical research designed to clarify the question has found no evidence to date that exposure to explicit sexual materials plays a significant role in the causation of delinquent or criminal behavior among youth or adults. The Commission cannot conclude that exposure to erotic materials is a factor in the causation of sex crime or sex delinquency." *Report of the Commission on Obscenity and Pornography* 27 (1970) (footnote omitted).

To the contrary, the Commission found that "on the positive side, explicit sexual materials are sought as a source of entertainment and information by substantial numbers of American adults. At times, these materials also appear to serve to increase and facilitate constructive communication about sexual matters within marriage." *Id,* at 53.

added that "if the State is only concerned about printed or filmed materials inducing antisocial conduct, we believe that in the context of private consumption of ideas and information we should adhere to the view that 'among free men, the deterrents ordinarily to be applied to prevent crime are education and punishment for violations of the law. . . .' *Whitney* v. *California,* 274 U. S. 357, 378 (1927) (Brandeis, J., concurring)." *Id.,* at 566–567.

Moreover, in *Stanley* we rejected as "wholly inconsistent with the philosophy of the First Amendment," *id.,* at 566, the notion that there is a legitimate state concern in the "control [of] the moral content of a person's thoughts," *id.,* at 565, and we held that a State "cannot constitutionally premise legislation on the desirability of controlling a person's private thoughts." *Id.,* at 566. That is not to say, of course, that a State must remain utterly indifferent to—and take no action bearing on—the morality of the community. The traditional description of state police power does embrace the regulation of morals as well as the health, safety, and general welfare of the citizenry. See, e. g., *Village of Euclid* v. *Ambler Realty Co.,* 272 U. S. 365, 395 (1926). And much legislation—compulsory public education laws, civil rights laws, even the abolition of capital punishment—is grounded, at least in part, on a concern with the morality of the community. But the State's interest in regulating morality by suppressing obscenity, while often asserted, remains essentially unfocused and ill defined. And, since the attempt to curtail unprotected speech necessarily spills over into the area of protected speech, the effort to serve this speculative interest through the suppression of obscene material must tread heavily on rights protected by the First Amendment.

In *Roe* v. *Wade,* 410 U. S. 113 (1973), we held constitutionally invalid a state abortion law, even though we were aware of

> *the sensitive and emotional nature of the abortion controversy, of the vigorous opposing views, even among physicians, and of the deep and seemingly absolute convictions that the subject inspires. One's philosophy, one's experiences, one's exposure to the raw edges of human existence, one's religious training, one's attitudes toward life and family and their values, and the moral standards one establishes and seeks to observe, are all likely to influence and to color one's thinking and conclusions about abortion.* Id., at 116.

Like the proscription of abortions, the effort to suppress obscenity is predicated on unprovable, although strongly held, assumptions about human behavior, morality, sex, and religion.[12] The existence of these assumptions cannot validate a statute that substantially undermines the guarantees of the First Amendment, any more than the existence of similar assumptions on the issue of abortion can validate a statute that infringes the constitutionally protected privacy interests of a pregnant woman.

---

[12] See Henkin, "Morals and the Constitution: The Sin of Obscenity," 63 *Col. L. Rev.* 391, 395 (1963).

If, as the Court today assumes, "a state legislature may . . . act on the . . . assumption that commerce in obscene books, or public exhibitions focused on obscene conduct, have a tendency to exert a corrupting and debasing impact leading to antisocial behavior," *ante,* at 90, then it is hard to see how state-ordered regimentation of our minds can ever be forestalled. For if a State, in an effort to maintain or create a particular moral tone, may prescribe what its citizens cannot read or cannot see, then it would seem to follow that in pursuit of that same objective a State could decree that its citizens must read certain books or must view certain films. Cf. *United States* v. *Roth,* 237 F. 2d 796, 823 (CA2 1956) (Frank, J., concurring). However laudable its goal—and that is obviously a question on which reasonable minds may differ—the State cannot proceed by means that violate the Constitution. The precise point was established a half century ago in *Meyer* v. *Nebraska,* 262 U. S. 390 (1923). . . .

In short, while I cannot say that the interests of the State—apart from the question of juveniles and unconsenting adults—are trivial or nonexistent, I am compelled to conclude that these interests cannot justify the substantial damage to constitutional rights and to this Nation's judicial machinery that inevitably results from state efforts to bar the distribution even of unprotected material to consenting adults. *NAACP* v. *Alabama,* 377 U. S. 288, 307, (1964); *Cantwell* v. *Connecticut,* 310 U. S., at 304. I would hold, therefore, that at least in the absence of distribution to juveniles or obtrusive exposure to unconsenting adults, the First and Fourteenth Amendments prohibit the State and Federal Governments from attempting wholly to suppress sexually oriented materials on the basis of their allegedly "obscene" contents. Nothing in this approach precludes those governments from taking action to serve what may be strong and legitimate interests through regulation of the manner of distribution of sexually oriented material.

The Moral Theory of Free Speech and Obscenity Law
David A. J. Richards

We turn now to a more concrete examination of the contribution of moral analysis to the clarification of constitutional law. Our initial focus will be on the moral analysis of the free speech clause of the First Amendment and the recent set of obscenity cases decided by the Supreme Court, especially *Miller* v. *California*[1] and *Paris Adult Theatre I* v. *Slaton*.[2] The examination of the constitutional law of obscenity, as established in *Miller* and *Paris Adult Theatre*, is a crucial test for this contractarian approach. These cases claim to identify a certain class of clearly communicative expressions which fail even to enter into the structure of First Amendment analysis. It is important to know whether the Court's view is fundamentally consistent with the moral theory underlying the First Amendment. If these difficult cases can be decisively analyzed, other cases may follow more easily. Accordingly, we undertake here the examination of these obscenity cases, drawing upon philosophical analysis, moral and constitutional theory, and the social sciences, where useful, as an elaborate example of the kind of reasoning that can, I believe, profitably be extended to other problems in First Amendment adjudication.

From *The Moral Criticism of Law*, copyright © 1977 by Dickinson Publishing Company, Inc. Reprinted by permission of the author and publisher. Footnotes have been renumbered.

[1] 413 U.S. 15 (1973).
[2] 413 U.S. 49 (1973).

We begin with a discussion of the moral theory underlying the First Amendment. Then, we turn to the examination of the notion of the obscene. The contours of the notion are not self-evident. In order to understand the law of obscenity, some precision must be given to this notion itself. Finally, the analysis will focus on the issue of the constitutionality of obscenity law.

The Moral Theory of the First Amendment

First, we develop further the suggestion that contractarian theory may significantly clarify the moral basis and proper interpretation of the First Amendment.

At this point, we should remind ourselves of the contractarian theory of justice elaborated earlier, and the principles of justice there formulated. [See pp. 44–56 of *The Moral Criticism of Law*.] We noted there that one reasonable solution to the problem of just constitutional design is a constitution providing that certain fundamental civil and human rights are to remain intact, notwithstanding the wishes of legislative majorities or popular leaders. Indeed, as suggested earlier, it is historically plausible that the First Amendment, among other constitutional provisions, is an early expression of a developing contractarian theory of justice. In this view, the moral foundation of constitutional democracy is not majority rule, but the principles of justice. Majority rule is justified only to the extent that it coheres with the principles of justice. Thus, the utilitarian political calculations of majority rule are limited by substantive benchmarks of justice; there are points beyond which the interests of the few may not be sacrificed to advance the interests of the many. Whatever its historic origins,[3] the spirit and explicit content of the First Amendment is, of course, at one with contractarian moral theory: freedom of speech, and of the press, and religious liberty are not to be abridged, popular wishes to the contrary notwithstanding.[4]

In interpreting and enforcing the First Amendment, courts must determine the proper standards under which their responsibility is to be discharged. On the basis of our formulation of applicable principles of justice, the constitutional notions of free speech and free press should be understood in terms of certain relevant requirements of the first principle of justice, namely, the greatest equal

---

[3]The technical legal history of free speech in England and America prior to the adoption of the First Amendment obviously renders doubtful any consensus on the specific application of the amendment; see L. Levy, *Legacy of Suppression: Freedom of Speech and Press in Early American History* 1–175 (1960). A consensus, to the extent it existed, was one of the generalities of a political compromise that concealed future divergences of interpretation.

[4]"Congress shall make no law respecting an establishment of religion, or prohibiting the free exercise thereof; or abridging the freedom of speech, or of the press; or the right of the people peaceably to assemble; and to petition the Government for a redress of grievances." U.S. Const. Amend I. J. S. Mill stated the underlying moral point dramatically: "If all mankind minus one were of one opinion, mankind would be no more justified in silencing that one person than he, if he had the power, would be justified in silencing mankind." J. S. Mill, *On Liberty* 21 (C. Shields ed. 1956).

liberty of communication compatible with a like liberty for all. Thus, all legal prohibitions and regulations which constrain liberty of communication in a manner incompatible with this idea should be constitutionally forbidden and invalid. But how are we to understand the concrete application of the equal liberty idea?[5]

One important point is that in applying the equal liberty principle, the basic liberties must be assessed as an interrelated system. The weights of each kind of liberty may depend on the specification of other kinds of liberty. The liberties of expression constitute both a right to communicate and a right to be the object of communication. Obviously, these liberties must be adjusted to one another in such a way as to best realize the underlying values of autonomous self-determination. The morally preferable adjustment is a liberty to communicate to any audience that is itself at liberty to choose to be or not to be an audience. Given this interpretation, the liberty to communicate and other liberties are to be assessed as a whole in the light of the principle requiring the greatest equal liberty compatible with a like liberty for all.

The crucial analytic question is whether institutions and practices governing human expression, assessed as a system,[6] violate or cohere with the idea of a system of greatest equal liberty compatible with a like liberty for all. For example, it is clear that procedural rules of order, time, and place which regulate a reasonable pattern of communications, cohere with this idea, for they enlarge the equal liberty of communication compatible with a like liberty for all.[7] Without such rules of order, time, and place, the liberty of communication of one will be used to violate the liberty of communication of another so that the system of liberties is not the greatest *equal* liberty compatible with a like liberty for all.

Similarly, the punishment of communications that are an indispensable part of actions designed to and capable of overthrowing the constitutional order—for example, communicating military secrets to the enemy—does not violate this equal liberty of communications, for such communications would help to overthrow the system of equal liberties. The proof that such communications do advance the overthrow of the constitutional order must, however, appeal to general principles of empirical induction and inference. No special principles of inference, not admissible in deciding on the principles of justice, are admissible in the interpretation of those principles. Thus, special a priori views regarding the relation of certain communications to the decline and fall of the constitutional order, not justified on generally acceptable empirical grounds, are not morally tolerable as reasons for limiting such communications.

Attempts by the state to prohibit certain contents of communication per se are fundamentally incompatible with the moral and constitutional principle of equal liberty. Notwithstanding the outrage felt by the majority toward certain

---

[5]For an interesting consideration of this general problem, see J. Feinberg, "Limits to the Free Expression of Opinion," J. Feinberg and H. Gross, *Philosophy of Law* 135–151.
[6]I take the notion of a system of free expression from T. Emerson, *The System of Freedom of Expression* (1970).
[7]See A. Meiklejohn, *Political Freedom* 21–28 (1960).

contents of communication, the equal liberty principle absolutely forbids the prohibition of such communications on the ground of such outrage alone. Otherwise, the liberty of expression, instead of the vigorous and potent defense of individual autonomy that it is, would be a pitifully meager permission allowing people to communicate only in ways to which no one has any serious objection. The interest of the few in free expression is not to be sacrificed on such grounds to the interest of the many. Conventional attitudes are not to be the procrustean measure of the exercise of human expressive and judgmental competence.

On this view, the constitutionally protected liberty of free expression is the legal embodiment of a moral principle which ensures to each person the maximum equal liberty of communication compatible with a like liberty for all. Importantly, if the First Amendment freedoms rest on a fundamental moral principle, they have no necessary justificatory relation to the liberty of equal voting rights. No doubt, both rights advance values of self-direction and autonomy, but a maximum equal liberty of self-expression is neither a necessary nor a sufficient condition of democratic voting rights or of the competent exercise of those rights. Voting rights may exist and be competently exercised in a regime where expression is not in general free, but is limited to a small class of talented technicians who circulate relevant data on policy issues to the electorate. Similarly, free expression may exist in a political aristocracy or in a democracy where voting rights are not competently exercised because of illiteracy or political apathy.

The independent status of the value of free expression shows that its value is not intrinsically political but rests on deeper moral premises regarding the general exercise of autonomous expressive and judgmental capacity and the good that this affords in human life. It follows that the attempt to limit the constitutional protection of free expression to the political[8] must be rejected on moral and constitutional grounds.[9]

The foregoing account makes clear that strong moral ideas are implicit in the First Amendment and that moral analysis may clarify the proper constitutional interpretation and application of those ideas. It is significant in this connection that the account here proposed clarifies many concrete features of First Amendment adjudications,[10] for example, the propriety of reasonable regulations of time, place, and procedure,[11] the insistence that majority dislike of protected expression has no

---

[8]See A. Meiklejohn, *supra* note 7. Meiklejohn attempted to defend his view by interpreting the political quite broadly. A. Meiklejohn, "The First Amendment Is an Absolute," 1961 *Sup. Ct. Rev.* 245, 255–257, 262–263.

[9]See Z. Chafee, Book Review, 62 *Harv. L. Rev.* 891, 896–898 (1949).

[10]As an explication, this account seems to have more explanatory power than other comparable general theories of the First Amendment. Unlike Meiklejohn's theory, it accounts for the fact that free expression is not limited to politics. See Meiklejohn, *supra* note 7. It also accounts for the clear and present danger test, unlike the work of Thomas Emerson. See T. Emerson, *supra* note 6; T. Emerson, *Toward a General Theory of the First Amendment* (1966).

[11]See, e.g., Cox v. Louisiana, 379 U.S. 536, 554–55 (1965); Poulos v. New Hampshire, 345 U.S. 395, 405 (1953); Kovacs v. Cooper, 336 U.S. 77 (1949).

constitutional weight,[12] the basis of the clear and present danger test,[13] and the refusal to limit the First Amendment to the political.[14] It is equally clear that this account provides a framework from which the case law may be crucially assessed both as regards proper extensions of First Amendment rights, such as rights of access to the media,[15] and the criticism of anomalies in existing case law which depart from its deepest moral strains.

The Concept of the Obscene

A satisfying philosophical explication of the notion of the obscene would clarify the notion itself, its connections to related notions (such as the pornographic, the indecent, and the immoral), its uses in speech, and its relations to fundamental attitudes which explain how the notion comes to have moving appeal to conduct. Initially, we must describe some general marks of the obscene. Then, a constructive account of the notion will be proposed, and, finally, an attempt will be made to connect the account to related notions, especially the pornographic.

The Marks of the Obscene

The etymology of *obscene* is obscure. The *Oxford English Dictionary* notes that the etymology is "doubtful,"[16] while *Webster's* suggests a derivation from the Latin *ob*, meaning *to, before, against*, and the Latin *caenum*, meaning *filth*.[17] Other commentators suggest alternative derivations from the Latin *obscurus*, meaning *concealed*,[18] or a derivation as a corruption of the Latin *scena* meaning *what takes place off stage*.[19] In the latter sense, blinding Gloucester on stage in *King Lear* would have been an obscenity for a Greek playwright like Sophocles (thus, Oedipus is blinded

---

[12]See, e.g., A Book Named "John Cleland's Memoirs of a Woman of Pleasure" v. Attorney General, 383 U.S. 413, 427 (1966) (Douglas, J., concurring); Kingsley International Pictures Corp. v. Regents, 360 U.S. 684, 688–89 (1959); Roth v. United States, 354 U.S. 476, 484 (1957); Terminiello v. Chicago, 337 U.S. 1, 3–5 (1949).

[13]See, e.g., Brandenburg v. Ohio, 395 U.S. 444 (1969); Dennis v. United States, 341 U.S. 494 (1951).

[14]See, e.g., Roth v. United States, 354 U.S. 476, 484 (1957) (all ideas with the slightest redeeming social value have First Amendment protection); Joseph Burstyn, Inc. v. Wilson, 343 U.S. 495 (1952).

[15]See J. Barron, "Access to the Press—a New First Amendment Right," 80 *Harv. L. Rev.* 1641 (1967).

[16]See 7 *Oxford English Dictionary* 0.26 (1961).

[17]See *Webster's Third New International Dictionary* 1557 (1965).

[18]A. Kaplan, "Obscenity as an Esthetic Category," 20 *Law & Contemp. Prob.* 544, 550 (1955).

[19]H. Ellis, *On Life and Sex* 175 (1962); G. Gorer, *The Danger of Equality* 218 (1966): W. Allen, "The Writer and the Frontiers of Tolerance," in *"To Deprave and Corrupt . . ."* 141, 147 (J. Chandos ed. 1962).

offstage), but it was not for an Elizabethan playwright like Shakespeare, who was imbued with the bloodthirstiness of Senecan tragedy.

The standard dictionary definition of *obscene* turns on notions of what is disgusting, filthy, or offensive to decency.[20] While contemporary legal discussions emphasize the applicability of *obscene* to depictions, it is clearly significantly applied to acts themselves. Shakespeare, for example, speaks of an obscene deed,[21] and Sartre discusses obscene movements of the body.[22] In the law, it is notable that the earliest English obscenity conviction was for obscene acts.[23] Judicial decisions[24] and legal and general[25] commentary emphasize the connections of the obscene to the notion of shame. It is clear that in European thought the notion of the obscene has long been connected to the scatological[26] and the sexually lascivious,[27] a connection emphasized in Anglo-American legal history.[28] This history also makes

---

[20]See notes 16 and 17 *supra*.

[21]"O, forfend it, God, that, in a Christian climate, souls refin'd should show so heinous, black, obscene a deed!" W. Shakespeare, *Richard II*, act 4, sc. 1. The deed in question is a subject's judging his king.

[22]J. P. Sartre, *Being and Nothingness* 401–402 (H. Barnes trans. 1956): cf. the notion of "the jest obscene," as used in Nitocris's condemnation of her son in Handel, *Belshazzar*, act I, sc. 4 (1744).

[23]*Sir Charles Sedley's Case*, 83 Eng. Rep. 1146 (K. B. 1663). Sir Charles Sedley was here convicted "for shewing himself naked in a balcony, and throwing down bottles (pist in) vi & armis among the people in Covent Garden, contra pacem and to the scandal of the Government," *Id.* at 1146–1147. Sedley's conduct was condemned for its intrinsic obscenity as well as on the four additional grounds of indecent exposure, blasphemy, throwing missiles containing urine, and inciting to the small riot that ensued. See L. M. Alpert, "Judicial Censorship of Obscene Literature," 52 *Harv. L. Rev.* 40, 41–43 (1938). One commentary on these events states that Sedley also excreted in public. See A. Craig, *The Banned Books of England* 23–24 (1962); D. Thomas, *A Long Time Burning* 81 (1969).

[24]Thus, the prurient interest test for obscenity, established in Roth v. United States, 354 U.S. 476, 487 (1957), and reaffirmed in Miller v. California, 413 U.S. 15, 24 (1973) and Paris Adult Theatre I v. Slaton, 413 U.S. 49 (1973) is defined in terms of "a shameful or morbid interest in nudity, sex, or excretion."

[25]See *Model Penal Code* §207.10, Comment at 1, 10, 29–31 (Tent. Draft No. 6 1957), and commentary thereon in L. B. Schwartz, "Morals Offenses and the Model Penal Code," 63 *Col. L. Rev.* 669 (1963), reprinted in Feinberg and Gross, *Philosophy of Law* 152–161. See also Kaplan, *supra* note 18, at 556.

[26]For example, Alexander Pope in his remarkable denunciations of Curl in *The Dunciad* uses "obscene" in excretory contexts. See A. Pope, *The Dunciad* 299, 300 (J. Sutherland ed. 1963) (first published 1728, 1743).

[27]For example, in Cavalli's characteristically lascivious opera *La Calisto* (ca. 1650), Calisto's amorous approach to the goddess Diana is rejected with "Taci, lascia, taci/ Qual, qual delirio osceno/ l'ingeno ti confonde?" meaning, "Silence, lascivious girl!/ What, what obscene delirium/ has come over your reason?" Cavalli, *La Calisto*, act I, sc. 1.

[28]For a useful general account, see Alpert, *supra* note 23. For accounts of English legal development, see D. Thomas, *supra* note 23; N. St. John-Stevas, *Obscenity and the Law* (1956). For the best general account of earlier American developments, see W. B. Lockhart and R. C. McClure, "Literature, the Law of Obscenity, and the Constitution," 38 *Minn. L. Rev.* 295 (1954).

clear the significant relation of the obscene to the notion of the morally corrupting. Many of these connections were summarized in the language of the Comstock Act, which, in forbidding the mailing of obscene material in interstate commerce in the United States, speaks of "obscene, lewd, or lascivious . . . publication[s]" and included in its prohibitions contraceptives and abortifacients or anything else "for any indecent or immoral use."[29]

The most significant class of speech acts involving the notion of the obscene is that class of epithets, known as *obscenities*, which relate to excretory or sexual functions.[30] Such expressions are, at least in reasonably well-educated circles, conventionalized ways of expressing attitudes of disgust and contempt which depend for their sometimes shocking and bracing effect on the impropriety of their use.[31] In circles, like the army, where the verbal obscenities are constantly employed, their function seems quite different;[32] there they are used as a kind of manly, transgression-braving vocabulary whose use is a criterion of intimate membership in the group. Related to this is the use of obscenities among intimate friends and even as a language of love.

The verbal obscenities demonstrate the relation of the obscene not only to shock and offense, but to the anxiety-producing loss of control. On hearing or using such expressions in reasonably well-educated circles, one has the sense of a loss of control, a sudden frustration, or an explosion of pique, which may surprise the speaker as much as the listener.

In the light of these functions and marks of the verbal obscenities, one can better understand the functions of literature which employs obscene contents, for example, some works of Swift[33] and Pope.[34] By employing contents known to be offensive to the conventional proprieties, such literature can express complex communicative intentions of bitter satire and burlesque in ways related to the capacity of the verbal obscenities to express disgust and contempt.[35] Similarly, one can understand the use of the obscene in literary humor as well as in the smutty joke and obscene witticism.[36] Obviously, such effects of the obscene are in some important way tied to attitudes, the existence of which accounts for these effects.

---

[29]Comstock Act §2, ch. 258, §2, 17 Stat. 598, 599 (1873), as amended, 18 U.S.C. 1461 (1970).

[30]See E. Sagarin, *The Anatomy of Dirty Words* (1962); Read, "An Obscenity Symbol," 9 *Am. Speech* 264 (1934).

[31]For the force of such expressions in psychoanalysis, see S. Ferenczi, *Sex in Psychoanalysis* 132–153 (E. Jones trans. 1950); cf. Stone, "On the Principal Obscene Word of the English Language," 33 *Int'l J. Psycho-Anal.* 30 (1954).

[32]See *Songs and Slang of the British Soldier 1914–1918*, at 15 (3d ed. Brophy & Partridge eds. 1931).

[33]See, e.g., J. Swift, *A Tale of a Tub*, in *Gulliver's Travels and Other Writings* 245, 327–329, 334–336 (L. Landa ed. 1960); J. Swift, *A Voyage to Lilliput*, in *id.* 3, 34–35.

[34]See A. Pope, *supra* note 26, at 299–300, 303–304, 306, 308–314.

[35]Cf. D. Thomas, *supra* note 23, at 273–274, 313–314 (1969); S. Sontag, *Styles of Radical Will* 35–73 (1969).

[36]Cf. S. Freud, *Wit and Its Relation to the Unconscious*, in *The Basic Writings of Sigmund Freud* 631, 692–697 (A. Brill trans. & ed. 1938).

An Explication of the Obscene

The concept of the obscene is identical with the concept of those actions, representations, works, or states which display an exercise of bodily or personal function which in certain circumstances constitutes an abuse of that function, as dictated by standards in which one has invested self-esteem, so that the supposed abuse of function is regarded as a demeaning object of self-contempt and self-disgust.[37]

On this view, the obscene is a subcategory of the objects of shame. Shame is, I believe, properly understood in terms of a fall from one's self-concept in the exercise of capacities which one desires to exercise competently. The objects of shame, thus, are explained by reference to the notions of personal competence and self-respect which are their bases. One feels ashamed because, for example, one has been cowardly, failing to exercise courageous self-control over fear when danger threatened. A characteristic mark of such failure is self-contempt or self-disgust.

The obscene identifies a special class of the possible objects of shame which are explained by reference to certain defined notions of competence in bodily or personal function. Thus, just as one explains to a child that it is an abuse and misuse of the function of a knife or fork to put either in the ear, so too one explains the proper exercise of bodily function. The use of the body is thought to have precise and sharply defined functions and ends. This idea, found widely among primitive peoples and the most ancient cultures,[38] including, significantly, ancient Judaism,[39] rigidly defines certain clear proprieties of bodily function as pure or clean. Failure to so exercise bodily function is unclean, polluting, an abomination, in short, obscene.[40]

The obscene, thus, is a conceptual residum of very ancient ways of thinking about human conduct. Human beings are thought of as clusters of strengths or virtues and corresponding weaknesses or vices, where virtues and vices are not conceived in narrow moral terms.[41] Obscenity within this view is a kind of vice, a wasting and abuse of the natural employment of bodily or personal function. Hence, a culture's definition of the obscene will indicate those areas of bodily or personal function in which the culture centrally invests its self-esteem and in which deviance provokes the deepest anxieties. For example, incompetence with respect to excretory function typically defines the frailest members of society, infants and the senile. Where frailty and declining powers are a source of anxiety, excretory impropriety is likely to be regarded as obscene. Moreover, where the sexual function is regarded as akin to the excretory function, as it easily may be,[42] sexual behavior will come to share this condemnation.

---

[37]I am indebted, for this idea of the relevance of the demeaning to the obscene, to criticisms of John Kleining.
[38]See M. Douglas, *Purity and Danger* (1966).
[39]See *id*. 41–57.
[40]See, e.g., *Leviticus* 11–15, 17–18.
[41]See Aristotle *Nicomachean Ethics* 116–251 (M. Ostwald trans. 1962).
[42]See notes 70 and 71 *infra* and accompanying text.

This explication is intended to apply cross-culturally.[43] To the extent people in different cultures take different attitudes to certain bodily or personal functions, those cultures will take different views of those things that are obscene, though the cultures share the concept of the obscene as an abuse of bodily or personal function. A striking example is provided by the Tahitians, who do not take the Western view of the competent exercise of sexual function, but do take a rather stringent view of eating; thus for Tahitians, displays of coitus are not obscene, but displays of eating are.[44] For us, aside from contexts of satirical humor,[45] eating conventional food would be obscene only in extreme circumstances of gluttonous self-indulgence[46] or in circumstances where eating is associated with aphrodisiacal allure.[47]

Similarly, this explication is true over time as well. For example, English society in the eighteenth century was apparently very tolerant of obscene literature, despite the fact that obscene libel had become a common law offense.[48] But in the nineteenth century, changing moral standards gave rise to groups like the Society for the Suppression of Vice and prosecutions for obscene libel increased rapidly.[49] Concern over the explosion of pornographic literature[50] finally received expression in English statutes.[51] In the same way, contemporary attitudes evince a shift in the application of the obscene; a growing modern usage applies the notion, for example, to violence and death and displays of violence and death (based on the idea, I believe, that these represent demeaning abuses of competences of the person),[52] but no longer applies the notion to sex or sexual displays.[53]

Significantly, this explication accounts for the application of *obscene* to acts as well as to depictions of acts. Both acts and depictions are obscene if they display

---

[43]Cf. Honigman, "A Cultural Theory of Obscenity," in *Sexual Behavior and Personality Characteristics* 31 (M. DeMartino ed. 1963).

[44]See W. LaBarre, "Obscenity: An Anthropological Appraisal," 20 *Law and Contemp. Prob.* 533, 541–542 (1955). Geoffrey Gorer cites the Trobriand Islanders as a people who finds public eating of solid food an obscenity; G. Gorer, *supra* note 19. For a discussion of the Indian idea that eating may be polluting, see M. Douglas, *supra* note 38, at 33–34.

[45]The suggestion of the reversal of the roles of eating and excretion (namely, that eating would be obscene and excretion a social occasion) is the subject of one scene of hilarious social satire in L. Bunuel's movie *Le Fantôme de la Liberté* (1974).

[46]E.g., the movie *La Grande Bouffe* (1974).

[47]E.g., the famous eating scene in the movie *Tom Jones* (1963).

[48]Rex v. Curl, 93 Eng. Rep. 849 (K.B. 1727).

[49]See N. St. John-Stevas, *supra* note 28, at 29–65.

[50]For a literary analysis of some notable examples of Victorian pornography, see S. Marcus, *The Other Victorians* (1966).

[51]E.g., the Customs Consolidating Act of 1853. 16 & 17 Vict., c. 107 (repealed by Customs Consolidating Act of 1876, 39 & 40 Vict., c. 36, §§42, 288); and Lord Campbell's Act of 1857, 20 & 21 Vict., c. 83 (repealed by Obscene Publications Act of 1959, 7 & 8 Eliz. 2, c. 66, §3(8)).

[52]In 1948, the Supreme Court expressly declined to find that depictions of violence could be obscene, Winters v. New York, 333 U.S. 507 (1948), but this holding seems quite questionable today in view of growing modern usage. My views on the obscenity of violence and death gratefully acknowledge helpful criticisms of Joel Feinberg.

[53]See note 63 *infra* and associated text.

certain exercises of bodily function; whether by the act itself or by depiction, our anxiety is aroused when we become aware of phenomena which threaten our self-esteem. It does not follow, of course, that obscene depictions are only of obscene acts. Normal heterosexual intercourse between a married couple is not typically viewed as obscene; but a public depiction of such intercourse would, by some people, be viewed as obscene. Nonetheless, there is little question that the obscenity of an act is a sufficient condition for the obscenity of a depiction of that act. Most cases of obscene depictions fall into this category. At one time obscenity convictions were granted for the mere sympathetic discussion of homosexuality or advocacy of birth control or abortion, apart from any pornographic representation of any kind.[54] The idea seems to have been that since homosexuality, birth control, and abortion were obscene, any favorable discussion of them was obscene. Even today, it is clear that courts are quickest to make or affirm judgments of obscenity with respect to depictions of sexual acts such as cunnilingus, fellatio, sodomy, sadomasochism, and bestiality that are regarded as obscene in themselves.[55] The view that these acts are obscene is the basis for judging their depiction to be obscene.

The connection between the obscenity of acts and depictions of acts distinguishes the obscene from the indecent. The distinctive mark of the indecent is the public exhibition of that which, while unobjectionable in private, is offensive and embarrassing when done in public.[56] The obscene, by contrast, may be and often is condemned whether or not it involves a public display.

Finally, this linkage between the act and its depiction accounts for the use of obscenities to express contempt and disgust. Since the obscene identifies a disgusting abuse of bodily function, it is wholly natural that it should be used to express disgust. It follows that if one does not find certain communicative contents obscene, one may tendentiously advocate the abandonment of speech acts using those contents to express disgust.[57]

The Obscene and the Pornographic

Pornography etymologically derives from the Greek *pornographos*, meaning *writing of harlots*, literally, writing concerning or descriptive of prostitutes in their

---

[54]See H. M. Hyde, *A History of Pornography* 3–8 (1964); N. St. John-Stevas, *supra* note 28, at 70–74, 98–103. See also notes 87, 88, and 89 *infra*.

[55]Compare, e.g., Paris Adult Theatre I v. Slaton, 413 U.S. 49, 52 (Burger, C. J., emphasized the occurrence of "scenes of simulated fellatio, cunnilingus, and group sex intercourse") and Mishkin v. New York, 383 U.S. 502, 508 (1965) (depictions of flagellation, fetishism, and lesbianism held obscene), with Sunshine Book Co. v. Summerfield, 355 U.S. 372 (1958) (per curiam), rev'd 249 F. 2d 114 (D.C. Cir. 1957), aff'd 128 F. Supp. 564 (D.D.C. 1955) (nudity per se not obscene). Cf. R. Kuh, *Foolish Figleaves?* 306–307 (1967) (suggesting that pictured bestiality and homosexuality are more obscene than comparable pictured heterosexuality.)

[56]See J. Feinberg, "'Harmless Immoralities' and Offensive Nuisances," in *Issues in Law and Morality* 83, 87 (N. Care and T. Trelogan eds. 1973).

[57]This proposal has been made with respect to sexual contents. See E. Sagarin, *supra* note 30,

profession.[58] Thus, the depictions of various forms of sexual intercourse on the walls of a certain building in Pompeii, intended as aphrodisiacs for the orgiastic bacchanales housed there, were literally *pornographos*.[59] Pornography in this sense is identified by its sexually explicit content, its depiction of varied forms of sexual intercourse, turgid genitalia, and so on.[60]

Pornography is neither conceptually nor factually identical with the obscene. Conceptually, the notion of sexually explicit, aphrodisiacal depictions is not the same idea as that of the abuse of a bodily or personal function. Many cultures, though sharing the fundamental concept of the obscene, do not regard pornography as obscene.[61] Individuals within our culture may find coprophagy (eating feces) obscene,[62] but do not find pornography obscene,[63] because they fail to take a certain attitude toward "proper" sexual function although they do have ideas about "proper" excretory function. For such people, viewing sex or depictions of sex as obscene is an unfortunate blending of the sexual and the excremental.[64]

If there is no necessary connection between the pornographic and the obscene, how did the connection between them arise?

One account of the sexual morality behind this connection is that of Catholic canon law which

> holds, as a basic and cardinal fact, that complete sexual activity and pleasure is licit and moral only in a naturally completed act in valid marriage. All acts which, of their psychological and physical nature, are designed to be preparatory to the complete act, take their licitness and their morality from the complete act. If, therefore, they are entirely divorced from the complete act, they are distorted, warped, meaningless, and hence immoral.[65]

at 9–12, 160–174. Lenny Bruce, according to the show, *The World of Lenny Bruce*, sc. 1 (1974), predicted the day when, pursuant to his view of the nonobscenity of sex, the erstwhile sexual obscenities would be used as forms of congratulation and good wishes.

[58]See, e.g., *Webster's Third New International Dictionary* 1767 (1966).

[59]See H. M. Hyde, *supra* note 54 at 1, 10.

[60]See, e.g., M. Peckham *Art and Pornography* 46–47 (1969); A. Kinsey, *Sexual Behavior in the Human Female* 671–672 (1953); E. Kronhausen and P. Kronhausen, *Pornography and the Law* 262, 265 (1959).

[61]See H. M. Hyde, *supra* note 54, at 30–58; D. Loth, *The Erotic in Literature* 41–68 (1961); M. Peckham, *supra* note 60, at 257–301: La Barre *supra* note 44, at 533–35.

[62]The example of coprophagy occurs in M. de Sade, *120 Days of Sodom*, in 2 *The Complete Marquis De Sade* 215, 222 (P. Gillette trans. 1966). De Sade suggests other examples, such as eating vomit, which someone might find obscene, even if he would not find pornography obscene. *Id.* 215.

[63]See R. Haney, *Comstockery in America* 58–59, 67–69, 75 (1960); D. Loth, *supra* note 61, at 208–233; L. Marcuse, *Obscene: The History of an Indignation* 307–327 (K. Gershon trans. 1965); M. Peckham, *supra* note 60, at 19–20; B. Russell, *Marriage and Morals* 93–117 (1929).

[64]See H. Ellis, *supra* note 19, at 21–37; E. Kronhausen and P. Kronhausen, *supra* note 60, at 167; B. Russell, *supra* note 63, at 106–107.

[65]H. Gardiner, "Moral Principles toward a Definition of the Obscene," 20 *Law & Contemp. Prob.* 560, 564 (1955).

This view of course derives from St. Augustine's classic conception that the only proper "genital commotion"[66] is one with the voluntary aim of reproduction of the species.[67] It follows from this view that only certain rigidly defined kinds of "natural" intercourse in conventional marriage are moral; "unnatural" forms of such intercourse are forbidden; extramarital and of course homosexual intercourse are forbidden. Further, all material that will induce to "genital commotion" not within marriage is forbidden. Pornography is obscene not only in itself, because it displays intercourse not within marriage, but also because it tempts to intercourse outside marriage or to masturbation, which are independently obscene acts because they are forms of sexual conduct that violate minimum standards of proper bodily function and thus cause disgust.

While this specific Catholic view is not the universal basis for the connection of the obscene and the pornographic, this general kind of view seems always present. Sexual function of certain rigidly defined kinds is alone the correct and competent exercise of sexual function. All other forms are marked by failure, weakness, and disgust. Masturbation in particular is a moral wrong.

Clearly this general notion, premised on supposed medical as well as theological facts, was behind the extraordinary explosion in obscenity legislation in England and the United States in the 1850s, 1860s, and 1870s. This legislation rested squarely on the remarkable Victorian medical view relating masturbation and sexual excess in general to insanity.[68] Pornography, being in part masturbation fantasy, was condemned on medical as well as theological grounds, so that Anthony Comstock, the father of the Comstock Act, could point with the support of medical authority to the fact that pornography's "most deadly effects are felt by the victims in the habit of secret vices."[69]

Significantly, Victorian medical literature and pornography[70] make transparent that sexual function was construed on the model of excretory function.[71] The

---

[66]This quaint phrase appears in Gardiner, *id.* 567.

[67]See, Augustine, *The City of God* 470–472 (M. Dods trans. 1950). St. Thomas is in accord with Augustine's view. Of the emission of semen apart from generation in marriage, he wrote, "after the sin of homicide whereby a human nature already in existence is destroyed, this type of sin appears to take next place, for by it the generation of human nature is precluded." T. Aquinas, *On the Truth of the Catholic Faith: Summa Contra Gentiles* 146 (V. Bourke trans. 1946).

[68]See A. Comfort, *The Anxiety Makers* (1970); J. Haller and R. Haller, *The Physician and Sexuality in Victorian America* 191–234 (1974); S. Marcus, *supra* note 50; E. H. Hare, "Masturbational Insanity: The History of an Idea," 108 *J. Mental Science* 1, 6–9 (1962).

[69]A. Comstock, *Traps for the Young* 136 (R. Bremner ed. 1967). See also *id.* 132–133, 139, 145, 169, 179, 205; A. Comstock, *Frauds Exposed* 388–389, 416, 437–438, 440–441 (1880; reprinted 1969).

[70]See S. Marcus, *supra* note 50, at 24–25, 233, 243.

[71]See H. Ellis, *supra* note 19, at 21–25. On the fundamental mistake involved in confusing sexual and excretory function, see W. Masters and V. Johnson, *Human Sexual Inadequacy* 10 (1970), who state: "Seemingly, many cultures and certainly many religions have risen and fallen on their interpretation and misinterpretation of one basic physiological fact. Sexual functioning is a natural physiological process, yet it has a unique facility that no other natural

proper exercise of sexual function was rigidly defined in terms of one mode, marital reproductive sexuality. Within that mode, the proper function was one of regularity and moderation. Thus, doctors condemned sexual excess within marriage[72] and deprecated infertile sexual activity within marriage as "conjugal onanism."[73] This rigid and narrow conception of sexual function was obviously profoundly opposed to pornography which would expose, in the words of one prominent Victorian court, "the minds of those hitherto pure . . . to the danger of contamination and pollution from the impurity it contains."[74]

Similar views regarding the evils of masturbation are echoed in contemporary writers who condemn pornography. Thus, D. H. Lawrence emphasized the corrosive effects of autoeroticism on the capacity for the central spiritual experience, for Lawrence, of sexual mutuality between partners.[75]

Whatever the form of theological, medical, or psychological belief underlying the association of the obscene and the pornographic, some such belief always prevails, so that there is a significant correlation between judgments of obscenity and the judgments that a certain work is both sexually arousing and quite unpleasant.[76]

The Constitutionality of Obscenity Law

It should now be possible to apply the foregoing explication of the obscene and the moral analysis of the First Amendment to the issue raised in *Miller* v. *California* and *Paris Adult Theatre I* v. *Slaton*—the constitutionally permissible concept of the obscene.

Miller reaffirmed the holding of *Roth* v. *United States* that obscene expression is not protected by the First Amendment. In addition, the Court, speaking through the Chief Justice, formulated a constitutional test for obscenity. The test is threefold:

> (a) whether "the average person, applying contemporary community standards" would find that the work, taken as a whole, appeals to the prurient interest . . . ; (b) whether the work depicts or describes, in a

physiological process, such as respiratory, bladder, or bowel function, can imitate. *Sexual responsivity can be delayed indefinitely or functionally denied for a lifetime.* No other basic physiological process can claim such malleability of physical expression."

[72]A. Comfort, *supra* note 68, at 57.

[73] *Id.* 155, 161.

[74]The Queen v. Hicklin, L. R. 3 Q.B. 359, 372 (1868).

[75]See D. H. Lawrence, *Sex, Literature, and Censorship* 64–81 (1953). For similar sentiments, see M. Mead, "Sex and Censorship in Contemporary Society," in *New World Writing*, 7, 19–21 (1953).

[76]See *United States Comm'n on Obscenity and Pornography, Report of the Comm'n on Obscenity and Pornography* 210–212 (GPO ed. 1979) [herinafter *Report*] cf. J. W. Higgins & M. B. Katzman, "Determinants in the Judgment of Obscenity," 125 *Am. J. Psychiat.* 1733 (1969).

patently offensive way, sexual conduct specifically defined by the applicable state law; and (c) whether the work, taken as a whole, lacks serious literary, artistic, political, or scientific value.[77]

This test imposes on states that wish to ban obscenity an obligation to formulate specific standards. Moreover, *Miller* limits the obscene to "representations or descriptions of ultimate sexual acts, normal or perverted, actual or simulated" or "of masturbation, excretory functions and lewd exhibition of the genitals."[78] In effect, only hard-core scatology and pornography may be banned.[79]

On the other hand, the *Miller* test permits censorship wherever the allegedly obscene work is without "serious" value.[80] Thus, a lighter burden is imposed on the prosecution than was imposed under the prior "utterly without redeeming social value" test.[81] Moreover, reliance on local standards,[82] within the bounds of the court's test, permits a variety of constitutionally permissible restrictions. Hence, a person's First Amendment rights may be restricted in one jurisdiction without appeal to a national standard.[83]

The *Miller* case involved a conviction for mailing unsolicited sexually explicit material, which is, of course, a problem of nonconsensual intrusion of offensive material. In *Paris Adult Theatre I* v. *Slaton*, however, a majority of the Court, again speaking through Chief Justice Burger, applied the *Miller* criteria for obscenity to an adult's fully informed and consensual access to obscene materials. The Court thus narrowly limited the holding of *Stanley* v. *Georgia*[84] to its facts. There the Court invalidated a state statute prohibiting the possession and private use in one's home of obscene (pornographic) materials on the grounds of infringing the constitutional right of privacy. In *Paris Adult Theatre*, and other cases decided concurrently, the Court made clear that the constitutional right of privacy as regards the use of obscene materials applies only to one's home, not to any theater, nor even to the transport of such materials in one's traveling bags for private use.[85]

Miller and *Paris Adult Theatre*, then, find obscenity, even for consenting adults, to be outside the protection of the First Amendment, but the analysis here presented suggests that the Court's decisions are wrong. An understanding of the

---

[77]413 U.S. at 24 (quoting Roth, 354 U.S. at 489).

[78]*Id.* 25. In Jenkins v. Georgia, 418 U.S. 153 (1974), the Court made clear the force of these requirements; the movie *Carnal Knowledge* could not constitutionally be found obscene, for the depictions therein are not sexually explicit within the meaning of the *Miller* tests.

[79]413 U.S. at 27–28.

[80]413 U.S. at 24–25.

[81]A Book Named "John Cleland's Memoirs of a Woman of Pleasure" v. Massachusetts, 383 U.S. 413, 419 (1966).

[82]413 U.S. at 30–34.

[83]The Court thus rejected the previously urged view that the standards to be applied were national, not local. E.g., Jacobellis v. Ohio, 378 U.S. 184, 192–193 (1974) (Brennan, J.).

[84]394 U.S. 557 (1969).

[85]United States v. Orito, 413 U.S. 139 (1973); United States v. 12 200-Ft. Reels of Film, 413 U.S. 123 (1973).

moral function of the First Amendment compels a conclusion contrary to the Court's; there should be a presumption that obscenity, like other forms of expression, falls within the protection of the First Amendment.

To summarize, obscene communications, it has been proposed, implicate the idea of the abuse of basic bodily functions, the proper exercise of which is an object of basic self-esteem and the improper use of which is an object of shame and disgust. A sufficient, though not a necessary, condition of the obscenity of a communication is that the act depicted be obscene.

On this view, the precise application of the notion of the obscene crucially depends on beliefs and attitudes involving precise and rigid definitions of the proper exercise of bodily functions. Thus, different cultures, with different beliefs and attitudes, may regard dissimilar acts or objects as obscene. Similarly, within a culture, individuals may apply the label *obscene* to different phenomena. In the United States, for example, many people regard pornography as obscene because it reflects, for them, an improper exercise of sexual function. But others, not sharing their beliefs and attitudes, do not regard pornography as obscene,[86] though they may think that other things, like depictions of coprophagy or gratuitous violence, are obscene.

An obscenity law, then, must be understood as a political expression of broader popular attitudes toward the putative proper and improper use of the body. It is no accident that such laws have been used to forbid the transport of abortifacient and contraceptive information[87] and dissemination of sex manuals[88] and to prosecute advocacy of contraception and population control.[89] The moral attitudes behind such laws, directed against a supposed "abuse" of the body, were founded on a compound of religious, psychological, and medical beliefs basic to which was a deep fear of masturbation.[90] Masturbation, it was believed, led directly to physical debility and even death,[91] as well as crime and civil disorder.[92]

In judicial interpretation of the notion of the obscene, courts implicitly decide on and enforce popular attitudes about bodily function. Whatever may be the constitutional legitimacy of regulating obscene acts, it is impossible to see how regulating obscene communications can avoid raising the deepest First Amend-

---

[86]See notes 61 to 64 *supra*.

[87]See note 29 *supra*; 18 U.S.C. §1461 (1964), as amended, 18 U.S.C. §1461 (1970) (mail); 18 U.S.C. §1462(c), as amended, 18 U.S.C. §1462(c) (1970) (interstate commerce).

[88]See, e.g., United States v. Chesman, 19 F. 497 (E.D. Mo. 1881).

[89]See, e.g., United States v. Bennett, 24 F. Cas, 1093, No. 14, 571 (C.C.S.D.N.Y. 1879); Regina v. Bradlaugh, 2 Q.B.D. 569 (1977), *rev'd on other grounds*, 3 A.B.D. 607 (1878).

[90]See text accompanying notes 65 to 74, *supra*.

[91]Comstock, for example, noted the case of a thirteen-year-old girl, in whose bureau he "found a quantity of the most debasing and foul-worded matter. The last heard from this child was she was in a dying condition, the result of habits induced by this foul reading," A. Comstock, *Traps for the Young* 139 (R. Bremner ed. 1967).

[92]Comstock cited a number of instances where, in his view, access to obscene material led to robbery, burglary, and murder. A. Comstock, *Frauds Exposed* 437–39 (1880, reprinted 1969). See also A. Comstock, *supra* note 91, at 132–33, 169, 179).

ment problems. Because judicial application of obscenity laws necessarily enforces a particular attitude, albeit presumably majoritarian, about the contents of communication, it seems to be obnoxious in principle to the central moral purpose of the First Amendment—to secure the greatest equal liberty of communication compatible with a like liberty for all. State prohibitions or regulations of communications are permissible, on this analysis, only to advance the system of greatest equal liberty. It is striking to compare this analysis with that adopted by the Court in *Roth* and reaffirmed in *Miller* and *Paris Adult Theatre*.

The Historical Status of Obscenity in American Law

The classical approach to interpretation of the First Amendment is taken in two analytical steps. First, one asks whether the federal or state prohibition or regulation applies to a communication of the sort protected by the "freedom of speech, or of the press" guaranteed by the First Amendment. Thus, displaying a red flag has been held to be a form of protected "speech,"[93] but burning draft cards is not a protected type of communication.[94] Assuming that protected speech is involved, one then asks whether the regulation or prohibition is justified by some clear or present danger that the state has a right to prevent,[95] or by some countervailing state interest which overbalances the interest in free speech.[96] The Supreme Court's consideration of the application of free speech standards to the publication of obscene materials has notably focused on the first step in the classic analytic approach, whether the obscene is protected speech at all.[97]

The initial and fundamental decision considering the First Amendment issue involved in the control of allegedly obscene materials was the consolidated case of *Roth v. United States* and *Albert v. California*.[98] Defining the obscene as "material which deals with sex in a manner appealing to the prurient interest,"[99] thus following the suggestions of the Model Penal Code,[100] the Court upheld the constitutionality of both the federal and California laws. The Court, speaking

---

[93]Stromberg v. California, 283 U.S. 359 (1931).

[94]United States v. O'Brien, 391 U.S. 367 (1968).

[95]See, e.g., Brandenburg v. Ohio, 395 U.S. 444, 447 (1969) (per curiam).

[96]Konigsberg v. State Bar, 366 U.S. 36 (1961); American Communications Association v. Douds, 339 U.S. 382 (1950).

[97]Where courts have reached the second step, they have uniformly failed to find sufficient clear and present danger that the state may prevent or some countervailing interest. See, e.g., Roth v. United States, 237 F. 2d 796, 801 (2d Cir. 1956) (Frank, J. concurring), aff'd 354 U.S. 476 (1957); Commonwealth v. Gordon, 66 Pa. D. & C. 101 (1949) (Bok, J.), aff'd sub nom. Commonwealth v. Feigenbaum, 166 Pa. Super. 120, 70 A. 2d 389 (1950).

[98]354 U.S. 476 (1957).

[99]*Id.* at 487.

[100]See note 25 *supra*.

through Justice Brennan, acknowledged that "All ideas having even the slightest redeeming social importance—unorthodox ideas, controversial ideas, even ideas hateful to the prevailing climate of opinion" are protected speech, but, on the basis of the "history of the First Amendment," it found that obscenity was not at all protected speech within the meaning of the First Amendment.[101] It is difficult to fathom how the Court supposed that the development of obscenity law in the United States, which postdates the adoption of the Bill of Rights, clarifies the purposes of the First Amendment.[102] Colonial legislatures in America appear to have been either unprovoked by[103] or indifferent to[104] obscenity. Justice Brennan cited only one example of preconstitutional obscenity law: an early Massachusetts law forbidding obscene or profane mockery of religious services.[105] This law, however, is more properly viewed as a religious establishment law than as a law against obscene literature or art in general, which is striking when contrasted with the Puritan propensity to supervise private conduct through the criminal law.[106] In any event, there appear to have been no prosecutions under this law,[107] and when Massachusetts set out to suppress the *Memoirs of a Woman of Pleasure* in 1821, it relied on the common law misdemeanor of obscene libel.[108] There appear to have been no prior prosecutions under the common law in Massachusetts either;[109] the earliest American prosecution for common law obscene libel was in 1815 in Pennsylvania.[110]

State laws regulating and prohibiting obscenity were adopted only after the passage of the First Amendment, as part of the nineteenth-century Anglo-American concern over pornography.[111] The earliest law was a Connecticut statute of 1821.[112] The first federal legislation was a customs statute passed in 1842.[113] Even with these laws, prosecutions were relatively few until after the Civil War[114] when the Committee for the Suppression of Vice, led by Anthony Comstock, took

[101]*Id.* at 484.

[102]Cf. O. J. Rogge, "The High Court of Obscenity," I, 41 *U. Col. L. Rev.* 1, 2–3 (1969).

[103]See M. F. Alschuler, "Origins of the Law of Obscenity," in United States Commission on Obscenity and Pornography, 2 *Technical Report* 65, 73–79 at 75 (GPO ed. 1971).

[104]See United States v. Roth, 237 F. 2d 796, 801, 806–809 (1956) (Frank, J., concurring).

[105]Act of Mar. 19, 1712, ch. 6, §19, 1 *Acts and Resolves of the Province of Mass. Bay* 682 (E. Ames & A. Goodell comps. 1869).

[106]See W. E. Nelson, "Emerging Notions of Modern Criminal Law in the Revolutionary Era," 42 *N.Y.U.L. Rev.* 450, 450–458 (1967).

[107]See Alschuler, *supra* note 103, at 75.

[108]Commonwealth v. Holmes, 17 Mass. 336, 338 (1821).

[109]See L. M. Alpert, "Judicial Censorship of Obscene Literature," 52 *Harv. L. Rev.* 40 at 53 (1938).

[110]Commonwealth v. Sharpless, 2 S. & R. 91 (Pa. 1815).

[111]Cf. text accompanying notes 48–51.

[112]Act of May, 1821, ch. 22, §69, [1821] Conn. Stat. Laws 165.

[113]Act of Aug. 30, 1842, ch. 270, §28, 5 Stat. 566.

[114]See W. B. Lockhart and R. C. McClure, *supra* note 28, at 295, 324.

up the cudgels for purity in earnest.[115] In short, the evidence for obscenity law contemporaneous with the passage of the First Amendment is tenuous at best. Indeed, in the court of appeals Judge Frank argued that the framers of the Constitution were rather tolerant of literature that later generations regarded as obscene.[116]

In any event, the existence at the time of the adoption of the First Amendment of laws, such as that against seditious libel, has never been supposed to conclude the question of the constitutionality of such laws.[117] The basis for the decision in *Roth* lies not in history but in policy.

The Propositional Nature of Obscenity

The policy behind the *Roth* decision was that "the lewd and obscene . . . are no essential part of any exposition of ideas, and are of such slight social value as a step to truth that any benefit that may be derived from them is clearly outweighed by the social interest in order and morality."[118] In effect, obscene speech was relegated by the Court to a class of clearly communicative employments of speech which the Court has held not to be "free speech" within the meaning of the First Amendment. Other members of that class are "fighting words," like the epithets "damned racketeer" and "damned fascist,"[119] libels,[120] and commercial uses of speech.[121]

It is quite clear that the *Roth* Court's observation applies most strongly to the use of verbal obscenities as epithets.[122] Obscene epithets are obviously nonpropositional; they are conventionalized ways of expressing attitudes of disgust or contempt, which depend for their effect on the impropriety of their use. The Court could not have meant, however, that such expressions are not speech, within

---

[115]For an account of the social history associated with this development, see P. Boyer, *Purity in Print: The Vice-Society Movement and Book Censorship in America* (1968).

[116]237 F. 2d at 806–809, *supra* note 97.

[117]See, e.g., Beauharnais v. Illinois, 343 U.S. 250, 272 (1952) (Black, J., dissenting), for the view that the First Amendment abolished seditious libel. Cf. Grosjean v. American Press Co., 297 U.S. 233, 248–249 (1936) (First Amendment prohibits taxes that restrict newspaper circulation, although such taxes were employed in England and America at the time of the adoption of the First Amendment).

[118]354 U.S. at 485 (quoting with approval Chaplinsky v. New Hampshire, 315 U.S. 568, 571–572 (1942)).

[119]Chaplinsky v. New Hampshire, 315 U.S. 568 (1942).

[120]See Gertz v. Robert Welch, Inc., 94 S. Ct. 2997, 3006–3007 (1974).

[121]See Pittsburgh Press Co. v. Pittsburgh Commission on Human Relations, 413 U.S. 376 (1973).

[122]In the quoted portion of Chaplinsky, text accompanying note 119 *supra*, the Court found support in Z. Chafee, *Free Speech in the United States* 150 (1941), 315 U.S. at 572 n. 5. By way of example, Chafee stated: "The man who swears in a street car is as much of a nuisance as the man who smokes there. Insults are punished like a threatening gesture, since they are liable to provoke a fight."

the meaning of the First Amendment, merely because they are nonpropositional. It is quite clear that many forms of supposedly obscene materials, which *Roth* would put wholly outside the protection of the First Amendment, are propositional; much hard-core pornography, for example, rather precisely describes certain acts in propositional terms. Conversely, nonpropositional expressions are not per se excluded from the protection of the First Amendment; even obscene epithets have been protected.[123] It is also clear that forms of art not expressible in words alone or in words at all, such as motion pictures, are within the protection of the First Amendment.[124] Indeed, in *Miller*, the Court conceded First Amendment protection to any work, even one with prurient appeal, that taken as a whole has "serious literary, artistic, political, or scientific value."[125] This concession suggests that the prohibition of dodecaphonic music or modern dance, although such art forms do not express formal propositions, would be unconstitutional. The First Amendment, thus, protects all communications, not just those in propositional form.

What, then, can the Supreme Court mean by saying in *Roth* and reaffirming in *Miller* and *Paris Adult Theatre* that the obscene does not express ideas and is not essential to their expression? The claim seems at bottom to be that obscene expression is essentially a *form* of saying something which can be equally well said without using that form. The obscene is like an unpleasant personal mannerism, for instance, a belligerent tone, that bears no real relation to the speaker's communicative intention. The idea is that the content of an obscene expression may be equally well expressed without being obscene; a pornographic depiction could be expressed in colorless medical language that does not appeal to prurient interest; or a novel dealing with the cruelties of sexuality without emotion may equally well express its point without certain vivid pornographic depictions.

But this view, once baldly stated, is clearly premised on a false philosophy of language as well as a false moral theory of the First Amendment. The meaning or communicative intention[126] of an obscene expression is inextricably intertwined with its obscene content. To remove the obscenity from an expression is precisely to remove an essential element of meaning. Verbal obscenities, for example, carry a very special meaning which cannot be captured in any other way. Consider reading the "Watergate tapes" transcripts with the expletives removed. At one point Nixon advised Haldeman and Ehrlichman to "use the most vicious libel lawyer there is; I'd sue every (expletive deleted) (unintelligible)."[127] It would surely impart a very different sense and reflect very differently on the mind of the President if he instead had said, "I'd sue every unsavoury scoundrel who criticized the Administration." Or consider Lenny Bruce's monologues with the obscenities

---

[123]Cohen v. California, 403 U.S. 15 (1971) ("Fuck the draft"), excerpted in Feinberg and Gross, *Philosophy of Law* 161–164.
[124]Jenkins v. Georgia, 418 U.S. 153 (1974); Joseph Burstyn, Inc. v. Wilson, 343 U.S. 495 (1952); see R. Randall, *Censorship of the Movies* 9–32 (1968).
[125]413 U.S. at 24.
[126]See S. Schiffer *Meaning* (1972); H. P. Grice, "Meaning," 66 *Philos. Rev.* 377 (1957).
[127]*The White House Transcripts* 737 (G. Gold ed. 1974).

removed; the comic and satiric meaning would not merely be modified, it would be completely transformed.[128] Similarly, the use of the obscene in literature —the depictions of excretion and the like in Pope[129] and Swift[130] come to mind —gives precise expression to the satirical disgust which is part of the complex communicative intentions of these works. To eliminate the obscene from such works, as in Bowdler's expurgations of Shakespeare,[131] impoverishes and distorts their meanings.

Hence, a prohibition of the obscene is a prohibition on a certain kind of meaning. It is fundamentally unreasonable to say, as the Supreme Court did in *Roth* and reaffirmed in *Miller* and *Paris Adult Theatre*, that this is not an essential form of speech within the meaning of the First Amendment. It is precisely that; by outlawing it, the Court makes criminal a certain content of communication.

If the Court does recognize the expressive function of the obscene, it must then be saying that this type of content in communication is without constitutional value. This view appears to be confirmed by either the test of obscenity employed in the *Roth* line of cases or that propounded in *Miller*. In *Roth*, Justice Brennan described obscenity as "utterly without redeeming social importance,"[132] and in *A Book Named "John Cleland's Memoirs of a Woman of Pleasure"* v. *Massachusetts*,[133] he specified that one part of the test for obscenity was whether or not the material was "utterly without redeeming social value."[134] Under this test, even material with a dominant appeal to a prurient interest in sex, and patently offensive to contemporary community standards, might not be illegally obscene, if it had any redeeming value. In *Miller*, however, Chief Justice Burger explicitly disavowed the "utterly without redeeming social value" test, permitting a finding of obscenity if the work "lacks serious literary, artistic, political, or scientific value."[135]

But by what criteria is value judged? It should be clear by now that there is no evidence, of a generally acceptable empirical kind, that hard-core pornography is without value.[136] On the contrary, various dispassionate empirical studies show that the use of hard-core pornographic materials has a significant and valued function in the life of many Americans.[137] In saying that the obscene is not constitutionally protected at all, and in identifying the obscene with the

---

[128]For the prosecutor's view of Bruce, see R. Kuh, *supra* note 55, at 175–211.
[129]See notes 26 and 35 *supra*.
[130]See note 34 *supra*.
[131]W. Shakespeare, *The Family Shakespeare* (T. Bowdler ed. 1807).
[132]354 U.S. at 484.
[133]383 U.S. 413 (1966).
[134]383 U.S. at 418.
[135]413 U.S. at 24–25.
[136]See, e.g., G. Gorer, *supra* note 19, at 217–231; *Report, supra* note 76, at 41, 154–163, 266–270; J. Money & R. Athanasiou, "Pornography: Review and Bibliographic Annotations," 115 *Am. J. Obstet. & Gyn.* 130, 143–146 (1973).
[137]See note 136 *supra;* M. Goldstein & H. Kant, *Pornography and Sexual Deviance* 147–153 (1973); N. Polsky, *Hustlers, Beats, and Others* 186–202 (1967); *Report, supra* note 76, at 128–134. The typical pornography users in America appear to be white, middle-aged, married males who had comparatively less sexual experience in adolescence than the norm. *Report, id.*

pornographic, the Court takes its standards of value from majority attitudes. In so doing, the Court violates the central moral value of the First Amendment, that majority attitudes per se are not a constitutionally valid basis for regulating or prohibiting expressive communications.

In an important sense, therefore, the Court's obscenity decisions are profoundly political and violate the ideal of neutral principles of constitutional adjudication, for the decision fails to deal evenhandedly with similarly situated claims. Thus, there is today in America substantial and growing disagreement regarding many questions of sexual and personal morality,[138] a few of which have already surfaced dramatically in major constitutional adjudications.[139] Part of this disagreement is over notions of proper sexual function, with serious arguments being proposed for major constitutional attacks on various statutes regulating sexual function.[140] The revaluation of the obscene is one aspect of this debate.[141] In this context, pornography can be seen as the unique medium of a vision of sexuality, a "pornotopia"[142]—a view of sensual delight in the erotic celebration of the body, a concept of easy freedom without consequences, a fantasy of timelessly repetitive indulgence. In opposition to the Victorian view that narrowly defines proper sexual function in a rigid way that is analogous to ideas of excremental regularity and moderation,[143] pornography builds a model of plastic variety and joyful excess in sexuality. In opposition to the sorrowing Catholic dismissal of sexuality as an unfortunate and spiritually superficial concomitant of propagation,[144] pornography affords the alternative idea of the independent status of sexuality as a profound and shattering ecstasy.[145]

Within the perspective of the evolving national debate over sexual morality and the Supreme Court's repeated support of an "uninhibited marketplace of ideas,"[146] it is difficult to see why the pornographic vision should not have a place in the marketplace of ideas beside other visions that celebrate the life of the

---

[138]See, e.g., R. Bell, *Premarital Sex in a Changing Society* (1966); *Beyond Monogamy* (J. Smith and L. Smith eds. 1974); Departmental Committee on Homosexual Offenses and Prostitution, *Report Cmnd. No. 247* (1957) (Wolfenden Report); D. Klaich, *Woman Plus Woman* (1974). Among the numerous books on the general topic of changing sexual morals are L. Lipton, *The Erotic Revolution* (1965); W. Reich, *The Sexual Revolution* (4th ed. rev. 1969).

[139]See, e.g., Roe v. Wade, 410 U.S. 113 (1973) (abortion); Griswold v. Connecticut, 381 U.S. 479 (1965) (contraception).

[140]See, e.g., W. Barnett, *Sexual Freedom and the Constitution* (1973); Special Student Contribution, *Homosexuality and the Law—An Overview*, 17 N.Y.L.F. 273, 295–299 (1971).

[141]See H. Ellis, *The Revaluation of Obscenity*, in *More Essays of Love and Virtue* 103–142 (1931); M. Ernst & W. Seagle, *To the pure* . . . 250–262 (1928); P. Goodman, "Pornography, Art, and Censorship," in *Perspectives on Pornography* 42 (D. Hughes ed. 1970).

[142]See S. Marcus, *supra* note 50, at 216, 268–2744 see also P. Michelson, *The Aesthetics of Pornography* 1–13, 233–241 (1971).

[143]See notes 68 to 76 *supra* and accompanying text.

[144]See notes 65 to 67 *supra* and accompanying text.

[145]Cf. S. Sontag, *supra* note 35, at 35–73 (1969).

[146]Red Lion Broadcasting Co. v. FCC, 395 U.S. 367, 390 (1969); Associated Press v. United States, 326 U.S. 1, 20 (1945). The marketplace concept is attributable to Justice Holmes, Abrams v. United States, 250 U.S. 616, 630 (1919) (Holmes, J., dissenting).

mind, the sanctity of ascetic piety, or the usefulness of prudent self-discipline.[147] In excluding the pornographic vision from the marketplace, the Court fundamentally fails to make a "morally neutral judgement . . . of obscene material,"[148] for in applying the concept of the obscene it affirms one moral and political view and denies another.

To argue from the social value of pornography is to meet the Court on its own terms and to dispute the outcome of its balancing test. One may equally reject the constitutional validity of the balancing approach itself; indeed, the contractarian moral theory of the First Amendment requires us to do so. The moral basis of the First Amendment is not merely a utilitarian calculus of the political usefulness of a debate on divergent points of view. Rather, the First Amendment rests more fundamentally on the moral liberties of expression, conscience, and thought; these liberties are fundamental conditions of the integrity and competence of a person in mastering his or her life and expressing this mastery to others. The freedom to determine the contents of one's communications is fundamental to this mastery. Without this freedom, one lacks a basic ingredient of self-determination.

There is no reason whatsoever to believe that the freedom to determine the sexual contents of one's communications or to be an audience to such communications is not as fundamental to this self-mastery as the freedom to decide upon any other communicative contents. On the contrary, one of the central aims of developing methods of sex therapy in our culture is to help couples in "learning to communicate . . . in an area that heretofore in our culture has been denied the dignity of freedom of communication."[149] That obscenity law has been a traditional instrument of this denial is explicit in the historic utility of obscenity laws for attacking sex education and instruction,[150] as well as in the recent attempts to ban pornography per se. The consequence of these assaults is not only a denial of a reasonable understanding of the varieties of pleasurable sexual function,[151] but also a crippling debasement of the human capacity to master one's sexual life in the light of independent judgment.

---

[147]One argument holds that pornographic materials are unequal combatants on the battlefield of truth and, accordingly, must be forbidden; otherwise the opposing ideas would have no fair chance. Given the panoply of rituals and traditions to which opposing ideas can and do appeal, it is difficult to credit this argument without putting restrictions on the appeal to rituals and traditions. Even assuming the argument deserves attention, its appeal rests on one of two unspoken, and morally unspeakable, assumptions: either the object of competition among conflicting ideas is not the victory of truth, at least if that truth is obscene, or any view that appeals to our baser instincts is presumptively less valuable than its innate competitive advantage would indicate. It should be obvious that these arguments are simply more manifestations of nonneutral principles of adjudication.

[148]Paris Adult Theatre I v. Slaton, 413 U.S. 49, 69 (1973).

[149]W. Masters and V. Johnson, *Human Sexual Inadequacy* 204 (1970).

[150]See notes 29, 87 to 89 *supra* and accompanying text.

[151]Thus, some popular sex manuals recommend the use of pornography, e.g., *The Joy of Sex* 208–209 (A. Comfort ed. 1972). Interestingly the Commission on Obscenity and Pornography adopted its proposal for the liberalization of obscenity law in light of its recommendations of the need for better sex education. *Report, supra* note 76, at 47–48, 58, 265–279. For an identical view, see B. Russell, *supra* note 63, at 93–117.

Viewed in this manner, it is clear that the obscene falls within the protection of the First Amendment and should be accorded whatever protection is given other forms of speech. The relevant constitutional question, therefore, is whether restrictions on the obscene are coherent with the principle of the greatest equal liberty of communication compatible with a like liberty for all.

Equal Liberty and the Protection of Moral Standards

First, the constitutional principle of equal liberty, as formulated and derived here, must be clearly understood. In deriving the principle, we observed that the value of free expression depended on the existence of developed capacities of rational choice. Thus, the principle is not intended to apply to persons presumably lacking rational capacities, such as children. In addition, the liberty of communication was so interpreted that the liberty of expression correlates with the liberty of others to choose to be or not to be an audience. It follows, therefore, that there should be no constitutional objection on free expression grounds to the reasonable regulation of the distribution of obscene materials to children.[152] Similarly, the state could prohibit the distribution of photographic pornography involving minors as subjects, because the child subjects could not have made a rational choice and their exploitation is not to be encouraged by permitting their exploiters to obtain the fruits of what is justifiably regarded as a crime. Nor is there any objection to the reasonable regulation of the obtrusive distribution of the obscene, in order to protect the liberty of persons not to be an audience, if they so choose.[153] But this argument is far different from the attempt, in *Paris Adult Theatre,* to justify the general prohibition of the obscene because of "the interest of the public in the quality of life and the total community environment, [and] the tone of commerce in the great city centers."[154] Any interest of this kind hardly justifies a general prohibition of all pornographic materials. At most, it would justify some form of regulatory zoning of the place of sale of such materials and some kind of restriction on their obtrusive sale.

Having formulated the relevant moral and constitutional principle to permit some reasonable restrictions on complete individual freedom, we must recall that any qualification of liberty of expression can be justified only on the basis of facts ascertainable by generally acceptable empirical methods. One quite relevant set of facts would be empirical support for the view that publication and use of

---

[152]There may, however, be good reason for believing that such laws are not justified as a matter of sound legislative policy. See, e.g., O. N. Larsen and M. E. Wolfgang, *Statements,* in *Report, supra* note 76, at 375–377.

[153]Cf. L. B. Schwartz, "Morals Offenses and the Model Penal Code," 63 *Colum. L. Rev.* 669, 681 (1963), reprinted in J. Feinberg and H. Gross, *Philosophy of Law* 152–161. The idea of reasonable avoidability rests on the moral idea that a person has no morally just complaint to the infliction of pain or offense which has been voluntarily and rationally undertaken. See . . . J. Feinberg, *supra* note 56, at 103–104.

[154]413 U.S. at 58.

obscene materials are "social poisons,"[155] leading directly to disease, death, crime, and social disorder—in short, the Victorian view.[156] Were these beliefs true, or even supported by substantial evidence, the principle of equal liberty would justify restrictions on obscene materials. In such circumstances the circulation of obscene materials would, of necessity, undermine the constitutional order of equal liberties. Certain of these Victorian beliefs, such as that regarding the evils of masturbation, are regarded today as medically ludicrous.[157] There remains an intuition, though, that pornography threatens the public safety. In *Paris Adult Theatre*, Chief Justice Burger advances this sort of argument, citing a minority report of the Commission on Obscenity and Pornography[158] that "indicates . . . at least an arguable correlation between obscene material and crime."[159] In a disingenuous manner the Court flatly ignores the great body of evidence that shows there to be no empirical basis for such a view.[160] Without the requisite empirical foundation, the supposed threat to the public safety provides no justification for restricting the circulation and use of obscene materials.

One set of facts for which there is evidence, however, seems to allow at least some prohibition of the obscene consistent with the equal liberty principle. These facts relate to those special circumstances where the use of verbal obscenities as direct personal insults is clearly likely to lead to physical violence, thus causing a breakdown of the relations of equal liberty. This quite specific set of facts, which justifies only a very narrow qualification to the constitutional protection of obscene speech, has, however, been supposed by the Supreme Court to place the obscene outside the protection of the First Amendment altogether.[161] This argument is certainly among the more unfortunate examples of bad judicial reasoning, for it

[155]The metaphor of poison was particularly favored by Anthony Comstock. See A. Comstock, *supra* note 92, at 388–389; A. Comstock *supra* note 91, at 174, 175, 179, 182, 206, 242.

[156]See notes 68 to 75 and accompanying text.

[157]See, e.g., A. Comfort, *supra* note 68, at 69–113. For statements of the normal and useful functions of masturbation, see *Sexual Behavior and Personality Characteristics* 239–276 (M. DeMartino ed. 1963). For statistical background, see P. Gebhard, J. Gagnon, W. Pomeroy, and C. Christenson, *Sex Offenders* 486–514 (1965); A. Kinsey, W. Pomeroy and C. Martin, *Sexual Behavior in the Human Male* 497–516 (1948); A. Kinsey, W. Pomeroy, C. Martin and P. Gebhard, *Sexual Behavior in the Human Female* 132–190 (1953).

[158]See M. A. Hill and W. C. Link, *Statements*, in *Report, supra* note 76, at 383, 385–386.

[159]413 U.S. at 58.

[160]See, e.g., P. Gebhard, J. Gagnon, W. Pomeroy and C. Christenson, *supra* note 157, at 403–409, 669–692; *Report, supra* note 76, at 215–243. Indeed, Denmark's experience was that repeal of its obscenity statute, as applied to consenting adults, *lowered* the rate of sex crimes. See *Report, supra* note 76, at 230–232; R. Ben-Veniste, "Pornography and Sex Crime: The Danish Experience," in United States Commission on Obscenity and Pornography, 7 *Technical Report* 245 (1971); B. Kutschinsky, "Towards an Explanation of the Decrease in Registered Sex Crimes in Copenhagen" in *id.*, 263.

[161]The Court's reliance in Roth on the quoted portion of Chaplinsky, 354 U.S. at 485, which in turn relies on Chafee's work, 315 U.S. at 572 n. 5, is misplaced. Chafee viewed these facts as justifying application of the "clear and present danger" test, or some variation thereof, but not as putting the obscene outside the protection of the First Amendment altogether. See Z. Chafee, *Government and Mass Communications* 49–61 (1947).

commits the obvious fallacy of overgeneralization and quite blatantly misuses authority to justify an unsupportable result.

It would appear, then, that no general prohibition of obscene communications seems justifiable on the basis of the facts capable of empirical confirmation. One final kind of argument, however, has been supposed by the Court to justify such a general prohibition, the argument from preserving moral standards. Having laid out his arguments from the "tone of commerce" and from "public safety," Justice Burger next proposes the general argument that society can forbid all access to pornographic materials in order to protect moral standards. The majority opinion cites *in extenso*[162] a statement of Professor Bickel to the effect that to allow people consensually to gather to view such materials, in a way not obtrusive on others,

> is to affect the world about the rest of us, and to impinge on other privacies [for] even supposing that each of us can, if he wishes, effectively avert the eye and stop the ear (which, in truth, we cannot), what is commonly read and seen and heard and done intrudes upon us all, want it or not.[163]

If the substance of this argument is that permitting any form of disapproved conduct between or among consenting adults violates the rights of privacy of those who disapprove of this conduct, it is surprising that it can be supposed by the Court to deserve any weight whatsoever.[164] We shall undertake shortly a general moral analysis of the constitutional notion of a right of privacy; but, even without anticipating that analysis here, it is natural to ask how, precisely, my right of privacy is violated by the consensual conduct of others? This argument claims that mere knowledge of the existence of certain disapproved conduct justifies legal prohibition of that conduct. As such it is an extension of the traditional argument, which we shall shortly examine, urged by Stephen[165] against Mill[166] and, more recently, by Devlin[167] against Hart.[168] But the traditional argument at least assumed that the condemned conduct had a weakening effect on society. At bottom, this argument rests on the crude moral confusion between an obtrusive offense and the offense derived from the mere knowledge of something. It must be rejected not only because it is intellectually indefensible, but also because its conclusions are morally outrageous. It would dilute the moral force of liberty

---

[162]413 U.S. at 59

[163]A. Bickel, 22 *Pub. Interest* 25–26 (1971); see also A. Bickel, *The Morality of Consent*, 73–74 (1975).

[164]If Bickel, on the other hand, means only to emphasize arguments about preserving the ambience of neighborhoods, the argument, as indicated earlier in the text, supports only some form of regulatory zoning, not an outright prohibition.

[165]See J. Stephen, *Liberty, Equality, Fraternity* 135–178, esp. 138–139 (R. White ed. 1967).

[166]J. S. Mill, *supra* note 4, at 91–113, esp. 100–101.

[167]P. Devlin, *The Enforcement of Morals* (1965).

[168]H. L. A. Hart, *Law, Liberty, and Morality* (1963).

into the empty and vapid idea that people be allowed to do that to which no one has any serious objection.[169] It would elevate every form of popular prejudice, bigotry, and intolerance, *without more*, into a moral basis for law. The Court has consistently and rightly rejected such arguments.[170] Majority attitudes per se, unsupported by reasoning of any intelligible kind, do not rise to the dignity of moral reasoning which can justify deprivations of liberty. They are merely intractable prejudices which the state should circumscribe where it is necessary to protect the system of equal liberties, rather than elevate into law.[171]

If this argument is wrong as applied to acts, it is even more palpably so as applied to communications. The First Amendment rests on the moral status and weight of freedom of expression. Notwithstanding the attitudes of the majority, free expression is granted to the most despised minorities who advance causes condemned by the majority. To appeal to the unfounded attitudes of the majority in order to restrict the free expression of the unpopular minority is precisely to withhold the value of free expression where it is most urgently required.

There is another form of this argument, however, that is not similarly objectionable in moral and constitutional principle, which the Court most likely had in mind.[172] According to this form of the argument, there are certain demonstrable moral virtues or character traits which citizens of a stable constitutional democracy must have. Because obscenity undermines these virtues, it leads to the breakdown of the constitutional order of equal liberties. Therefore, it is justifiable to prohibit obscenity on grounds of the equal liberty principle.[173]

While this argument has the general form of an acceptable moral and constitutional argument for limiting free speech, it is fundamentally circular, and its empirical premises are not, in fact, supported by evidence. Its circularity derives from unexamined assumptions. For example, it identifies the virtues required for democratic citizenship with the virtues specified by a quite special, religiously informed sexual morality that regards pornography as repugnant to its narrow

---

[169]Cf. *id.*, at 46–47.

[170]See, e.g., Roe v. Wade, 410 U.S. 113 (1973) (abortion); Eisenstadt v. Baird, 405 U.S. 438 (1972) (contraception for unmarried persons); Loving v. Virginia, 388 U.S. 1 (1967) (miscegenation); Griswold v. Connecticut, 381 U.S. 479 (1965) (contraception); Brown v. Board of Education, 347 U.S. 483 (1954) (segregated education).

[171]R. M. Dworkin, "Lord Devlin and the Enforcement of Morals," 75 *Yale L. J.* 986 (1966).

[172]See 413 U.S. at 59–60, where the court refers to the maintenance of a "decent society."

[173]For one statement of this view, see I. Kristol, "Pornography, Obscenity and the Case for Censorship," *New York Times*, Mar. 28, 1971, §6 (Magazine), at 24, reprinted in Feinberg and Gross, *Philosophy of Law* 165–171. See also H. Clor, *Obscenity and Public Morality* (1969); W. Berns, "Pornography vs. Democracy: The Case for Censorship," 22 *Pub. Interest* 3 (1971); G. Elliot, "Against Pornography," *Harper's Mag.*, March 1965, at 51; E. van den Haag, in *Censorship: For and Against* 143 (1971); E. van den Haag, "Quia Ineptum," in *To Deprave and Corrupt* 109 (J. Chandos ed. 1962). For a general statement of this approach to the analysis of First Amendment adjudications, see W. Berns, *Freedom, Virtue and the First Amendment* 228–257 (1965). For the great classical statements of the position today defended by these authors, see Plato, *Republic* (F. Cornford trans. 1945) 321–359; J.-J. Rousseau, *Letter to M. D'Alembert on the Theatre* (A. Bloom trans. 1960).

definition of proper sexual function.[174] It also assumes that pornography disconnects sex and love in a damaging way.[175] However, there is no reason whatsoever to identify the virtues of democratic citizenship—public spiritedness, civic responsibility, democratic tolerance, mutual respect—with the virtue of rigid abstinence from pornographic material.[176] Indeed, there is no consensus in our culture that such abstinence is a virtue,[177] even some religiously informed sexual moralities are now tolerant of such obscene materials.[178] Further, unless one begs the question and assumes that love is properly defined by one narrow view of its proper expression, there is little empirical reason to suppose that pornography disconnects sex and love in a damaging way. On the contrary, some suppose that pornography may be a healthy influence, expressing a frank understanding of the integrated relation of emotion and its bodily expressions.[179]

Surely good citizenship is compatible with many sexual styles and moralities. Indeed, one might justly suppose that the virtues of democratic tolerance and mutual respect are fostered by practicing tolerance toward different sexual moralities and by insistence on maintaining constitutional liberties of free speech for all groups.

In any event, sexual moralities and pornography cannot be treated as unified phenomena. Different behaviors and materials appeal to different tastes. Even if the Court should conclude that one class of materials, sadistic obscenity, for example, does have a deleterious effect on some fundamental democratic virtue, such as mutual respect, that conclusion would have no bearing on other types of obscene materials, such as depictions of cunnilingus, that have no ramifications for democratic virtues. Furthermore, although it is plausible that sadistic materials imply a lack of mutual respect in sexual relations,[180] in order to justify the suppression of even sadistic materials, the Court would have to find that attitudes in sexual fantasy cause destructive civic attitudes and behavior. According to the "outlet" theory of aggressive fantasy, however, quite the contrary would be true.[181]

---

[174]Namely, a certain kind of disciplined, child-rearing, marital heterosexuality. See, e.g., text accompanying notes 65 to 67.

[175]See Kristol, *supra* note 173, at 24, 112.

[176]For a similar distinction, see R. McKeon, R. Merton and W. Gellhorn, *The Freedom to Read* 23–24 (1957).

[177]See note 63, *supra*.

[178]See, e.g., A Book Named "John Cleland's Memoirs of a Woman of Pleasure" v. Massachusetts, 383 U.S. 413, 433 (app. to opinion of Douglas, J., concurring; an address by a clergyman urging that *Fanny Hill* is a moral piece of literature); cf. Jones, Statement in *Report*, *supra* note 76.

[179]See *supra* note 151.

[180]Cf. the claim of feminists that much pornography is demeaning to women. See, in general, K. Millett, *Sexual Politics* (1970).

[181]For example, de Sade himself, when released from the torments of his prison life, refused to use legal power to seek vengeance on his tormenters and was notable in his time for advocating abolition of the death penalty. G. Gorer, *supra* note 19, at 210.

In fact, there is no generally accepted empirical evidence that access to pornography in general has an adverse effect on character traits.[182] People's capacity for responsible behavior and moral sensitivity does not seem to be affected by access to pornography. Nor is there any evidence that access to pornography causes social or cultural breakdown.[183] Without evidence on these matters, the argument from preserving civil virtues is untenable.

In depending on such an argument to support its decision, then, the majority of the Court must be erecting some special notion of sexual morality into constitutional law. But on what constitutional basis does it do so? There are, no doubt, certain sexual moralities, based on special religious perceptions,[184] which sharply condemn access to pornography. Such perceptions, however, are not constitutionally admissible in interpreting the application of the equal liberty principle;[185] they run contrary to the moral basis of the First Amendment, including the express prohibitions of the establishment of religion clause of the First Amendment.[186] Accordingly, such perceptions cannot be the basis of a constitutional justification of limitations on free speech. To the extent that the Court's acquiescence in general prohibitions of pornography depends solely on such perceptions, it violates the fundamental moral rationale of the free speech and free press clause of the First Amendment and raises serious independent constitutional questions under that amendment's establishment of religion clause.

Finally, Justice Burger argues that just as there is no conclusive evidence to support many laws, such as antitrust, securities regulation, and educational support laws, which have been held to be constitutionally justifiable, so the absence of evidence to support the obscenity laws cannot be used to attack their constitutionality. This argument confuses the lack of conclusive evidence with the lack of any evidence whatsoever. There is certainly evidence of a general theoretical and factual kind for the laws and institutions that Burger cites; there is no comparable evidence regarding the effects of obscenity. Burger's argument invites acquiescence in the most intractable prejudices, dismissing all evidence as irrelevant. It undermines the whole idea of rationality in legislation, substituting a notion of tradition that is a mask for ignorance and intolerance. The invalidity of this argument is even more extreme in the light of the values underlying the First Amendment. Because the principle of equal liberty is fundamental to a moral

---

[182]See *Report, supra* note 76, at 202.

[183]See, e.g., H. L. A. Hart, "Social Solidarity and the Enforcement of Morals," 35 *U. Chi. L. Rev.* 1 (1967).

[184]E.g., the claim of Charles H. Keating, Jr., that it suffices to condemn pornography that it is against God's law. C. H. Keating, *Statement*, in *Report, supra* note 76, 511, 515, 547.

[185]For an attempt to incorporate such perceptions into the derivation of the equal liberty requirements, see H. Gardiner, *supra* note 65, at 564–568. For a refusal by a Catholic to take this move, see J. C. Murray, "Literature and Censorship," in *The First Freedom* 215 (R. Downs ed. 1960).

[186]See Epperson v. Arkansas, 393 U.S. 97 (1968); W. Barnett, *supra* note 140; L. Henkin, "Morals and the Constitution: The Sin of Obscenity," 63 *Colum. L. Rev.* 391 (1963).

theory of society, a higher burden of proof than is required in ordinary economic legislation is surely appropriate to justify legislation restricting that liberty. Yet, the Court allows the abridgement of equal liberty in the absence of any substantial evidence and on the basis of appeals to majority attitudes—precisely what the First Amendment forbids.

Women Fight Back
Susan Brownmiller

Critics of the women's movement, when they are not faulting us for being slovenly, straggly haired, construction-booted, whiny sore losers who refuse to accept our female responsibilities, often profess to see a certain inexplicable Victorian primness and antisexual prudery in our attitudes and responses. "Come on, gals," they say in essence, "don't you know that your battle for female liberation is part of our larger battle for sexual liberation? Free yourselves from all your old hang-ups! Stop pretending that you are actually offended by those four-letter words and animal noises we grunt in your direction on the street in appreciation of your womanly charms. When we plaster your faceless naked body on the cover of our slick magazines, which sell millions of copies, we do it in sensual obeisance to your timeless beauty—which, by our estimation, ceases to be timeless at age twenty or thereabouts. If we feel the need for a little fun and go out and rent the body of a prostitute for a half hour or so, we are merely engaging in a mutual act between two consenting adults, and what's it got to do with you? When we turn our movie theaters into showcases for pornographic films and convert our bookstores to outlets for mass-produced obscene smut, not only should you marvel at the wonders of our free-enterprise system, but you should applaud us for pushing back the barriers of repressive middle-class morality, and for our strenuous defense of all the civil liberties you hold so dear, because we have made obscenity

From *Against Our Will: Men, Women and Rape* (New York: Simon & Schuster, 1975), pp. 389–396. Copyright © 1975 by Susan Brownmiller. Reprinted by permission of Simon & Schuster, a Division of Gulf & Western Corporation.

the new frontier in defense of freedom of speech, that noble liberal tradition. And surely you're not against civil liberties and freedom of speech, now, are you?"

The case against pornography and the case against toleration of prostitution are central to the fight against rape, and if it angers a large part of the liberal population to be so informed, then I would question in turn the political understanding of such liberals and their true concern for the rights of women. Or to put it more gently, a feminist analysis approaches all prior assumptions, including those of the great, unquestioned liberal tradition, with a certain open-minded suspicion, for all prior traditions have worked against the cause of women and no set of values, including that of tolerant liberals, is above review or challenge. After all, the liberal *politik* has had less input from the feminist perspective than from any other modern source; it does not by its own considerable virtue embody a perfection of ideals, it has no special claim on goodness, rather, it is most receptive to those values to which it has been made sensitive by others.

The defense lawyer mentality had such a hold over the liberal tradition that when we in the women's movement first began to politicize rape back in 1971, and found ourselves on the side of the prosecutor's office in demanding that New York State's rape laws be changed to eliminate the requirement of corroborative proof, the liberal establishment as represented by the American Civil Liberties Union was up in arms. Two years later the ACLU had become sensitized to the plight of rape victims under the rules of law, thanks to the lobbying efforts of feminist lawyers, and once this new concern for rape victims was balanced against the ACLU's longstanding and just concern for the rights of all defendants, the civil-liberties organization withdrew its opposition to corroboration repeal. This, I believe, was a philosophic change of significant proportions, and perhaps it heralds major changes to come. In any event, those of us who know our history recall that when the women's liberation movement was birthed by the radical left, the first serious struggle we faced was to free ourselves from the structures, thought processes, and priorities of what we came to call the *male* left—and so if we now find ourselves in philosophic disagreement with the thought processes and priorities of what has been no less of a male liberal tradition, we should not find it surprising.

Once we accept as basic truth that rape is not a crime of irrational, impulsive, uncontrollable lust, but is a deliberate, hostile, violent act of degradation and possession on the part of a would-be conqueror, designed to intimidate and inspire fear, we must look toward those elements in our culture that promote and propagandize these attitudes, which offer men, and in particular, impressionable, adolescent males, who form the potential raping population, the ideology and psychologic encouragement to commit their acts of aggression *without awareness, for the most part, that they have committed a punishable crime,* let alone a moral wrong. The myth of the heroic rapist that permeates false notions of masculinity, from the successful seducer to the man who "takes what he wants when he wants it," is inculcated in young boys from the time they first become aware that being a male means access to certain mysterious rites and privileges, including the right to buy a woman's body. When young men learn that females may be bought for a price, and that acts of sex command set prices, then how should they not also conclude that that which may be bought may also be taken without the civility of a monetary exchange?

That there *might* be a connection between prostitution and rape is certainly not a new idea. Operating from the old (and discredited) lust, drive and relief theory, men have occasionally put forward the notion that the way to control criminal rape is to ensure the ready accessibility of female bodies at a reasonable price through the legalization of prostitution, so that the male impulse might be satisfied with ease, efficiency and a minimum of bother. Alas for these androcentric pragmatists, even Dr. Kinsey could unearth "no adequate data to prove the truth or falsity" of such a connection. Twenty years after Kinsey others of a similar mind were still trying, although the evidence still suggested that men who make frequent use of brothels are several years older than men who are usually charged with criminal rape. To my mind the experience of the American military in Vietnam, where brothels for GIs were officially sanctioned, even incorporated into the base-camp recreation areas, should prove conclusively that the availability of sex for a small price is no deterrent to the decision to rape, any more than the availability of a base-camp shooting range is a deterrent to the killing of unarmed civilians and children.

But my horror at the idea of legalized prostitution is not that it doesn't work as a rape deterrent, but that it institutionalizes the concept that it is man's monetary right, if not his divine right, to gain access to the female body, and that sex is a female service that should not be denied the civilized male. Perpetuation of the concept that the "powerful male impulse" must be satisfied with immediacy by a cooperative class of women, set aside and expressly licensed for this purpose, is part and parcel of the mass psychology of rape. Indeed, until the day is reached when prostitution is totally eliminated (a millennium that will not arrive until men, who create the demand, and not women who supply it, are fully prosecuted under the law), the false perception of sexual access as an adjunct of male power and privilege will continue to fuel the rapist mentality.

Pornography has been so thickly glossed over with the patina of chic these days in the name of verbal freedom and sophistication that important distinctions between freedom of political expression (a democratic necessity), honest sex education for children (a societal good) and ugly smut (the deliberate devaluation of the role of women through obscene, distorted depictions) have been hopelessly confused. Part of the problem is that those who traditionally have been the most vigorous opponents of porn are often those same people who shudder at the explicit mention of any sexual subject. Under their watchful, vigilante eyes, frank and free dissemination of educational materials relating to abortion, contraception, the act of birth, and female biology in general is also dangerous, subversive and dirty. (I am not unmindful that a frank and free discussion of rape, "the unspeakable crime," might well give these righteous vigilantes further cause to shudder.) Because the battle lines were falsely drawn a long time ago, before there was a vocal women's movement, the anti-pornography forces appear to be, for the most part, religious, Southern, conservative and right-wing, while the pro-porn forces are identified as Eastern, atheistic and liberal.

But a woman's perspective demands a totally new alignment, or at least a fresh appraisal. The majority report of the President's Commission on Obscenity and Pornography (1970), a report that argued strongly for the removal of all legal restrictions on pornography, soft and hard, made plain that 90 percent of all pornographic material is geared to the male heterosexual market (the other 10 percent is geared to the male homosexual taste), that buyers of porn are "predominantly white, middle-class, middle-aged married males" and that the graphic depictions, the meat and potatoes of porn, are of the naked female body and of the multiplicity of acts done to that body.

Discussing the content of stag films, "a familiar and firmly established part of the American scene," the commission report dutifully, if foggily, explained, "Because pornography historically has been thought to be primarily a masculine interest, the emphasis in stag films seems to represent the preferences of the middle-class American male. Thus male homosexuality and bestiality are relatively rare, while lesbianism is rather common."

The commissioners in this instance had merely verified what purveyors of porn have always known: hard-core pornography is not a celebration of sexual freedom; it is a cynical exploitation of female sexual activity through the device of making all such activity, and consequently all females, "dirty." Heterosexual male consumers of pornography are frankly turned on by watching lesbians in action (although never in the final scenes, but always as a curtain raiser); they are turned off with the sudden swiftness of a water faucet by watching naked men act upon each other. One study quoted in the commission report came to the unastounding conclusion that "seeing a stag film in the presence of male peers bolsters masculine esteem." Indeed. The men in groups who watch the films, it is important to note, are *not* naked.

When male response to pornography is compared to female response, a pronounced difference in attitude emerges. According to the commission, "Males report being more highly aroused by depictions of nude females, and show more interest in depictions of nude females that [do] females." Quoting the figures of Alfred Kinsey, the commission noted that a majority of males (77 percent) were "aroused" by visual depictions of explicit sex while a majority of females (68 percent) were not aroused. Further, "females more often than males reported 'disgust' and 'offense.'"

From whence comes this female disgust and offense? Are females sexually backward or more conservative by nature? The gut distaste that a majority of women feel when we look at pornography, a distaste that, incredibly, it is no longer fashionable to admit, comes, I think, from the gut knowledge that we and our bodies are being stripped, exposed and contorted for the purpose of ridicule to bolster that "masculine esteem" which gets its kick and sense of power from viewing females as anonymous, panting playthings, adult toys, dehumanized objects to be used, abused, broken and discarded.

This, of course, is also the philosophy of rape. It is no accident (for what else could be its purpose?) that females in the pornographic genre are depicted in two cleanly delineated roles: as virgins who are caught and "banged" or as nymphomaniacs who are never sated. The most popular and prevalent pornographic fantasy combines the two: an innocent, untutored female is raped and "subjected to unnatural practices" that turn her into a raving, slobbering nymphomaniac, a dependent sexual slave who can never get enough of the big, male cock.

There can be no "equality" in porn, no female equivalent, no turning of the tables in the name of bawdy fun. Pornography, like rape, is a male invention, designed to dehumanize women, to reduce the female to an object of sexual access, not to free sensuality from moralistic or parental inhibition. The staple of porn will always be the naked female body, breasts and genitals exposed, because as man devised it, her naked body is the female's "shame," her private parts the private property of man, while his are the ancient, holy, universal, patriarchal instrument of his power, his rule by force over *her*.

Pornography is the undiluted essence of anti-female propaganda. Yet the very same liberals who were so quick to understand the method and purpose behind the mighty propananda machine of Hitler's Third Reich, the consciously spewed-out anti-Semitic caricatures and obscenities that gave an ideological base to the Holocaust and the Final Solution, the very same liberals who, enlightened by blacks, searched their own conscience and came to understand that their tolerance of "nigger" jokes and portrayals of shuffling, rolling-eyed servants in movies perpetuated the degrading myths of black inferiority and gave an ideological base to the continuation of black oppression—these very same liberals now fervidly maintain that the hatred and contempt for women that find expression in four-letter words as expletives and in what are quaintly called "adult" or "erotic" books and movies are a valid extension of freedom of speech that must be preserved as a Constitutional right.

To defend the right of a lone, crazed American Nazi to grind out propaganda calling for the extermination of all Jews, as the ACLU has done in the name of free speech, is, after all, a self-righteous and not particularly courageous stand, for American Jewry is not currently threatened by storm troopers, concentration camps and imminent extermination, but I wonder if the ACLU's position might change if, come tomorrow morning, the bookstores and movie theaters lining Forty-second Street in New York City were devoted not to the humiliation of women by rape and torture, as they currently are, but to a systematized, commercially successful propaganda machine depicting the sadistic pleasures of gassing Jews or lynching blacks?

Is this analogy extreme? Not if you are a woman who is conscious of the ever-present threat of rape and the proliferation of a cultural ideology that makes it sound like "liberated" fun. The majority report of the President's Commission on Obscenity and Pornography tried to pooh-pooh the opinion of law enforcement agencies around the country that claimed their own concrete experience with offenders who were caught with the stuff led them to conclude that pornographic material is a causative factor in crimes of sexual violence. The commission maintained that it was not possible at this time to scientifically prove or disprove such a connection.

But does one need scientific methodology in order to conclude that the anti-female propaganda that permeates our nation's cultural output promotes a climate in which acts of sexual hostility directed against women are not only tolerated but ideologically encouraged? A similar debate has raged for many years over whether or not the extensive glorification of violence (the gangster as hero; the loving treatment accorded bloody shoot-'em-ups in movies, books and on TV) has a causal effect, a direct relationship to the rising rate of crime, particularly among youth. Interestingly enough, in this area—nonsexual and not specifically related to abuses against women—public opinion seems to be swinging to the position that explicit violence in the entertainment media does have a deleterious effect; it makes violence commonplace, numbingly routine and no longer morally shocking.

More to the point, those who call for a curtailment of scenes of violence in movies and on television in the name of sensitivity, good taste and what's best for our children are not accused of being pro-censorship or against freedom of speech. Similarly, minority group organizations, black, Hispanic, Japanese, Italian, Jewish, or American Indian, that campaign against ethnic slurs and demeaning portrayals in movies, on television shows and in commercials are perceived as waging a just political fight, for if a minority group claims to be offended by a specific portrayal, be it Little Black Sambo or the Frito Bandido, and relates it to a history of ridicule and oppression, few liberals would dare to trot out a Constitutional argument in theoretical opposition, not if they wish to maintain their liberal credentials. Yet when it comes to the treatment of women, the liberal consciousness remains fiercely obdurate, refusing to be budged, for the sin of appearing square or prissy in the age of the so-called sexual revolution has become the worst offense of all.

Tinker v. *Des Moines Independent Community School District*, 393 U.S. 503 (1969)

[This case involved school children wearing black armbands to school as a "symbolic" protest to the Vietnam War. The U.S. Supreme Court held this action to be "closely akin to 'pure speech'," and entitled to First Amendment protection. Included here is the opinion of the Court and the dissent of Mr. Justice Black. Case citations have been edited and footnotes have been renumbered.]

Opinion of the Court.

Mr. Justice Fortas delivered the opinion of the Court.

Petitioner John F. Tinker, 15 years old, and petitioner Christopher Eckhardt, 16 years old, attended high schools in Des Moines, Iowa. Petitioner Mary Beth Tinker, John's sister, was a 13-year-old student in junior high school.

In December 1965, a group of adults and students in Des Moines held a meeting at the Eckhardt home. The group determined to publicize their objections to the hostilities in Vietnam and their support for a truce by wearing black armbands during the holiday season and by fasting on December 16 and New Year's Eve. Petitioners and their parents had previously engaged in similar activities, and they decided to participate in the program.

The principals of the Des Moines schools became aware of the plan to wear armbands. On December 14, 1965, they met and adopted a policy that any student wearing an armband to school would be asked to remove it, and if he refused he would be suspended until he returned without the armband. Petitioners were aware of the regulation that the school authorities adopted.

On December 16, Mary Beth and Christopher wore black armbands to their schools. John Tinker wore his armband the next day. They were all sent home and suspended from school until they would come back without their armbands. They did not return to school until after the planned period for wearing armbands had expired—that is, until after New Year's Day.

This complaint was filed in the United States District Court by petitioners, through their fathers, under § 1983 of Title 42 of the United States Code. It prayed for an injunction restraining the respondent school officials and the respondent members of the board of directors of the school district from disciplining the petitioners, and it sought nominal damages. After an evidentiary hearing the District Court dismissed the complaint. It upheld the constitutionality of the school authorities' action on the ground that it was reasonable in order to prevent disturbance of school discipline. 258 F. Supp. 971 (1966). The court referred to but expressly declined to follow the Fifth Circuit's holding in a similar case that the wearing of symbols like the armbands cannot be prohibited unless it "materially and substantially interferes with the requirements of appropriate discipline in the operation of the school." *Burnside* v. *Byars,* 363 F. 2d 744, 749 (1966).[1]

On appeal, the Court of Appeals for the Eighth Circuit considered the case *en banc.* The court was equally divided, and the District Court's decision was accordingly affirmed, without opinion. 383 F. 2d 988 (1967). We granted certiorari. 390 U.S. 942 (1968).

I

The District Court recognized that the wearing of an armband for the purpose of expressing certain views is the type of symbolic act that is within the Free Speech Clause of the First Amendment. See *West Virginia* v. *Barnette,* 319 U.S. 624 (1943); *Stromberg* v. *California,* 283 U.S. 359 (1931). Cf. *Thornhill* v. *Alabama,* 310 U.S. 88 (1940); *Edwards* v. *South Carolina,* 372 U.S. 229 (1963); *Brown* v. *Louisiana,* 383 U.S. 131 (1966). As we shall discuss, the wearing of armbands in the circumstances of this case was entirely divorced from actually or potentially disruptive conduct by those participating in it. It was closely akin to "pure speech" which, we have repeatedly held, is entitled to comprehensive protection under the First Amendment. Cf. *Cox* v. *Louisiana,* 379 U.S. 536, 555 (1965); *Adderley* v. *Florida,* 385 U.S. 39 (1966).

---

[1] In Burnside, the Fifth Circuit ordered that high school authorities be enjoined from enforcing a regulation forbidding students to wear "freedom buttons." It is instructive that in Blackwell v. Issaquena County Board of Education, 363 F. 2d 749 (1966), the same panel on the same day reached the opposite result on different facts. It declined to enjoin enforcement of such a regulation in another high school where the students wearing freedom buttons harassed students who did not wear them and created much disturbance.

First Amendment rights, applied in light of the special characteristics of the school environment, are available to teachers and students. It can hardly be argued that either students or teachers shed their constitutional rights to freedom of speech or expression at the schoolhouse gate. This has been the unmistakable holding of this Court for almost 50 years. In *Meyer* v. *Nebraska,* 262 U.S. 390 (1923), and *Bartels* v. *Iowa,* 262 U.S. 404 (1923), this Court, in opinions by Mr. Justice McReynolds, held that the Due Process Clause of the Fourteenth Amendment prevents States from forbidding the teaching of a foreign language to young students. Statutes to this effect, the Court held, unconstitutionally interfere with the liberty of teacher, student, and parent.[2] . . .

In *West Virginia* v. *Barnette, supra,* this Court held that under the First Amendment, the student in public school may not be compelled to salute the flag. Speaking through Mr. Justice Jackson, the Court said:

> *The Fourteenth Amendment, as now applied to the States, protects the citizen against the State itself and all of its creatures—Boards of Education not excepted. These have, of course, important, delicate, and highly discretionary functions, but none that they may not perform within the limits of the Bill of Rights. That they are educating the young for citizenship is reason for scrupulous protection of Constitutional freedoms of the individual, if we are not to strangle the free mind at its source and teach youth to discount important principles of our government as mere platitudes. 319 U.S., at 637.*

On the other hand, the Court has repeatedly emphasized the need for affirming the comprehensive authority of the States and of school officials, consistent with fundamental constitutional safeguards, to prescribe and control conduct in the schools. See *Epperson* v. *Arkansas,* 393 U.S. 97, 104 (1968); *Meyer* v. *Nebraska, supra,* at 402. Our problem lies in the area where students in the exercise of First Amendment rights collide with the rules of the school authorities.

---

[2]Hamilton v. Regents of Univ. of Cal., 293 U.S. 245 (1934), is sometimes cited for the broad proposition that the State may attach conditions to attendance at a state university that require individuals to violate their religious convictions. The case involved dismissal of members of a religious denomination from a land grant college for refusal to participate in military training. Narrowly viewed, the case turns upon the Court's conclusion that merely requiring a student to participate in school training in military "science" could not conflict with his constitutionally protected freedom of conscience. The decision cannot be taken as establishing that the State may impose and enforce any conditions that it chooses upon attendance at public institutions of learning, however violative they may be of fundamental constitutional guarantees. See, e.g., West Virginia v. Barnette, 319 U.S. 624 (1943); Dixon v. Alabama State Board of Education, 294 F. 2d 150 (C.A. 5th Cir. 1961); Knight v. State Board of Education, 200 F. Supp. 174 (D. C. M. D. Tenn. 1961); Dickey v. Alabama State Board of Education, 273 F. Supp. 613 (D. C. M. D. Ala. 1967). See also Note, "Unconstitutional Conditions," 73 *Harv. L. Rev.* 1595 (1960); Note, "Academic Freedom," 81 *Harv. L. Rev.* 1045 (1968).

II

The problem posed by the present case does not relate to regulation of the length of skirts or the type of clothing, to hair style, or deportment. Cf. *Ferrell* v. *Dallas Independent School District*, 392 F. 2d 697 (1968); *Pugsley* v. *Sellmeyer*, 158 Ark. 247, 250 S. W. 538 (1923). It does not concern aggressive, disruptive action or even group demonstrations. Our problem involves direct, primary First Amendment rights akin to "pure speech."

The school officials banned and sought to punish petitioners for a silent, passive expression of opinion, unaccompanied by any disorder or disturbance on the part of petitioners. There is here no evidence whatever of petitioners' interference, actual or nascent, with the schools' work or of collision with the rights of other students to be secure and to be let alone. Accordingly, this case does not concern speech or action that intrudes upon the work of the schools or the rights of other students.

Only a few of the 18,000 students in the school system wore the black armbands. Only five students were suspended for wearing them. There is no indication that the work of the schools or any class was disrupted. Outside the classrooms, a few students made hostile remarks to the children wearing armbands, but there were no threats or acts of violence on school premises.

The District Court concluded that the action of the school authorities was reasonable because it was based upon their fear of a disturbance from the wearing of the armbands. But, in our system, undifferentiated fear or apprehension of disturbance is not enough to overcome the right to freedom of expression. Any departure from absolute regimentation may cause trouble. Any variation from the majority's opinion may inspire fear. Any word spoken, in class, in the lunchroom, or on the campus, that deviates from the views of another person may start an argument or cause a disturbance. But our Constitution says we must take this risk, *Terminiello* v. *Chicago*, 337 U.S. 1 (1949); and our history says that it is this sort of hazardous freedom—this kind of openness—that is the basis of our national strength and of the independence and vigor of Americans who grow up and live in this relatively permissive, often disputatious, society.

In order for the State in the person of school officials to justify prohibition of a particular expression of opinion, it must be able to show that its action was caused by something more than a mere desire to avoid the discomfort and unpleasantness that always accompany an unpopular viewpoint. Certainly where there is no finding and no showing that engaging in the forbidden conduct would "materially and substantially interfere with the requirements of appropriate discipline in the operation of the school," the prohibition cannot be sustained. *Burnside* v. *Byars, supra*, at 749.

In the present case, the District Court made no such finding, and our independent examination of the record fails to yield evidence that the school authorities had reason to anticipate that the wearing of the armbands would substantially interfere with the work of the school or impinge upon the rights of other students. Even an official memorandum prepared after the suspension that listed the reasons for the ban on wearing the armbands made no reference to the anticipation of such disruption.[3]

On the contrary, the action of the school authorities appears to have been based upon an urgent wish to avoid the controversy which might result from the expression, even by the silent symbol of armbands, of opposition to this Nation's part in the conflagration in Vietnam.[4] It is revealing, in this respect, that the meeting at which the school principals decided to issue the contested regulation was called in response to a student's statement to the journalism teacher in one of the schools that he wanted to write an article on Vietnam and have it published in the school paper. (The student was dissuaded.[5])

It is also relevant that the school authorities did not purport to prohibit the wearing of all symbols of political or controversial significance. The record shows that students in some of the schools wore buttons relating to national political campaigns, and some even wore the Iron Cross, traditionally a symbol of Nazism. The order prohibiting the wearing of armbands did not extend to these. Instead, a particular symbol—black armbands worn to exhibit opposition to this Nation's involvement in Vietnam—was singled out for prohibition. Clearly, the prohibition of expression of one particular opinion, at least without evidence that it is necessary to avoid material and substantial interference with schoolwork or discipline, is not constitutionally permissible.

In our system, state-operated schools may not be enclaves of totalitarianism. School officials do not possess absolute authority over their students. Students

---

[3]The only suggestions of fear of disorder in the report are these:

"A former student of one of our high schools was killed in Viet Nam. Some of his friends are still in school and it was felt that if any kind of a demonstration existed, it might evolve into something which would be difficult to control."

"Students at one of the high schools were heard to say they would wear armbands of other colors if the black bands prevailed."

Moreover, the testimony of school authorities at trial indicates that it was not fear of disruption that motivated the regulation prohibiting the armbands; the regulation was directed against "the principle of the demonstration" itself. School authorities simply felt that "the schools are no place for demonstrations," and if the students "didn't like the way our elected officials were handling things, it should be handled with the ballot box and not in the halls of our public schools."

[4]The District Court found that the school authorities, in prohibiting black armbands, were influenced by the fact that "the Viet Nam war and the involvement of the United States therein has been the subject of a major controversy for some time. When the arm band regulation involved herein was promulgated, debate over the Viet Nam war had become vehement in many localities. A protest march against the war had been recently held in Washington, D.C. A wave of draft card burning incidents protesting the war had swept the country. At that time two highly publicized draft card burning cases were pending in this Court. Both individuals supporting the war and those opposing it were quite vocal in expressing their views." 258 F. Supp., at 972–973.

[5]After the principals' meeting, the director of secondary education and the principal of the high school informed the student that the principals were opposed to publication of his article. They reported that "we felt that it was a very friendly conversation, although we did not feel that we had convinced the student that our decision was a just one."

in school as well as out of school are "persons" under our Constitution. They are possessed of fundamental rights which the State must respect, just as they themselves must respect their obligations to the State. In our system, students may not be regarded as closed-circuit recipients of only that which the State chooses to communicate. They may not be confined to the expression of those sentiments that are officially approved. In the absence of a specific showing of constitutionally valid reasons to regulate their speech, students are entitled to freedom of expression of their views. As Judge Gewin, speaking for the Fifth Circuit, said, school officials cannot suppress "expressions of feelings with which they do not wish to contend." *Burnside v. Byars, supra,* at 749.

In *Meyer v. Nebraska, supra,* at 402, Mr. Justice McReynolds expressed this Nation's repudiation of the principle that a State might so conduct its schools as to "foster a homogeneous people." He said:

> *In order to submerge the individual and develop ideal citizens, Sparta assembled the males at seven into barracks and intrusted their subsequent education and training to official guardians. Although such measures have been deliberately approved by men of great genius, their ideas touching the relation between individual and State were wholly different from those upon which our institutions rest; and it hardly will be affirmed that any legislature could impose such restrictions upon the people of a State without doing violence to both letter and spirit of the Constitution.*

This principle has been repeated by this Court on numerous occasions during the intervening years. In *Keyishian v. Board of Regents,* 385 U.S. 589, 603, Mr. Justice Brennan, speaking for the Court, said:

> "The vigilant protection of constitutional freedoms is nowhere more vital than in the community of American schools." Shelton v. Tucker [364 U.S. 479], at 487. The classroom is peculiarly the "marketplace of ideas." The Nation's future depends upon leaders trained through wide exposure to that robust exchange of ideas which discovers truth "out of a multitude of tongues, [rather] than through any kind of authoritative selection."

The principle of these cases is not confined to the supervised and ordained discussion which takes place in the classroom. The principal use to which the schools are dedicated is to accommodate students during prescribed hours for the purpose of certain types of activities. Among those activities is personal intercommunication among the students.[6] This is not only an inevitable part of the

---

[6]In Hammond v. South Carolina State College, 272 F. Supp. 947 (D.C.S.C. 1967), District Judge Hemphill had before him a case involving a meeting on campus of 300 students to express their views on school practices. He pointed out that a school is not like a hospital or a

process of attending school; it is also an important part of the educational process. A student's rights, therefore, do not embrace merely the classroom hours. When he is in the cafeteria, or on the playing field, or on the campus during the authorized hours, he may express his opinions, even on controversial subjects like the conflict in Vietnam, if he does so without "materially and substantially interfer[ing] with the requirements of appropriate discipline in the operation of the school" and without colliding with the rights of others. *Burnside v. Byars, supra*, at 749. But conduct by the student, in class or out of it, which for any reason—whether it stems from time, place, or type of behavior—materially disrupts classwork or involves substantial disorder or invasion of the rights of others is, of course, not immunized by the constitutional guarantee of freedom of speech. Cf. *Blackwell v. Issaquena County Board of Education,* 363 F. 2d 749 (C. A. 5th Cir. 1966).

Under our Constitution, free speech is not a right that is given only to be so circumscribed that it exists in principle but not in fact. Freedom of expression would not truly exist if the right could be exercised only in an area that a benevolent government has provided as a safe haven for crackpots. The Constitution says that Congress (and the States) may not abridge the right to free speech. This provision means what it says. We properly read it to permit reasonable regulation of speech-connected activities in carefully restricted circumstances. But we do not confine the permissible exercise of First Amendment rights to a telephone booth or the four corners of a pamphlet, or to supervised and ordained discussion in a school classroom.

If a regulation were adopted by school officials forbidding discussion of the Vietnam conflict, or the expression by any student of opposition to it anywhere on school property except as part of a prescribed classroom exercise, it would be obvious that the regulation would violate the constitutional rights of students, at least if it could not be justified by a showing that the students' activities would materially and substantially disrupt the work and discipline of the school. Cf. *Hammond v. South Carolina State College,* 272 F. Supp. 947 (D.C.S.C. 1967) (orderly protest meeting on state college campus); *Dickey v. Alabama State Board of Education,* 273 F. Supp. 613 (D.C.M.D. Ala. 1967) (expulsion of student editor of college newspaper). In the circumstances of the present case, the prohibition of the silent, passive "witness of the armbands," as one of the children called it, is no less offensive to the Constitution's guarantees.

As we have discussed, the record does not demonstrate any facts which might reasonably have led school authorities to forecast substantial disruption of or material interference with school activities, and no disturbances or disorders on the school premises in fact occurred. These petitioners merely went about their ordained rounds in school. Their deviation consisted only in wearing on their sleeve a band of black cloth, not more than two inches wide. They wore it to exhibit

jail enclosure. Cf. *Cox v. Louisiana*, 379 U.S. 536 (1965); *Adderley v. Florida*, 385 U.S. 39 (1966). It is a public place, and its dedication to specific uses does not imply that the constitutional rights of persons entitled to be there are to be gauged as if the premises were purely private property. Cf. *Edwards v. South Carolina*, 372 U.S. 229 (1963); *Brown v. Louisiana*, 383 U.S. 131 (1966).

their disapproval of the Vietnam hostilities and their advocacy of a truce, to make their views known, and, by their example, to influence others to adopt them. They neither interrupted school activities nor sought to intrude in the school affairs or the lives of others. They caused discussion outside of the classrooms, but no interference with work and no disorder. In the circumstances, our Constitution does not permit officials of the State to deny their form of expression.

We express no opinion as to the form of relief which should be granted, this being a matter for the lower courts to determine. We reverse and remand for further proceedings consistent with this opinion.

Reversed and remanded.

Mr. Justice Black, Dissenting

The Court's holding in this case ushers in what I deem to be an entirely new era in which the power to control pupils by the elected "officials of state supported public schools . . ." in the United States is in ultimate effect transferred to the Supreme Court.[7] The Court brought this particular case here on a petition for certiorari urging that the First and Fourteenth Amendments protect the right of school pupils to express their political views all the way "from kindergarten through high school." Here the constitutional right to "political expression" asserted was a right to wear black armbands during school hours and at classes in order to demonstrate to the other students that the petitioners were mourning because of the death of United States soldiers in Vietnam and to protest that war which they were against. Ordered to refrain from wearing the armbands in school by the elected school officials and the teachers vested with state authority to do so, apparently only seven out of the school system's 18,000 pupils deliberately refused to obey the order. One defying pupil was Paul Tinker, 8 years old, who was in the second grade; another, Hope Tinker, was 11 years old and in the fifth grade; a third member of the Tinker family was 13, in the eighth grade; and a fourth member of the same family was John Tinker, 15 years old, an 11th grade high school pupil. Their father, a Methodist minister without a church, is paid a salary by the American Friends Service Committee. Another student who defied the school order and insisted on wearing an armband in school was Christopher Eckhardt, an 11th grade pupil and a petitioner in this case. His mother is an official in the Women's International League for Peace and Freedom.

As I read the Court's opinion it relies upon the following grounds for holding unconstitutional the judgment of the Des Moines school officials and the two courts below. First, the Court concludes that the wearing of armbands is "symbolic speech" which is "akin to 'pure speech'" and therefore protected by the

---

[7]The petition for certiorari here presented this single question: "Whether the First and Fourteenth Amendments permit officials of state supported public schools to prohibit students from wearing symbols of political views within school premises where the symbols are not disruptive of school discipline or decorum."

First and Fourteenth Amendments. Secondly, the Court decides that the public schools are an appropriate place to exercise "symbolic speech" as long as normal school functions are not "unreasonably" disrupted. Finally, the Court arrogates to itself, rather than to the State's elected officials charged with running the schools, the decision as to which school disciplinary regulations are "reasonable."

Assuming that the Court is correct in holding that the conduct of wearing armbands for the purpose of conveying political ideas is protected by the First Amendment, cf., e.g., *Giboney* v. *Empire Storage & Ice Co.*, 336 U.S. 490 (1949), the crucial remaining questions are whether students and teachers may use the schools at their whim as a platform for the exercise of free speech—"symbolic" or "pure"—and whether the courts will allocate to themselves the function of deciding how the pupils' school day will be spent. While I have always believed that under the First and Fourteenth Amendments neither the State nor the Federal Government has any authority to regulate or censor the content of speech, I have never believed that any person has a right to give speeches or engage in demonstrations where he pleases and when he pleases. This Court has already rejected such a notion. In *Cox* v. *Louisiana,* 379 U.S. 536, 554 (1965), for example, the Court clearly stated that the rights of free speech and assembly "do not mean that everyone with opinions or beliefs to express may address a group at any public place and at any time."

While the record does not show that any of these armband students shouted, used profane language, or were violent in any manner, detailed testimony by some of them shows their armbands caused comments, warnings by other students, the poking of fun at them, and a warning by an older football player that other, nonprotesting students had better let them alone. There is also evidence that a teacher of mathematics had his lesson period practically "wrecked" chiefly by disputes with Mary Beth Tinker, who wore her armband for her "demonstration." Even a casual reading of the record shows that this armband did divert students' minds from their regular lessons, and that talk, comments, etc., made John Tinker "self-conscious" in attending school with his armband. While the absence of obscene remarks or boisterous and loud disorder perhaps justifies the Court's statement that the few armbanded students did not actually "disrupt" the classwork, I think the record overwhelmingly shows that the armbands did exactly what the elected school officials and principals foresaw they would, that is, took the students' minds off their classwork and diverted them to thoughts about the highly emotional subject of the Vietnam war. And I repeat that if the time has come when pupils of state-supported schools, kindergartens, grammar schools, or high schools, can defy and flout orders of school officials to keep their minds on their own schoolwork, it is the beginning of a new revolutionary era of permissiveness in this country fostered by the judiciary. The next logical step, it appears to me, would be to hold unconstitutional laws that bar pupils under 21 or 18 from voting, or from being elected members of the boards of education.[8]

[8]The following Associated Press article appeared in the Washington *Evening Star*, January 11, 1969, p. A–2, col. 1:
"Bellingham, Mass. (AP)—Todd R. Hennessy, 16, has filed nominating papers to run for

The United States District Court refused to hold that the state school order violated the First and Fourteenth Amendments. 258 F. Supp. 971. Holding that the protest was akin to speech, which is protected by the First and Fourteenth Amendments, that court held that the school order was "reasonable" and hence constitutional. There was at one time a line of cases holding "reasonableness" as the court saw it to be the test of a "due process" violation. Two cases upon which the Court today heavily relies for striking down this school order used this test of reasonableness, *Meyer* v. *Nebraska*, 262 U.S. 390 (1923), and *Bartels* v. *Iowa*, 262 U.S. 404 (1923). The opinions in both cases were written by Mr. Justice McReynolds; Mr. Justice Holmes, who opposed this reasonableness test, dissented from the holdings as did Mr. Justice Sutherland. This constitutional test of reasonableness prevailed in this Court for a season. It was this test that brought on President Franklin Roosevelt's well-known Court fight. His proposed legislation did not pass, but the fight left the "reasonableness" constitutional test dead on the battlefield, so much so that this Court in *Ferguson* v. *Skrupa*, 372 U.S. 726, 729, 730, after a thorough review of the old cases, was able to conclude in 1963:

> *There was a time when the Due Process Clause was used by this Court to strike down laws which were thought unreasonable, that is, unwise or incompatible with some particular economic or social philosophy....*
>
> *The doctrine that prevailed in* Lochner, Coppage, Adkins, Burns, *and like cases—that due process authorizes courts to hold laws unconstitutional when they believe the legislature has acted unwisely —has long since been discarded.*

The *Ferguson* case totally repudiated the old reasonableness-due process test, the doctrine that judges have the power to hold laws unconstitutional upon the belief of judges that they "shock the conscience" or that they are "unreasonable," "arbitrary," "irrational," "contrary to fundamental 'decency,'" or some other such flexible term without precise boundaries. I have many times expressed my opposition to that concept on the ground that it gives judges power to strike down any law they do not like. If the majority of the Court today, by agreeing to the opinion of my Brother Fortas, is resurrecting that old reasonableness-due process test, I think the constitutional change should be plainly, unequivocally, and forthrightly stated for the benefit of the bench and bar. It will be a sad day for the country, I believe, when the present-day Court returns to the McReynolds due process concept. Other cases cited by the Court do not, as implied, follow the McReynolds reasonableness doctrine. *West Virginia* v. *Barnette*, 319 U.S. 624, clearly rejecting the "reasonableness" test, held that the Fourteenth Amendment made the First applicable to the States, and that the two forbade a State to *compel* little schoolchildren to salute the United States flag when they had

town park commissioner in the March election.
"'I can see nothing illegal in the youth's seeking the elective office,' said Lee Ambler, the town counsel. 'But I can't overlook the possibility that if he is elected any legal contract entered into by the park commissioner would be void because he is a juvenile.'
"Todd is a junior in Mount St. Charles Academy, where he has a top scholastic record."

religious scruples against doing so.[9] Neither *Thornhill v. Alabama,* 310 U.S. 88; *Stromberg v. California,* 283 U.S. 359; *Edwards v. South Carolina,* 372 U.S. 229; nor *Brown v. Louisiana,* 383 U.S. 131, related to schoolchildren at all, and none of these cases embraced Mr. Justice McReynolds' reasonableness test; and *Thornhill, Edwards,* and *Brown* relied on the vagueness of state statutes under scrutiny to hold them unconstitutional. *Cox v. Louisiana,* 379 U.S. 536, 555, and *Adderley v. Florida,* 385 U.S. 39, cited by the Court as a "compare," indicating, I suppose, that these two cases are no longer the law, were not rested to the slightest extent on the *Meyer* and *Bartels* "reasonableness-due process-McReynolds" constitutional test.

I deny, therefore, that it has been the "unmistakable holding of this Court for almost 50 years" that "students" and "teachers" take with them into the "schoolhouse gate" constitutional rights to "freedom of speech or expression." Even *Meyer* did not hold that. It makes no reference to "symbolic speech" at all; what it did was to strike down as "unreasonable" and therefore unconstitutional a Nebraska law barring the teaching of the German language before the children reached the eighth grade. One can well agree with Mr. Justice Holmes and Mr. Justice Sutherland, as I do, that such a law was no more unreasonable that it would be to bar the teaching of Latin and Greek to pupils who have not reached the eighth grade. In fact, I think the majority's reason for invalidating the Nebraska law was that it did not like it or in legal jargon that it "shocked the Court's conscience," "offended its sense of justice," or was "contrary to fundamental concepts of the English-speaking world," as the Court has sometimes said. See, e.g., *Rochin v. California,* 342 U.S. 165, and *Irvine v. California,* 347 U.S. 128. The truth is that a teacher of kindergarten, grammar school, or high school pupils no more carries into a school with him a complete right to freedom of speech and expression than an anti-Catholic or anti-Semite carries with him a complete freedom of speech and religion into a Catholic church or Jewish synagogue. Nor does a person carry with him into the United States Senate or House, or into the Supreme Court, or any other court, a complete constitutional right to go into those places contrary to their rules and speak his mind on any subject he pleases. It is a myth to say that any person has a constitutional right to say what he pleases, where he pleases, and when he pleases. Our Court has decided precisely the opposite. See, e.g., *Cox v. Louisiana,* 379 U.S. 536, 555; *Adderley v. Florida,* 385 U.S. 39.

In my view, teachers in state-controlled public schools are hired to teach there. Although Mr. Justice McReynolds may have intimated to the contrary in

[9]In Cantwell v. Connecticut, 310 U.S. 296, 303–304 (1940), this Court said:
"The First Amendment declares that Congress shall make no law respecting an establishment of religion or prohibiting the free exercise thereof. The Fourteenth Amendment has rendered the legislatures of the states as incompetent as Congress to enact such laws. The constitutional inhibition of legislation on the subject of religion has a double aspect. On the one hand, it forestalls compulsion by law of the acceptance of any creed or the practice of any form of worship. Freedom of conscience and freedom to adhere to such religious organization or form of worship as the individual may choose cannot be restricted by law. On the other hand, it safeguards the free exercise of the chosen form of religion. Thus the Amendment embraces two concepts—freedom to believe and freedom to act. The first is absolute but, in the nature of things, the second cannot be. Conduct remains subject to regulation for the protection of society.

Meyer v. Nebraska, supra, certainly a teacher is not paid to go into school and teach subjects the State does not hire him to teach as a part of its selected curriculum. Nor are public school students sent to the schools at public expense to broadcast political or any other views to educate and inform the public. The original idea of schools, which I do not believe is yet abandoned as worthless or out of date, was that children had not yet reached the point of experience and wisdom which enabled them to teach all of their elders. It may be that the Nation has outworn the old-fashioned slogan that "children are to be seen not heard," but one may, I hope, be permitted to harbor the thought that taxpayers send children to school on the premise that at their age they need to learn, not teach.

The true principles on this whole subject were in my judgment spoken by Mr. Justice McKenna for the Court in *Waugh v. Mississippi University* in 237 U.S. 589, 596–597. The State had there passed a law barring students from peaceably assembling in Greek letter fraternities and providing that students who joined them could be expelled from school. This law would appear on the surface to run afoul of the First Amendment's freedom of assembly clause. The law was attacked as violative of due process and of the privileges and immunities clause and as a deprivation of property and of liberty, under the Fourteenth Amendment. It was argued that the fraternity made its members more moral, taught discipline, and inspired its members to study harder and to obey better the rules of discipline and order. This Court rejected all the "fervid" pleas of the fraternities' advocates and decided unanimously against these Fourteenth Amendment arguments. The Court in its next to the last paragraph made this statement which has complete relevance for us today:

> *It is said that the fraternity to which complainant belongs is a moral and of itself a disciplinary force. This need not be denied. But whether such membership makes against discipline was for the State of Mississippi to determine. It is to be remembered that the University was established by the State and is under the control of the State, and the enactment of the statute may have been induced by the opinion that* membership in the prohibited societies divided the attention of the students and distracted from that singleness of purpose which the State desired to exist in its public educational institutions. *It is not for us to entertain conjectures in opposition to the views of the State and annul its regulations upon disputable considerations of their wisdom or necessity. (Emphasis supplied.)*

It was on the foregoing argument that this Court sustained the power of Mississippi to curtail the First Amendment's right of peaceable assembly. And the same reasons are equally applicable to curtailing in the States' public schools the right to complete freedom of expression. Iowa's public schools, like Mississippi's university, are operated to give students an opportunity to learn, not to talk politics by actual speech, or by "symbolic" speech. And, as I have pointed out before, the record amply shows that public protest in the school classes against the Vietnam war "distracted from that singleness of purpose which the State [here Iowa] desired to exist in its public educational institutions." Here the Court should accord Iowa educational institutions the same right to determine for themselves to what extent free expression should be allowed in its schools as it accorded Mississippi with reference to freedom of assembly. But even if the record were silent as to protests against the Vietnam war distracting students from their assigned class work, members of this Court, like all other citizens, know, without being told, that the disputes over the wisdom of the Vietnam war have disrupted and divided this country as few other issues ever have. Of course students, like other people, cannot concentrate on lesser issues when black armbands are being ostentatiously displayed in their presence to call attention to the wounded and dead of the war, some of the wounded and the dead being their friends and neighbors. It was, of course, to distract the attention of other students that some students insisted up to the very point of their own suspension from school that they were determined to sit in school with their symbolic armbands.

Change has been said to be truly the law of life but sometimes the old and the tried and true are worth holding. The schools of this Nation have undoubtedly contributed to giving us tranquility and to making us a more law-abiding people. Uncontrolled and uncontrollable liberty is an enemy to domestic peace. We cannot close our eyes to the fact that some of the country's greatest problems are crimes committed by the youth, too many of school age. School discipline, like parental discipline, is an integral and important part of training our children to be good citizens—to be better citizens. Here a very small number of students have crisply and summarily refused to obey a school order designed to give pupils who want to learn the opportunity to do so. One does not need to be a prophet or the son of a prophet to know that after the Court's holding today some students in Iowa schools and indeed in all schools will be ready, able, and willing to defy their teachers on practically all orders. This is the more unfortunate for the schools since groups of students all over the land are already running loose, conducting break-ins, sit-ins, lie-ins, and smash-ins. Many of these student groups, as is all too familiar to all who read the newspapers and watch the television news programs, have already engaged in rioting, property seizures, and destruction. They have picketed schools to force students not to cross their picket lines and have too often violently attacked earnest but frightened students who wanted an education that the pickets did not want them to get. Students engaged in such activities are apparently confident that they know far more about how to operate public school systems than do their parents, teachers, and elected school officials. It is no answer to say that the particular students here have not yet reached such high points in their demands to attend classes in order to exercise their political pressures. Turned loose with lawsuits for damages and injunctions against their teachers as they are here, it is nothing but wishful thinking to imagine that young, immature students will not soon believe it is their right to control the schools rather than the right of the States that collect the taxes to hire the teachers for the benefit of the pupils. This case, therefore, wholly without constitutional reasons in my judgment, subjects all the public schools in the country to the whims and caprices of their loudest-mouthed, but maybe not their brightest, students. I, for one, am not fully persuaded that school pupils are wise enough, even with this Court's expert help from Washington, to run the 23,390 public school systems[10] in our 50 States. I wish, therefore, wholly to disclaim any purpose on my part to hold that the Federal Constitution compels the teachers, parents, and elected school officials to surrender control of the American public school system to public school students. I dissent.

[10]*Statistical Abstract of the United States* (1968), Table No. 578, p. 406.

Symbolic Conduct and Freedom of Speech
Fred R. Berger[1]

Civil disobedience is no longer the live topic it was in the United States during the 1960s. As the Vietnam war ended, and the civil rights struggle gave way to more intractable racial difficulties, public discussion of civil disobedience virtually died out. Civil disobedience long predated the sixties, however, and it will continue to be a mode of protest, resistance, or political change as long as governments exist. Moreover, there is much unfinished business in the area of the political and legal philosophy of American institutions which bears on civil disobedience. Despite years of litigation involving conscience-motivated disobedience, there still is no clearcut jurisprudence of civil disobedience to which the American legal system is committed. This is especially true of protest that involves symbolic conduct. The courts have been faced with claims to First Amendment protection of such conduct as distributing literature,[2] soliciting donations for a religious group,[3] parading,[4] picketing,[5] burning a flag,[6] wearing black armbands to

---

[1] I would like to thank Mary Vencill for research and critical assistance without which this essay could not have been written. I would also like to thank Richard Wasserstrom for suggestions that have helped to clarify certain important points.

[2] Lovell v. City of Griffin, 303 U.S. 444 (1938).

[3] Cantwell v. Connecticut, 310 U.S. 296 (1940).

[4] There are a great many cases bearing on this issue. See, e.g., Shuttlesworth v. City of Birmingham, 382 U.S. 87 (1965).

[5] The classic case is Thornhill v. Alabama, 310 U.S. 88 (1940). The development and recent history of picketing doctrine is outlined in Thomas I. Emerson, *The System of Freedom of Expression* (New York: Random House, 1970), pp. 435–49.

[6] Street v. New York, 394 U.S. 576 (1969).

school,[7] burning a draft card,[8] sitting-in at a segregated lunch counter,[9] and so on. Although the Supreme Court has at times shown admirable sensitivity to the claims of the protestors, it has also shown a remarkable flexibility in the decisions it has taken. The results have appeared to some observers quite anomalous or even bordering on the contradictory.

Part of the difficulty with the Court's position arises from an inadequate theoretical position. It has sometimes employed a distinction between "pure speech" and "speech plus" as a tool for deciding cases involving symbolic conduct. "Speech plus," presumably, cannot have the same protections afforded speech proper. We shall explore some difficulties with this treatment.

In this essay I shall seek: (1) to show up the inadequacy of the speech-conduct distinction; (2) to illuminate the nature of symbolic conduct; (3) to provide a philosophical justification for bringing symbolic conduct under First Amendment purview; (4) to answer some of the chief objections to doing so; and (5) to indicate the sorts of legal doctrines needed to intelligently deal with symbolic conduct. Some of this work has been done by others.[10] My intention is to present the issues in outline or capsule form, and to stress points that others have missed or have not dealt with. I maintain that the same criteria should apply to symbolic conduct and so-called pure speech. Just as one cannot be free to say anything one wants, wherever and whenever one wants, so too one cannot engage in symbolic conduct in any form, whenever and wherever one wants. However, the grounds for distinguishing the acceptable from the unacceptable cases should be the same for both conventional and symbolic communication.

I. The Nature of Symbolic Conduct

Symbolic conduct is a subject to which surprisingly little attention has been given. Moreover, there is one special form of symbolic conduct which, in my opinion, has very great importance in the contemporary world and which has not been adequately discussed in the literature.

---

[7]Tinker v. Des Moines Independent Community School District, 393 U.S. 503 (1969).
[8]United States v. O'Brien, 391 U.S. 367 (1968).
[9]See Garner v. Louisiana, 368 U.S. 157, 201–202 (1961), where the issue was posed clearly by Justice Harlan. The relevant passage is quoted below, in note 11.
[10]Some of the works I have found especially helpful are: Harry Kalven, Jr., "The Concept of the Public Forum: Cox v. Louisiana," *The Supreme Court Review, 1965*, ed. P. Kurland (Chicago: University of Chicago Press, 1966), pp. 1–32; Dean Alfange, Jr., "Free Speech and Symbolic Conduct: The Draft-Card Burning Case," *The Supreme Court Review, 1968*, ed. P. Kurland (Chicago: University of Chicago Press, 1969), pp. 1–52; Lawrence R. Velvel, "Freedom of Speech and the Draft-Card Burning Cases," *Kansas Law Review XVI* (1968), pp. 149–79; James E. Leahy, "'Flamboyant Protest,' the First Amendment and the Boston Tea Party," *Brooklyn Law Review* XXXVI (Winter 1970), pp. 185–211; and Melville B. Nimmer, "The Meaning of Symbolic Speech Under the First Amendment," *UCLA Law Review* XXI (October 1973), pp. 29–62. Nimmer's article has the most extensive treatment of the nature of symbolic conduct.

In contemporary philosophical circles theories of "speech acts" are very popular. Such theories emphasize how, in engaging in *speech*, we perform certain acts, e.g., promising, insulting, contracting, etc. What is wanted is a theory that explains how, in engaging in *other* acts, e.g., burning a draft card, we accomplish what is done by speech acts, and why, sometimes, we do it *better* that way. Although I cannot provide such a theory, I shall indicate some ways in which actions may be symbolic and thus communicate ideas. One kind of symbolic action—a "demonstration" of an evil—I think is particularly important.

The simplest form of symbolic action takes place when what are normally noncommunicative acts are mingled with conventional speech or with conventional nonverbal symbols, e.g., banners, placards, flags, etc. Here, the nonverbal devices convey at least part of the message and give added meaning to the behavior. A group might, for example, wear black armbands in a sit-in at a police station to protest the shooting of a member of the group.

Special problems are raised if there is a temporal gap in the behavior and the appearance of the conventional symbols or speech. For example, one might have burned one's draft card during the Vietnam War and later marched to the draft board with the ashes to confront the state with the deed. At first glance, it appears there are *two* acts committed—the burning of the draft card, which is not communicative (it may have been done in secret), and the later announcement of the deed. Only the latter, some persons would say, counts as speech.

Such an approach seems overly hasty, for there are at least two important reasons for regarding the series of actions as aspects of one complex act, which, as a whole, carries the communicative force of the protest. First, the full impact of the conventional speech is tied in essential ways to the defiance of statute embodied in the earlier aspect of the complex. Second, the act was done (I am supposing), in part *as* an aspect of the attempt to confront the state in a dramatic way with its alleged iniquity. In other words, the force, effectiveness, and importance attached to the communication are altered and enhanced through the commission of the nonverbal act, and this was part of the actor's intention. By virtue of its properties, the nonverbal act influences the character of the communication and thus acquires communicative force. It does not have this force performed alone, but then the conventional speech does not fully convey its message when performed alone, either. So, though one can distinguish the nonverbal activities, from another perspective they are part of a chain of activities that together constitute the full communicative act.

If this reasoning seems implausible, consider that we would not find it acceptable as a defense in a murder case for the defendant to claim that all he did was to set an alarm clock, if we knew that the clock was connected to a bomb and that the defendant knew this and set the alarm with the intention of exploding the bomb and killing someone. It is the intended connections between what (from another point of view) appear as discrete events that justify us in part in identifying a single act of murder. Perhaps more a propos, we can note that the movements of our vocal chords, lips, and tongues are different from one another and from the sounds we make. We do not, however, separate any of these from the protected act of speaking, simply because if they occurred alone they would not convey any message. The sorts of acts we are talking of may be seen as a necessary means of conveying a message with full force, clarity, and urgency.

Alternatively, these cases, and a spectrum of others, could be characterized as ones in which objects or actions normally not symbolic are *given* a symbolic function. Presumably, any thing, action, or event can be arbitrarily assigned a meaning, but it is clear that the symbolic function usually requires that the "symbol" bear some relation to the object of the protest. For example, a draft card had a clear, obvious connection to the conduct of a war that protestors opposed. On the other hand, political assassination, though sometimes done with communicative purpose or effect, is not well suited for that purpose because the audience cannot readily identify the policies or programs being protested and is drawn away from the "message" by the nature of the deed.

There is one special kind of symbolic conduct that relies heavily on its connection with the protested injustice. This is an extremely important form of civil disobedience in contemporary society, and it has not been sufficiently recognized. These are statute-violating acts that *demonstrate,* in their commission, the protested injustice or policy. Such acts have sometimes been of great historical importance. When Gandhi marched to the sea and extracted a bit of salt from it—a violation of British colonial law—he was *demonstrating* the nature, extent, and burden of English colonial oppression and of the laws buttressing it. He showed that even so simple and harmless an act as making salt from sea water was made a crime in order to guarantee an open market for English salt manufacturers. Moreover, the Salt Acts were not the most oppressive laws Gandhi was protesting; his civil disobedience was doubly symbolic in that it pointed to the many ways in which colonial rule stifled native initiative and industry to turn British profits.

Similarly, when black students in the United States refused to leave segregated lunch counters, they were demonstrating that, even in such matters as getting a cup of coffee in a department store, they were discriminated against. And, of course, the lunch counter sit-ins were symbolic of the various affronts to human dignity supported by racist local governments. A demonstration of this kind may be a more meaningful appeal to the electorate than conventional speech, and, indeed, these and other demonstrations helped pave the way for legislation and changed attitudes that decades of speeches, petitions, legal marches, etc., had been unable to accomplish.[11]

The impact of a demonstration, and thus its importance, is very much a function of the manner in which it serves to communicate ideas. A demonstration is

[11]In the case of Garner v. Louisiana, 368 U.S. 157, 201–202, Justice Harlan remarked:
"We would surely have to be blind not to recognize that petitioners were sitting at these counters, where they knew they would not be served, in order to demonstrate that their race was being segregated in dining facilities in this part of the country.
Such a demonstration, in the circumstances of these two cases, is as much a part of the "free trade in ideas" as is verbal expression, more commonly thought of as "speech." It, like speech, appeals to good sense and to "the power of reason as applied through public discussion" just as much as, if not more than, a public oration delivered from a soapbox at a street corner."

very like what Charles Peirce called an *icon* or *iconic sign*: "a sign that represents its Object in resembling it."[12] The kinds of civil disobedience I am discussing create, through the violation of statute or orders of public officials, situations that have features in common with the protested wrong by virtue of being an instance of it. A demonstration *shows* people the injustice and signifies patterns of which it is an instance. With today's potential for media coverage, this can be a significant means of enlightening a complacent public—through either apprising it of facts or getting it to better appreciate facts of which it is already aware. The general public could readily identify with the situation of young blacks at the lunch counters and was literally confronted with injustices of which it previously had only an intellectual grasp.

In summary, there appear to be two general conditions for an act to be communicative or symbolic: (1) It has features (of the kinds indicated) that suit it for conveying ideas, and (2) the actor intends (perhaps among other things) to communicate ideas in that way.

II. The Argument for Protection

Does the democratic idea of freedom of expression give grounds for according special protection to symbolic conduct—e.g., under the umbrella of the First Amendment of the Constitution of the United States? I shall argue that it does.

First, let us concentrate on the point, purpose, and values that provide the rationale for the First Amendment. Freedom of speech, press, and assembly reflect the democratic principles that all citizens are sources of ideas and political influence, that all citizens have a right to participate in their governance, that freedom of expression is essential to the preservation and furtherance of other freedoms, and that certain kinds of liberties are crucial to a sense of dignity and self-determination. Moreover, the First Amendment is clearly intended to foster open, unfettered, informed debate—an obvious prerequisite for the determination of public policy and the election of public officials.[13]

Furthermore, to the extent that being oneself openly and honestly involves expressing oneself in one's own way, mutual respect for one another as persons dictates freedom of expression as something deserving of protection, in as

---

[12]Charles S. Peirce, *Values in a Universe of Chance*, ed. Philip P. Wiener (Garden City, N.Y.: Doubleday, 1958), p. 368. Cf. also, Charles W. Morris: "A sign is iconic to the extent to which it itself has the properties of its denotata." (*Signs, Language, and Behavior* [New York: George Braziller, 1946], p. 349.) Morris' work is an attempt to develop a general theory of signs that would have application to, among other things, the issues raised here. Even if one is unwilling to accept his behavioral approach, or his specific kind of behaviorism, there is a great deal in the book that is useful to problems of this kind.

[13]All of the underlying values I have mentioned have been cited by the courts at some time or other in connection with the First Amendment. A helpful discussion of these is in Thomas I. Emerson, *Toward a General Theory of the First Amendment* (New York: Random House, 1967), ch. I. Emerson has useful discussions of the sorts of First Amendment cases I have in mind in his monumental study, *The System of Freedom of Expression*.

many ways as is consistent with civic life. Democracy correctly professes to incorporate respect for persons as a value, and the protection of the right of free speech is one important way in which this is done.

If we take seriously the values underlying freedom of speech, there is no reason to limit its ambit to conventional modes of communication. And, indeed, the Supreme Court has not always insisted on a narrow interpretation of the legal term *speech*, certifying the free speech rights of persons wearing armbands; displaying banners, flags, or placards; holding parades; picketing; etc.

Moreover, there are reasons why, in the contemporary world, unconventional communications have increasing importance. With contemporary media technology, we are literally bombarded with communications of conventional kinds—a situation that has a numbing effect. Also, the "normal" techniques are too often controlled or monopolized by special groups. During the Vietnam War, the successive presidential administrations had continual access to sizable audiences, whereas critics were fortunate to be able to *buy* extremely expensive media time. When one bears in mind that administration platforms dealing with that issue were too often employed for implanting misleading or false beliefs, and for impugning the patriotism and honesty of the opposition, it is apparent that any countercommunication had an uphill battle to fight.[14] In such circumstances, shock tactics may be required.

We should add that many who have cause to protest in our society are unconventional persons who require unconventional modes to feel they are freely and fully expressing their views effectively. To the extent that freedom of speech is a form of respect for autonomous individuals, we should allow maximum tolerance to the need of individuals to express themselves in the manner *they* feel best suits their message. And, to the extent we are willing to take this stance, we will regard restrictions as to time, place, and manner as possible interferences with speech.

Finally, we must note that the conventional, or "normal" channels for mass communication can prove extremely costly and require considerable

---

[14]To cite just one example, President Nixon asserted in a news conference on June 29, 1972, that, at the end of the French-Indochinese conflict, "15,000 French were never accounted for," indicating that the Vietnamese Communists had not released prisoners and that he would not remove American troops from Vietnam and let that happen to American POWs. Within days, the French government disputed the President's claim, stating that "we are certain that the North Vietnamese gave us back all the prisoners they had." It was further pointed out that, though there were approximately 6,200 troops unaccounted for, they were, for the most part, "Nazi SS officers who fled to Indochina to join the French Foreign Legion," and on whom no records had been kept. (San Francisco *Sunday Examiner and Chronicle,* July 2, 1972, Sec. A, p. 4.) It is a further irony that, very close to the time of the President's statement, a couple of cases were being decided in the Supreme Court concerning groups who, two years before, had tried to buy time on television to criticize presidential policies on Vietnam, and had been denied. Cf. Business Executives Move for Vietnam Peace v. FCC, and Democratic National Committee v. FCC, 450 F. 2d 642 (1971), for an appellate ruling on the case. Though the Court of Appeals held that these groups did have a right to be heard, the Supreme Court reversed the ruling, thus leaving dissenting groups at the mercy of the media even if they were able to raise the money for a presentation of their views. Cf. Columbia Broadcasting System, Inc. v. Democratic National Committee, 412 U.S. 94 (1972).

sophistication and knowledge for effective utilization. This is true of the process by which redress is to be had for legal as well as for social wrongs.

III. Objections and Replies

Though most persons with an interest in freedom of speech acknowledge some force to these arguments, many are unwilling to accept the general proposition that symbolic conduct is entitled to First Amendment protection. The chief objection is that recognition of such a principle would expand too broadly the range of activity that would be protected. "We cannot accept the view," Chief Justice Warren wrote in one of the draft-card burning cases, "that an apparently limitless variety of conduct can be labelled *speech* whenever the person engaging in the conduct intends thereby to express an idea."[15] The perceived defects of this expansion vary.

Professor Carl Cohen has argued that, in such cases as sitting-in, blocking traffic, etc., the "specific act . . . is not the sort of thing that requires constitutional protection." To insist that such an act is speech because the actor intends it to be, and "in spite of its specific nature, which is obvious and undeniable," is to bring any sort of action under the First Amendment, which was not its original or "proper present" intention.[16]

Such an argument is beside the point. It is not claimed that trespasses, burning cards or flags, interferences with traffic, and so on, are per se the sorts of things that require constitutional protection. It is *communication* that must be protected. Moreover, it is not claimed that such acts become communicative simply because the actor intends them to be. Rather, they become communicative acts for that reason *and* the fact that they have features that suit them for the conveying of ideas. I have tried to indicate some of these, and Professor Cohen has listed several such features in another place in his book.[17] There is no good reason the courts cannot, at least under certain circumstances, investigate and take note of acts of such kinds and recognize the important communicative role they sometimes play in our social and political life. Finally, we should note that Cohen's point that these acts, in their "specific" descriptions, are not intended to be protected would destroy protection for all speech. Lip movements and the making of sounds are not specifically encompassed within the First Amendment. It is the functional connection of these with the production of communicative speech and the dissemination of ideas that is crucial. Where such a functional connection can be strongly made for acts with other specific descriptions, fidelity to the values for which protection is required makes it incumbent to extend protection to such acts.

---

[15]United States v. O'Brien, 391 U.S. 367, 376 (1968).
[16]Carl Cohen, *Civil Disobedience, Conscience, Tactics, and the Law* (New York: Columbia University Press, 1971), pp. 188–89.
[17]*Ibid.*, p. 53. Cohen correctly points out that symbolic force may be conveyed by the location or time of the act as well as by "the *nature* of the disobedient act."

A second variation on the theme was expressed by former Justice Fortas:

The Supreme Court of the United States has said, over and over, that the words of the First Amendment mean what they say. But they mean what they say and not something else. They guarantee freedom to speak and freedom of the press—not freedom to club people or to destroy property. The First Amendment protects the right to assemble and to petition, but it requires—in plain words—that the right be peaceably exercised.[18]

A related, and perhaps more appealing, objection would stress the dangers to civil rights of *impartially* protecting symbolic conduct without regard to the protestor's political views. Impartial administration of the First Amendment requires protecting the expression of views of those with whom we disagree. If we protect as First Amendment activity a sit-in that protests racial discrimination, then, it may be argued, impartiality requires that we also protect those who seek to block attempts at racial equality.[19]

Such views will seem plausible only if one insists on ignoring important differences between such acts as clubbing people and destroying property, and (for example) making a spoonful of salt or remaining at a lunch counter when asked to leave. The second version will appeal only if we fail to distinguish acts that infringe no basic political and moral rights from those that do. Not all cases of statute-violating acts threaten the lives, property, or basic rights of others. There is simply no reason why the courts cannot recognize this fact; they could consistently protect symbolic conduct that poses no serious dangers while permitting punishment of conduct that does.

This point also bears on my final objection, raised also by Professor Cohen, which holds that an expansive view on symbolic conduct and the First Amendment would grant excessive autonomy to individuals, permitting anyone to ignore the law whenever the person claims his or her violation of law is a protest. This, Cohen thinks, is an absurd result and not in keeping with First Amendment principles. Cohen's objection is that the courts will balance interests *only* when there is a "natural" and "unavoidable" conflict between the two. Thus, there is a natural and unavoidable conflict between an individual's interest in being protected from injurious, libelous speech, and freedom of speech. Generally speaking, there is no such natural and unavoidable conflict between, say, prohibitions on trespass and freedom of speech. If, however, symbolic conduct is given First Amendment protection, the "natural and unavoidable conflict" requirement would fall away; protestors would be able to force on the courts *their* choice of which interests must be balanced against freedom of speech:

---

[18] Abe Fortas, *Concerning Dissent and Civil Disobedience* (New York: Signet, 1968), p. 34.

[19] For a rather extreme statement of such a view, which seems to imply that the law cannot make *any* such distinctions, see the statement by former Solicitor General Irwin Griswold in "Dissent—1968," *Tulane Law Review* XLII (1968), pp. 733–34. Griswold could see no legal difference between stopping a troop train and firing shots into a civil rights leader's home.

> But if any deliberate violation of a trespass statute chosen by the protestor to be a political act must be balanced against the larger need to protect free speech, then the deliberate violation of any statute, major or minor, if intended as a protest, will have also to be so balanced and may claim the same protection. To accept [the] argument, in short, is to allow a First Amendment defense for any statute violation whatever, if it could reasonably be argued that the violation was intended as some form of protest. This would carry the extension of First Amendment guarantees to the point of absurdity, giving that Amendment as a protective weapon to whomever might wish to stage an illegal protest, whatever its form. . . .
>
> This is not to say that where the interests of free speech conflict with property or other interests of lesser importance the latter should prevail, but only that unless there is a natural or normal conflict of community interests, such a balancing need not be undertaken.[20]

It is important to note that Cohen's argument, if it is to have prima facie plausibility, is directed against an extreme view not taken in this paper, namely, that First Amendment rights are absolute against all other interests. Indeed, all his mention of balancing interests is a smokescreen, for the position he is attacking in fact rejects balancing. If it asserts that all protest activity is speech *and* that the free speech guarantee *always* overrides contrary statutes "major or minor," then any further "balancing" is otiose. The account for which I have been arguing rejects so simplistic a view. It recognizes the fact that symbolic conduct can pose immediate dangers to important interests that citizens have, and that sometimes those dangers can be very great. Accepting symbolic conduct as protected speech need not commit one to asserting such a right holds even when according it protection in the circumstances of its occurrence would invade important rights of others.

Moreover, granting a certain amount of legal autonomy to citizens, conditioned on the circumstances and the dangers its exercise poses, would not have the absurd result Cohen claims. Once the disobedient can show that the action is a significant communicational act, he or she can then argue that it *is* the kind of thing the Constitution is meant to protect,[21] and the fact that it is unusual, or not normal, cannot by itself defeat the claim. The free speech guarantee is considerably weakened if excluded from its ambit are the remarkable, the unusual, and the unconventional. The choice exercised by the protestor should be put in proper perspective. That choice is of the *manner* of the exercise of the right. And, surely, freedom of speech is compromised if a fair measure of choice as to manner is not protected. There must be some limits, but they are not marked by what is a "normal" manner of expression.

[20] Cohen, *Civil Disobedience, Conscience, Tactics, and the Law*, pp. 190–92.

[21] Note that the relevant notion of intention is that of "oblique intention." For example, the Framers could not have known of the coming of radio and television; yet it is clear the First Amendment is "meant" to have some applications to the media—the Founders did mean to protect the communication of ideas.

At this stage, it is important to note that all the objections considered above have a feature in common. They all assume some fundamental difference between symbolic conduct and conventional speech hinging on the fact that physical activity is involved in the former but not in the latter—thus, the Supreme Court's distinction between "pure speech" and "speech plus." Not only is this view mistaken, but rigid adherence to it will make inexplicable First Amendment doctrine dealing with uncontested aspects of "pure speech."

As we have seen earlier, even conventional speech involves physical activity—the movement of one's vocal chords and mouth, the movements of one's hands, writing on paper, etc. As is the case with symbolic conduct, what gives these movements communicative force are the intended connections among them, the signs used, and the conveyance of ideas. Moreover, the deliverance of speech and writing involves a physical context. Speech always occurs in a given *place*, at a given *time*. Written or printed material consists of physical objects that must be distributed in a place, at a time, etc. All communication arises in, or as a result of, physical activity. What makes "pure speech" seem different from symbolic speech (when it is not merely the nature of the symbols employed that is the basis of the distinction) is that the sorts of physical activity involved—moving one's lips, etc.—do not normally impinge on others' rights or pose dangers to others. But—and this is of central importance—when the physical aspects of conventional speech *do* affect the interests and rights of others, regulation is in order. Even a defender of an "absolute" right of free speech agrees that one has no First Amendment right to give political speeches in a hospital operating room.[22] This is "pure speech," but properly proscribed because it poses a real and immediate danger to important interests of others.

I am urging, then, that a solution to the question of the legal doctrines needed to deal with symbolic conduct must be part of a unified theory of freedom of expression that makes no essential distinction between symbolic and conventional speech.[23] Though I cannot present and argue for the doctrines needed, I do want to make some points that bear on the selection of such doctrines.

IV. Legal Doctrines Needed

The choice of principles to govern First Amendment regulation must recognize an important, if imprecise, distinction between regulation of speech because of its *content*, and regulation of the *activity* of engaging in speech.

---

[22] Alexander Meiklejohn, *Political Freedom: The Constitutional Powers of the People* (New York: Oxford University Press, 1965), p. 25. Somewhat paradoxically, Meiklejohn's "absolutist" position is consonant with the arguments I am making, as he makes an important (if arguable) distinction between the *regulation* of speech and the *abridgment* of speech. See also his essay "The First Amendment Is an Absolute," *The Supreme Court Review, 1961*, ed. Philip B. Kurland (Chicago: University of Chicago Press, 1962), pp. 245–66.

[23] I am not holding that no distinctions can be made, only that, *from the point of view of the objectives of the First Amendment*, there is no important distinction between the two.

Prosecutions based on such concepts as defamation, libel, invasion of privacy, and incitement to crime are all based in part on the nature of the speech involved. Although we like to think freedom of speech is perfectly neutral as to content, in fact, each such prosecution necessarily inquires into what was said, and, in some cases, even into whether what was said was true or false. Such exemptions from First Amendment protection constitute specifiable classes of cases in which certain interests of persons are endangered by what is said and in which the values underlying free speech are not significantly furthered. Principles are needed for picking out such classes, but once identified, the principles for regulating protected speech will not necessarily apply to these cases.[24]

In cases where the *activity* is to be regulated, the interests of others may be endangered directly or through danger to the institutions in which persons have an interest. The conflict will normally be posed by a person engaging in speech in a context which, prima facie, constitutes a violation of an official statute, directive, or order that is directed at protecting or furthering interests other than interests in engaging in speech.[25] What is needed are guidelines for adjudicating these conflicts. The clear and present danger rule was one attempt to come up with such guidelines, the balancing of interests test another.

The Supreme Court in the *O'Brien* draft-card burning case set out the following criteria:

> a government regulation is sufficiently justified if it is within the constitutional power of the Government; if it furthers an important or substantial governmental interest; if the governmental interest is unrelated to the suppression of free expression; and if the incidental restriction on alleged First Amendment freedoms is no greater than is essential to the furtherance of that interest.[26]

At least one commentator has pointed out that an additional and important criterion was used in the case of *Tinker*, involving students wearing black armbands to school. The Court held that "where there is no finding and no showing that engaging in any of the forbidden conduct would 'materially and substantially interfere with the requirements of appropriate discipline in the operation of the school,' the prohibition cannot be sustained."[27] If one combines these points with

---

[24]In effect, the Supreme Court has classed pornography and obscenity with the "exemption" cases. (See, e.g., Paris Adult Theatre I v. Slaton, 413 U.S. 49.) This is an extremely questionable move. It is unclear that there are significant, real "harms" involved, and there are serious problems with identifying material as falling into the categories of pornography and obscenity without endangering First Amendment values. See David A. J. Richards, *The Moral Criticism of Law* (Encino and Belmont, Calif.: Dickenson Publishing Company, 1977), pp. 56–77; and my own essay "Pornography, Sex and Censorship," *Social Theory and Practice* IV (Spring 1977), pp. 183–209.

[25]As Nimmer points out, the legislation *may* be directed at protecting "anti-speech" interests. See "The Meaning of Symbolic Speech Under the First Amendment," especially pp. 44–46. My own treatment of the legal doctrines is very much influenced by Nimmer's.

[26]United States v. O'Brien, 391 U.S. 367, 377 (1968).

[27]Tinker v. Des Moines Independent Community School District, 393 U.S. 503, 509 (1969).

the thrust of the clear and present danger rule that proscribed speech activity must pose a likely and imminent danger to interests it is appropriate for government to protect, criteria emerge that can form the basis of the legal doctrines needed to regulate speech—conventional *and* symbolic: (1) The speech activity must endanger interests the government may properly protect. (2) The interest protected must be important or substantial. (3) The government interest must be unrelated to the suppression of free speech. (4) The government regulation employed to further that interest must in fact do so, and not unnecessarily infringe speech. (5) The speech activity must present a likely danger of a material and substantial degree to the interests that government seeks to protect.

Much needs to be said concerning the interpretation of these points, and additional criteria may be needed. Moreover, ultimate clarification could only come from applying the principles to actual cases. These points do, however, provide a basis for the development of the needed legal doctrines. They are drawn from existing legal adjudication, and they can be applied to both conventional and symbolic speech.

The Enemy Within:
The American Nazis and Symbolic Conduct
Nat Hentoff

One night in the late 1960s, South Vietnam's ambassador to the United States, having been invited to speak at New York University, tried to do so but was received in the manner accorded dissidents in Saigon. Shouting and stamping made the words of Thieu's emissary inaudible; water laced with imprecations was poured over him; and the ambassador was otherwise manhandled while learning how a free society functions.

Some of his suppressors were authoritarian "revolutionaries," and that was no surprise. As has been shown in other contexts—Stalinists and storm troopers, Mark Rudd and Tom Charles Huston—all yearning totalitarians are fundamentally the same. However, among others who roaringly silenced the Vietnamese ambassador that night were unaffiliated anti-war activists characterizing themselves as true egalitarians. And it was with them in mind that I wrote here of how the assault on Thieu's vassal had revealed the attackers were beginning to resemble those they took so much pride in calling their enemies. . . .

Now, in 1977, in a domestic war, or rather skirmish, the phenomenon recurs of decent people so intent on crushing a foul enemy that they are coming, in small but distinct ways, to resemble that enemy.

As detailed last week, the village of Skokie, just north of Chicago, has gone to court, many courts, to prevent the National Socialist Party of America from

From "The Enemy Within," *The Village Voice* (New York), August 8, 1977. Reprinted by permission of The Village Voice. Copyright © The Village Voice, Inc., 1978.

demonstrating anywhere in the village where some 40,000 of the 70,000 residents are Jews. (And 7,000 of those Jews are survivors of Hitler). At the moment, the homegrown Nazis have been banned by the Illinois Appellate Court from assembling and speaking in Skokie as long as they insist on wearing or displaying swastikas. The Nazis and their counsel, the American Civil Liberties Union, keep maintaining that the swastika is symbolic speech and so must be fully protected by the First Amendment.

The future of the swastika in Skokie will not be decided for some time. . . .

Meanwhile, in Skokie, consider what these good folk have done to themselves in their zeal to entirely shut the village off from Nazi free expression. On May 3, Skokie passed a set of ordinances imposing criminal penalties on certain forms of speech and assembly. Without mentioning the Nazis by name, the ordinances first require that no parade or assembly involving more than 50 persons can be held unless there is at least 30 days notice for a demonstration permit—and unless a $350,000 insurance policy is obtained by the demonstrators. The latter, covering public liability and property damage, costs anywhere from $100 to $900, depending on the risk. You also have to find an underwriter willing to insure you, and that is not always possible.

Also prohibited, under any circumstances, is any demonstration that will "incite violence, hatred, abuse, or hostility toward a person or group of persons by reason or reference to racial, ethnic, national, or religious affiliation." There's more in the ordinances, and it all transmogrifies Skokie into a village so sterilized to avoid controversy that it could almost be in Czechoslovakia.

The lengthy notice for a permit prevents ad hoc demonstrations, yet free speech often must be timely to be effective. The blanket definition of the kinds of "incitement" now banished from Skokie suffocates the First Amendment. And the insurance provision turns the Bill of Rights into a document disfavoring the lower economic classes. Suppose you don't have $100 or $900?

There is an escape clause. Skokie's governing body can waive any or all of these ordinances, if they so choose, for a particular demonstration. Terrific. As far as free speech is concerned, Skokie has become a tiny fascist state. Henceforth, a few people will decide what all the people in the village can safely hear. Given a town of their own, the National Socialist Party would do the same thing.

These ordinances will be challenged in court by the ACLU and will probably be struck down. Though you never know. But will Skokie itself ever fully recover its sense of liberty? How deep was that sense to begin with?

Before the courts' injunctions against the Nazis, some 18 Jewish organizations met in Skokie and planned a counterdemonstration in which 12,000 to 15,000 people were expected to participate on the same day some 30 to 50 Nazis were to appear for half an hour in front of the Village Hall. At the meeting of the Jewish organizations, also attended by village officals, it was made clear that the counterdemonstration would be peaceful so long as the Nazis did *not* appear. Otherwise, it was stated, there could well be bloodshed.

See, said the village officials, we won't be able to control the incited crowds so we must get an injunction against the Nazis. However, as the ACLU pointed out, "If the village was so sure that certain hostile groups would be hard to control, it is difficult to understand why the village did not seek an injunction against *those* persons to prohibit *their* unlawful activities." (Emphasis added.) Unless, of course, Skokie, through fear of free speech, is now under mob rule where violence and the threat of violence prevail over individual liberties.

In sour fact, this is indeed what Skokie has become.

To the once free, now fear-shackled people of that village, I commend an opinion in a 1961 case concerning George Lincoln Rockwell's right to speak in a New York City park. Said Judge Charles Breitel: "The unpopularity of views, their shocking quality, their obnoxiousness, and even their alarming impact is not enough [to prohibit speech]. Otherwise, the preacher of any strange doctrine could be stopped: the anti-racist himself could be suppressed if he undertakes to speak in 'restricted 'areas; and one who asks the public schools be open indiscriminately to all ethnic groups could be lawfully suppressed, if only he chose to speak where persuasion is most needed."

It is from this indivisibility of liberty that Skokie, having become its own enemy, has chosen to secede.

Affirmative Promotion of Freedom of Expression: Radio and Television
Thomas I. Emerson

The most challenging problems in First Amendment theory today lie in the prospect of using law affirmatively to promote more effective functioning of the system of freedom of expression. The traditional premises of the system are essentially laissez-faire in character. They envisage an open marketplace of ideas, with all persons and points of view having equal access to the means of communication. In supporting this system the First Amendment has played a largely negative role: it has operated to protect the system against interference from the government. Thus the issues have turned for the most part upon reconciling freedom of expression with other social interests that the government seeks to safeguard. The development of legal doctrine has been primarily in the evolution of a series of negative commands. A realistic view of the system of freedom of expression in this country today, however, discloses serious deficiencies that call for a different kind of First Amendment approach.

There are numerous reasons for the failures now threatening the existence of the system. Probably the most significant is the overpowering monopoly over the means of communication acquired by the mass media. Two international news services, Associated Press and United Press International, furnish most of the international news. In 1967, out of 1,547 cities with daily newspapers, there were competing dailies in only 64. Three gigantic networks, ABC, CBS, and NBC, determine most of what is seen in American homes on television. In 1966,

From *The System of Freedom of Expression*, copyright © 1970 by Thomas I. Emerson. Reprinted by permission of Random House, Inc. Footnotes have been renumbered.

thirty-five advertisers supplied over 50 percent of television's total advertising income. In 1967, newspapers held interests in a third of the VHF stations and in 22 percent of the UHF stations. In the same year some twenty-five Congressmen or their families owned interests in radio and television properties, and about a half of the members of Congress were members of law firms that represented broadcasters. The economics of radio and television press inevitably in the direction of programs that appeal to the lowest common denominator of a mass audience. The consequence of all this is that the expression emanating from the mass media tends to represent a single, generally bland, point of view.[1]

Other factors are less overwhelming, but still important. Modern government, by virtue of its size, resources, control of information, and links to the mass media, plays a more dominant and narrowing role in the system. The issues in a technical age grow constantly more complex, and there is at the same time a bewildering mass of information on some subjects and a frustrating paucity of information on others. Costs of all methods of communication steadily rise, beyond the means of the individual or the ordinary group. The growth of voluntary associations on a mass scale, while solving some problems, adds to the disadvantage of the non-belonging person or the less powerful organization.

The result is that the system is choked with communications based upon the conventional wisdom and becomes incapable of performing its basic function. Search for the truth is handicapped because much of the argument is never heard or heard only weakly. Political decisions are distorted because the views of some citizens never reach other citizens, and feedback to the government is feeble. The possibility of orderly social change is greatly diminished because those persons with the most urgent grievances come to believe the system is unworkable and merely shields the existing order. Under these circumstances it becomes essential, if the system is to survive, that a search be made for ways to use the law and legal institutions in an affirmative program to restore the system to effective working order.

In general, the government must affirmatively make available the opportunity for expression as well as protect it from encroachment. This means that positive measures must be taken to assure the ability to speak despite economic or other barriers. It also means that greater attention must be given to the right of the citizen to hear varying points of view and the right to have access to information upon which such points of view can be intelligently based. Thus, equally with the right and ability to speak, such an approach would stress the right to hear and the right to know.

[1]The figures are taken from Bryce W. Rucker, *The First Freedom* (Carbondale: Southern Illinois University Press, 1968). See also Dan Lacy, *Freedom and Communications* (Urbana: University of Illinois Press, 2d ed. 1965); James R. Wiggins, *Freedom or Secrecy* (New York: Oxford University Press, rev. ed. 1964); Charles A. Reich, "Making Free Speech Audible," *The Nation*, Feb. 8, 1965, p. 138; and other materials cited in Thomas I. Emerson, David Haber and Norman Dorsen, *Political and Civil Rights in the United States* (Boston: Little, Brown & Co., 3d ed. 1967), pp. 900–901 (cited hereafter in this chapter as *Political and Civil Rights in the United States*).

In terms of First Amendment theory the issues fall into two categories. In the first situation the government relies upon some existing power as the basis for regulation designed to improve operation of the system of freedom of expression. Thus the Federal Government may seek, through use of the commerce power, to require broadcasting stations to give equal time to all political candidates; or a State may, under its general police powers, require disclosure of the sources of campaign contributions. The question is whether, since such a regulation impinges upon freedom of expression, it is permissible under the First Amendment. This issue, however, is not like the question that arises when the government places restrictions upon expression in order to protect or advance some other kind of social interest outside the system of freedom of expression. As an affirmative measure the regulation has its impact entirely within the system; it is designed to make the system work better, not to limit expression in order to promote a conflicting interest. Hence the ordinary First Amendment tests—bad tendency, incitement, clear and present danger, balancing of opposing interests, and full protection—are not applicable. The problem must be resolved in terms of whether there has been an "abridgment" of freedom of expression, and the tests must be framed in terms of accommodation of interests within the system, nondiscrimination, promotion rather than deterrence of expression, and the like.[2]

A second kind of problem arises when governmental power to facilitate operation of the system is sought in the First Amendment itself. Such affirmative power of the First Amendment may be invoked in two forms. In one it is self-executing and enforceable by the courts as a constitutional mandate. Thus the claim that a local board of education must make a school building available for public meetings would rest upon the principle that the First Amendment of its own force requires such action. In its other form the affirmative power of the First Amendment manifests itself as the basis for legislation. This might be Federal legislation enacted directly by virtue of the First Amendment, or Federal legislation enacted under Section 5 of the Fourteenth Amendment, which makes the First Amendment applicable to the States. Such uses of the First Amendment as an affirmative power are, of course, rare. But some development of the law has begun in this direction. Here again the applicable tests are quite different from those employed in traditional situations in which the First Amendment is invoked purely as a negative right against government interference.

Apart from the task of developing suitable First Amendment doctrine, grave administrative and procedural problems are posed by any effort to employ governmental authority to facilitate operation of the system of freedom of expression. The attempt to use governmental power to achieve some limited objective, while at the same time keeping the power under control, is always a risky enterprise. Nowhere is this truer than in the area of freedom of expression. Nevertheless there is no alternative. The weaknesses of the existing system are so

---

[2]The issues are much the same as those that arise in maintaining traffic controls over the right of expression, discussed in Chapter IX [see, *The System of Freedom of Expression* (New York: Random House, Inc., 1970).]

profound that failure to act is the more dangerous course. Moreover, the government is already deeply involved at many points, some of great importance, as in its regulation of radio and television. The same kind of movement may be found in other areas of individual rights today, such as the development of the affirmative aspects of the equal protection clause. The only prudent course, then, is to formulate principles and devise techniques that use social power to facilitate freedom of expression while holding the instrument of that power in check.[3] . . .

Regulation of Privately Owned Media: Radio and Television

The government can also promote the system of freedom of expression through regulation of the privately owned media of communication, with a view to expanding and enriching their output. As noted above, the greatest distortions in our system of free expression have developed in the mass media, and the efforts to eliminate these distortions have created many of the most difficult and controversial questions. The principal goals of regulation are (1) to create a greater diversity in the expression communicated by the media, and (2) to give a greater number of individuals and groups access to the media. The two objectives are of course closely related.

Government regulation along these lines has advanced furthest in radio and television. These two offer special problems. In the first place radio and television are probably the most influential media of communication in our society today. They present, on a selective basis as all communications do, not only information but ideas, attitudes, impressions and fantasies. They pervade the home, the automobile, and many public places. Secondly, radio and television are, by almost unanimous agreement, a "wasteland." The economic, political and social factors that make them so are sufficiently entrenched to discourage expectation of change on the initiative of the industry itself. Thirdly, government involvement in radio and television has always, and necessarily, been extensive. Because they are limited access media, and in any event require elaborate engineering coordination by the government, offical controls have permeated the field from the beginning.

A solution of the radio and television problem might have been attempted through government ownership and control of all broadcasting facilities. This has

---

[3]The first comprehensive effort to consider the question of affirmative promotion of a system of freedom of expression was made in Zechariah Chafee, Jr., *Government and Mass Communications* (Chicago: University of Chicago Press, 1947; reprinted Hamden, Conn.: Archon Books, 1965). A recent discussion that has aroused a good deal of interest is Jerome A. Barron, "Access to the Press—A New First Amendment Right," *Harvard Law Review*, Vol. 80 (1967), p. 1641, and "An Emerging First Amendment Right of Access to the Media?" *George Washington Law Review*, Vol. 37 (1969), p. 487. Materials and references dealing with many of the problems discussed in this chapter may be found in Donald M. Gillmor and Jerome A. Barron, *Mass Communication Law: Cases and Comment* (St. Paul, Minn.: West Publishing Co., 1969). See also Charles A. Reich, "The Law of the Planned Society," *Yale Law Journal*, Vol. 75 (1966), p. 1227; Louis H. Mayo, "The Limited Forum," *George Washington Law Review*, Vol. 22 (1954), p. 261.

been the approach in most other parts of the world. To the extent that a physical scarcity of facilities is involved, the First Amendment would probably not have prevented this arrangement. But serious First Amendment problems would be posed over the right of access to the media by private individuals and groups, and by the government's use of the monopoly in itself participating in the system of freedom of expression. These issues are not wholly different from those which actually have arisen and are discussed below.

In any event the United States chose, rather than government ownership and control, a different method of regulation. When the unregulated transmission of radio signals had brought about a state of chaos in the nineteen-twenties, Congress passed the Federal Radio Act of 1927 establishing a system of licensing to be administered by the Federal Radio Commission. The statutory scheme was revised and expanded by the Federal Communications Act of 1934, which still remains the basic legislation. Under the Federal Communications Act in its present form the Federal Communications Commission, successor to the earlier Commission, is empowered to grant licenses, for not more than three years but renewable, to applicants for broadcasting facilities on the basis that such grant will serve the "public interest, convenience, or necessity." Section 3(h) expressly provides that licensees shall not become "common carriers." There are specific prohibitions against obscenity, profanity and lotteries. Section 315 makes provision for "equal time" for political candidates and, as amended in 1959, requires broadcasters to "operate in the public interest and to afford reasonable opportunity for the discussion of conflicting views on issues of public importance." Section 326 declares that the Federal Communications Commission has no "power of censorship," nor power to interfere with "the right of free speech." These provisions are the only ones that deal directly with programs or access.[4]

The licensing system that has developed under the Federal Communications Act has several significant features. It is predicated upon the fact that there is a scarcity of physical facilities, that is, wavelengths, and that allocation of those facilities is therefore necessary. The franchise to operate a broadcasting station, often worth millions, is awarded free of charge to enterprises selected under the standard of "public interest, convenience, or necessity." Although licenses must be renewed every three years, renewals are given in all but isolated cases. The commercial sector of broadcasting, which is the dominant sector, obtains its income largely not from the listener, but from advertisers. All of this adds up to the fact that, although the broadcasting industry bears some resemblance to a traditional laissez-faire system, it has basic features that are quite different.

The main First Amendment issues grow out of the attempts by the government to regulate the media in three principal ways:

---

[4]Federal Radio Act of 1927, 44 Stat. 1162 (1927); Federal Communications Act of 1934, 48 Stat. 1064, 47 U.S.C. §151 ff. The provisions forbidding obscenity, profanity and lotteries are 18 U.S.C. §§1464 and 1304. For the background of the legislation see Justice Frankfurter's opinion in National Broadcasting Co. v. United States, 319 U.S. 190 (1943), Justice White's opinion in Red Lion Broadcasting Co. v. FCC, 395 U.S. 367 (1969), and materials referred to below.

(1) Some of the controls are directed toward the character of the ownership and control of broadcasting facilities, principally with the aim of assuring independence and diversity among those who own and operate the facilities. These regulations deal with multiple ownership of stations, ownership by newspapers or other media, relation of the station to the networks, and the like. Some are concerned with the financial resources of the licensee, his relation to the community, and similar matters.

(2) Other controls are designed to achieve variety and relevance in programming. Such regulations attempt to obtain balance between different types of programs, inclusion of diverse and controversial subjects in the programs, and the presentation of varying points of view. They are incorporated in the program balance policies of the Federal Communications Commission and in the fairness doctrine.

(3) The third type of control is concerned with access to broadcasting facilities by individuals and groups wishing to use the medium. The main regulations of this kind are the equal time rule and the fairness doctrine.

The constitutional basis for these various controls has been a matter of high dispute. The Federal Communications Commission and the broadcasting industry have been at loggerheads, commentators have disagreed, and the courts were slow to clarify the situation. Finally, in the *Red Lion* decision in 1969 the Supreme Court came forth with a comprehensive theory.[5]

1. Development of First Amendment Theory in Court Decisions

The Supreme Court had dealt with the Federal Communications Act in a significant number of cases, but until *Red Lion* it had addressed itself directly to First Amendment issues in only one—*National Broadcasting Co. v. United States*. That decision, rendered in 1943, constituted the landmark case for over twenty-

---

[5] A collection of materials and references on the problem may be found in *Political and Civil Rights in the United States*, ch. VIII. Later material includes Jerome A. Barron, *op. cit. supra* note 3; Harry Kalven, Jr., "Broadcasting, Public Policy and the First Amendment," *Journal of Law and Economics*, Vol. 10 (1967), p. 15; Glen O. Robinson, "The FCC and the First Amendment: Observations on 40 Years of Radio and Television Regulation," *Minnesota Law Review*, Vol. 52 (1967), p. 67; Fred W. Friendly, *Due to Circumstances Beyond Our Control* (New York: Random House, 1967); Roscoe L. Barrow, "The Equal Opportunities and Fairness Doctrines in Broadcasting: Pillars in the Forum of Democracy," *Cincinnati Law Review*, Vol. 37 (1968), p. 447: Louis L. Jaffe, "The Fairness Doctrine, Equal Time, Reply to Personal Attacks, and the Local Service Obligation: Implications of Technological Change," *Cincinnati Law Review*, Vol. 37 (1968), p. 550.

We are not concerned here with the validity under the First Amendment of restrictions imposed on radio and television for the purpose of protecting social interests outside the system of freedom of expression. These matters have been discussed previously in connection with libel, privacy, obscenity and the like. See also the discussion in Robinson, *op. cit. supra*, pp. 98–111.

five years. The specific issue involved was the validity of the FCC's Chain Broadcasting Regulations, which undertook to regulate the relations of individual broadcasting stations to the networks with a view to lessening the dependence of the single station upon the chain. The regulations were attacked upon a number of fronts, including that they constituted a violation of the First Amendment. The Supreme Court, voting five to two, upheld them. Justice Frankfurter, who wrote for the majority, dealt with the First Amendment at the end of a long opinion, saying only:

> *Freedom of utterance is abridged to many who wish to use the limited facilities of radio. Unlike other modes of expression, radio inherently is not available to all. That is its unique characteristic, and that is why, unlike other modes of expression, it is subject to governmental regulation. Because it cannot be used by all, some who wish to use it must be denied. But Congress did not authorize the Commission to choose among applicants upon the basis of their political, economic or social views, or upon any other capricious basis. If it did, or if the Commission by these Regulations proposed a choice among applicants upon some such basis, the issue before us would be wholly different. The question here is simply whether the Commission, by announcing that it will refuse licenses to persons who engage in specified network practices (a basis for choice which we hold is comprehended within the statutory criterion of "public interest"), is thereby denying such persons the constitutional right of free speech. The right of free speech does not include, however, the right to use the facilities of radio without a license. The licensing system established by Congress in the Communications Act of 1934 was a proper exercise of its power over commerce. The standard it provided for the licensing of stations was the "public interest, convenience, or necessity." Denial of a station license on that ground, if valid under the Act, is not a denial of free speech.*[6]

Justice Frankfurter thus made clear that radio broadcasting can be regulated without infringing the First Amendment because, unlike "other modes of expression," the facilities are limited. He concluded that any regulation which met the standard of "public interest, convenience, or necessity" was "not a denial of free speech." There was, however, an exception: the Commission could not choose among applicants "on the basis of their political, economic or social views, or upon any other capricious basis." Justice Frankfurter's opinion was, to say the least, unsatisfactory. It did not explain why the scarcity factor eliminated First Amendment issues, on what theory the exception was made, why the exception was limited to applicants, or numerous other questions that lurked in the problem.

---

[6]National Broadcasting Co. v. United States, 319 U.S. 190, 226–227 (1943). Justices Murphy and Roberts dissented, without mentioning First Amendment issues. Justices Black and Rutledge did not participate.

Following the *National Broadcasting* case there were scattered lower Federal court opinions, upholding various actions of the Commission against First Amendment challenges, but they did little to elucidate the issue.[7]

Under these conditions wide differences of opinion on the subject persisted. The broadcasting industry clung to its position that radio broadcasting was similar to newspaper publishing and entitled to the same First Amendment protection. The FCC adopted the broad view that the licensee was in effect a public trustee bound to operate its station in accordance with the public interest. It recognized First Amendment limitations, but never made very plain how or why they applied. Commentators argued for these and various other positions.[8]

The *Red Lion* decision involved two cases, each challenging aspects of the FCC fairness doctrine. The fairness doctrine, in the words of Justice White's opinion, required that the "broadcaster must give adequate coverage to public issues . . . and coverage must be fair in that it accurately reflects the opposing views." Originally a policy of the FCC in applying the "public interest, convenience, or necessity" standard, the rule was written into the statute by Congress in its 1959 amendment of Section 315. One special feature of the fairness doctrine was that when a personal attack had been made in a broadcast upon a person involved in a public issue, the broadcaster must give that person an opportunity to respond. There was also a rule requiring any broadcaster who endorsed one candidate in a political editorial to offer the other candidates time to reply. The Court of Appeals for the District of Columbia had upheld the personal attack rule, but the Court of Appeals for the Seventh Circuit had invalidated regulations embodying both the personal attack rule and the political editorial rule. The Supreme Court unanimously upheld both rules.[9]

Justice White began his analysis of the First Amendment issues, as had Justice Frankfurter, with the scarcity of physical facilities for broadcasting: "only a tiny fraction of those with resources and intelligence can hope to communicate by radio at the same time if intelligible communication is to be had, even if the entire radio spectrum is utilized in the present state of commercially acceptable technology." For this reason the government must allocate frequencies, and therefore "it is idle to posit an unabridgeable First Amendment right to broadcast comparable to the right of every individual to speak, write, or publish." "No one

---

[7]The lower Federal court cases are summarized in the Kalven and Robinson articles, *op. cit. supra* note 5, and in Roscoe L. Barrow, "The Attainment of Balanced Program Service in Television," *Virginia Law Review*, Vol. 52 (1966), pp. 633, 644–652. See also the lower court decisions in Red Lion, and Banzhaf v. FCC., 405 F.2d 1082 (D.C. Cir. 1968), cert. denied 396 U.S. 842 (1969).

[8]The broadcasting industry's view may be found in W. Theodore Pierson, "The Need for Modification of Section 326," *Federal Communications Bar Journal*, Vol. 18 (1963), p. 15. The FCC's theories are discussed in Robinson, *op. cit. supra* note 5, pp. 142–144; Barron, *op. cit. supra* note 3, pp. 1664–1665. For Commissioner Loevinger's dissent from the F.C.C. view see Kalven, *op. cit. supra* note 5, pp. 18–19. See also the briefs in the *Red Lion* case in the Supreme Court.

[9]Red Lion Broadcasting Co. v. FCC., 395 U.S. 367, 377 (1969). Justice Douglas did not participate.

has a First Amendment right to a license," he went on, "or to monopolize a radio frequency." He then explained the constitutional status of the broadcaster in the following terms:

> By the same token, as far as the First Amendment is concerned those who are licensed stand no better than those to whom licenses are refused. A license permits broadcasting, but the licensee has no constitutional right to be the one who holds the license or to monopolize a radio frequency to the exclusion of his fellow citizens. There is nothing in the First Amendment which prevents the Government from requiring a licensee to share his frequency with others and to conduct himself as a proxy or fiduciary with obligations to present those views and voices which are representative of his community and which would otherwise, by necessity, be barred from the airwaves.[10]

In extending the protection of the First Amendment to the broadcast situation, Justice White continued, "it is the right of the viewers and listeners, not the right of the broadcasters, which is paramount." He repeated: "It is the right of the public to receive suitable access to social, political, aesthetic, moral, and other ideas and experiences which is crucial here." The fairness doctrine, he concluded, gives effect to this First Amendment right of the public. It simply forces the licensee to share a scarce resource with "those who have a different view." Justice White completed the constitutional picture by adding that the provisions of Section 315 requiring equal time for candidates were valid on the same grounds and, reaffirming *National Broadcasting*, declared that the FCC "neither exceeded its powers under the statute nor transgressed the First Amendment in interesting itself in general program format and the kinds of programs broadcast by licensees."[11]

Justice White's answers to two contentions advanced by the broadcasters throw additional light on the Supreme Court's position. It had been "strenuously argued" that "if political editorials or personal attacks will trigger an obligation in broadcasters to afford the opportunity for expression to speakers who need not pay for time and whose views are unpalatable to the licensees, then broadcasters will be irresistibly forced to self-censorship and their coverage of controversial public issues will be eliminated or at least rendered wholly ineffective." To this Justice White replied that such a possibility "is at best speculative," that the "fairness doctrine in the past has had no such overall effect," and that "if the present licensees should suddenly prove timorous, the Commission is not powerless to insist that they give adequate and fair attention to public issues." Justice White also examined the contention that a scarcity of broadcast facilities no longer existed. Relying mainly on the increasing demand for competing uses of the frequency spectrum, from marine, aviation, amateur, military and common carrier users, he concluded: "Nothing in this record, or in our own researches, convinces us that the

[10] 395 U.S. at 388, 389.
[11] 395 U.S. at 390, 391, 395.

resource is no longer one for which there are more immediate and potential uses than can be accommodated, and for which wise planning is essential."[12]

The *Red Lion* decision marked an important advance in First Amendment theory concerned with affirmative promotion of the system of freedom of expression. Certain implications of the decision, and some wider perspectives on the problem, require further consideration.

2. *The Theory of Radio and Television Control*

In attempting to formulate a satisfactory theory of the First Amendment in its application to the regulation of radio and television two initial concepts must be given brief attention. First, it has sometimes been argued that the public as a whole "owns" the airways and the government may therefore allocate their use on such terms as are in the general interest, subject only to constitutional prohibitions against discriminatory or arbitrary action. This theory, much like the Frankfurter opinion in *National Broadcasting*, fails to come to grips with the real issues. It could equally well be said that the public "owns" the streets and parks, and that consequently individuals have no right to use them for purposes of expression except on the government's own terms. Moreover, the problem is not solved simply by bringing into the picture the doctrine of unconstitutional conditions—that if the government extends the privilege of using the airways to private individuals or groups it cannot attach conditions that violate the First Amendment. Surely the affirmative power of the First Amendment demands that the government make available for general use, as a constitutional right, the most significant medium in our whole system of freedom of expression. The government cannot maintain a monopoly of the airways any more than it can maintain a monopoly of the streets, or of printing presses. Starting from this point, then, the First Amendment issues begin to grow far more complex than the "public ownership" theory envisages.

The second concept that needs initial clarification is the doctrine of prior restraint. On the face of it the requirement that any person obtain a license before engaging in communication by broadcasting is the baldest kind of prior restraint. The conditions for obtaining a license, moreover, go far beyond the time, place and manner regulations that have been upheld in other permit systems. Even if it is conceded, under *Times Film* [*Times Film Corp.* v. *Chicago*, 355 U.S. 35 (1957)], that the doctrine of prior restraint is subject to some exceptions, the Supreme Court has in *Freedman* v. *Maryland* insisted upon procedural safeguards that are totally lacking in the Federal Communications Commission licensing system. How, then, does one reconcile radio and television licensing with the doctrine of prior restraint? The Supreme Court has ignored this problem. There would seem to be two possible answers. One is that the factor of limited facilities necessitates a modification of the prior restraint rule. The other is that public "ownership" of the

[12]395 U.S. at 392–393, 399.

airwaves justifies or requires this kind of prior restraint and that First Amendment rights are protected through other methods. These suggested answers bring us to the major issues.

There can be no doubt that the scarcity of facilities is a major consideration in the application of the First Amendment to radio and television regulation. The essential point is that the scarcity is physical, rather than economic. This condition takes radio and television out of the traditional laissez-faire system that is the basis of the First Amendment's application to the press, publishing, and other types of media. The open marketplace may control access to such media in a distorted way, but it is the traditional means of control and, while the government may attempt to expand the marketplace, it cannot totally usurp its function. In radio and television, however, the open market condition brings only physical chaos. Not everybody can be accommodated. The government, therefore, has a different function, and that function is to bring initial order into the system by regulating access to limited facilities.

When broadcasting controls were first initiated there was no question whatever that the physical facilities were in fact limited. Since that time there has been a significant expansion in available facilities, owing to the development of FM in radio, UHF in television, and CATV. Indeed, the number of radio and television stations in operation came to exceed by far the number of daily newspapers. In 1966, for example, there were 5,881 radio and 721 television stations, compared with 1,751 newspapers. Moreover, there were some frequencies, particularly UHF television channels in the lesser market areas, still unallocated. It is contended that the major factor now limiting the number of radio and television stations is not physical but economic. On the basis of these considerations the broadcasters urged in *Red Lion* that the scarcity factor can no longer serve as justification for radio and television controls different from those applicable to the press and other media.[13]

The developments just recounted, however, would not appear to change the basic scarcity factor. As Justice White argued in *Red Lion* there are growing demands from industrial, military, and other users for available frequencies. Moreover, the total number of radio and television stations operating in the country does not signify there is no longer a shortage of facilities in specific areas, particularly centers of dense population. Nor does reliance upon the total number of stations take into account the possibility of an untapped demand for diversity. Furthermore, to the extent that economic considerations restrict the number of stations now, those factors could easily change. More important than all of these considerations, however, is the fact that the scarcity of facilities should not be measured by the number of *stations* allowed to broadcast but by the number of *individuals or groups* who wish to use the facilities, or would use them if they were more readily available. The real problem is whether there is a scarcity as to potential users, not as to stations operating at a profit under present conditions. In this sense

[13]Materials dealing with the problem of scarcity in available frequencies are cited in Red Lion, 395 U.S. at 397. The figures on the number of radio and television stations and newspapers are from U.S. Bureau of the Census, *Statistical Abstract of the United States* (Washington, D.C., G.P.O., 87th ed. 1966), p. 523.

a more significant comparison would be not with the number of newspapers, but with the number of printing presses. In these terms there remains a serious scarcity and one that is likely to persist.[14]

Once it is assumed that a scarcity of broadcasting facilities exists the next question becomes, what follows from that? The question can be answered on two levels. In purely common-sense terms it would seem to follow that, if the government must choose among applicants for the same facilities, it should choose on some sensible basis. The only sensible basis is the one that best promotes the system of freedom of expression. Since a laissez-faire system does not select the users, and the government is forced to do so, it would be intolerable, and actually inconsistent with the First Amendment, for the government to choose in another way. Consequently all three kinds of regulations listed above would be valid under the First Amendment if they in fact promoted the system of freedom of expression.

The question can also be answered on a deeper level, which leads into a public agency or trustee theory. If broadcasting facilities are physically limited, then the government is obliged by the First Amendment to permit citizens to use the facilities without discrimination. This would be true whether the affirmative power of the First Amendment compelled the government to make them available, or whether the government just did so as a matter of policy. The obligation flows both from the First Amendment's right to communicate and its right to hear. Under either concept it would be a violation of the constitutional guarantee for the government to give a monopoly to any person or group. The licensee therefore can only be considered as the agent of the government, or trustee of the public, in a process of further allocation. Hence the licensee would have no direct First Amendment rights of his own, except as to his own expression. The First Amendment right would run from the individual or group seeking to engage in expression, or seeking to listen, to the government; not from the licensee (except as to his own expression) to the government. This would mean that there could be no censorship of the actual user of the facilities, but there could be controls over the licensee to assure that he made a fair allocation of the limited facilities both to users and to listeners. Only through such a system, indeed, would the requirements of the First Amendment be met.

This is essentially the position the Supreme Court reached in *Red Lion*. Justice White found the force of the First Amendment to lie in the right of the public to hear, and he ignored the right of the ordinary citizen to use broadcasting facilities to speak. But he did conclude that the broadcaster had only the First Amendment rights of a "proxy or fiduciary," with an obligation "to present those views and voices which are representative of his community."[15]

---

[14]For the argument that no scarcity of facilities now exists see John Paul Sullivan, "Editorials and Controversy: The Broadcaster's Dilemma," *George Washington Law Review*, Vol. 32 (1964), pp. 719, 759; Robinson, *op. cit. supra* note 5, pp. 157–161. For the counter argument see Jerome A. Barron, "In Defense of 'Fairness': A First Amendment Rationale for Broadcasting's 'Fairness Doctrine,'" *University of Colorado Law Review*, Vol. 37 (1964), pp. 31, 39–41. Professor Kalven seems to accept the scarcity theory. See Kalven, *op. cit. supra* note 5, pp. 34, 37. The issue is of course, at least temporarily, disposed of by Red Lion.

[15]The Court's position was not greatly different from that taken by the FCC, but the

Along either path from the physical scarcity factor, it is necessary to proceed further and to outline, at least in a general way, the kinds of limitation which the First Amendment would impose upon government operation of such a licensing system. The *Red Lion* decision did not move very far in this direction. It found the fairness doctrine a reasonable method of sharing a scarce resource, and it brushed off as "speculative" the broadcasters' contention that the fairness doctrine would result in reduced coverage of controversial issues. But it did not pursue the questions further.

The basic issue would be whether the government control "abridged" freedom of expression. It might do so in at least two ways:

(1) The regulations might, as a substantive matter, diminish rather than expand the amount of expression, lessen rather than increase diversity, or in similar respects harm rather than promote the system of freedom of expression. The broadcasters made this claim in *Red Lion*. Such a judgment would at times be difficult to make, or for a court to document. But it should be noted that the issue is not the broad one of whether in an abstract way the product of the system is "better" on some particular scale of values. The government cannot control the content of individual expression, or normally try to purify the system, or favor one person over another. Its powers are limited to removing obstructions in the system. It therefore must confine itself to increasing the number of participants in the system, enlarging the diversity of the expression, or removing obstacles to effective working of the system. All this must be carried out, of course, in light of the basic functions of the system.

(2) The regulations might, as an administrative matter, operate to smother freedom of expression through the power of surveillance, threats of informal sanction, or other form of harassment available to government officials because of the regulatory mechanism. This kind of limitation is likewise hard to measure. The government presence is always inhibiting. The courts would probably find it unduly repressive only in exceptional circumstances. It remains a meaningful limitation, however, and in the course of time might be given more specific content. In general, like the doctrine of *Freedman* v. *Maryland*, it would give the courts supervisory power over the practical details of administering the controls.[16]

Quite apart from the scarcity factor in radio and television facilities, it is possible to fashion a theory of control out of affirmative concepts of the First Amendment. The regulations we are here concerned with are not those designed to restrict expression on behalf of other social interests. They are intended to promote the system of free expression through encouraging wider participation by those who wish to communicate and greater diversity for those who wish to hear. In general the affirmative features of the First Amendment would permit this. The ordinary negative limits of the First Amendment, as applied to government restrictions seeking to safeguard other social interests, would not be relevant. Rather, in this context the negative limitations—the measure of "abridge"—would

commission had never spelled it out or accepted its implications. See also Barron, *op. cit. supra* note 14, pp. 43–45, and *op. cit. supra* note 3, pp. 1663–1665.

[16]*Freedman* v. *Maryland*, 380 U.S. 51 (1965), discussed in Chapter XIII [see *The System of Freedom of Expression*].

be those just set forth as controlling when the government power was based on the scarcity theory.

Such a doctrine of First Amendment power and limitation is far-reaching and entails obvious dangers. Applied to the press, for example, it might authorize controls over newspaper coverage that would be highly questionable. In the area of radio and television, however, the government is already heavily involved with the task of preventing electrical interference and solving similar engineering problems. Thus the regulations have a different substantive and administrative impact and would not necessarily constitute an abridgment of free expression in the same way as comparable regulations in other areas not already heavily weighted by government controls.

The application of these principles, whether derived from the scarcity factor theory or the pure affirmative theory, would involve detailed and complex factual judgments. Regulations in the first category—those directed towards the character of ownership and control by licensees—would probably have the least difficulty in passing First Amendment muster. A regulation limiting the number of stations one enterprise may own, or forbidding ownership of a broadcasting station by a newspaper, or forbidding a network to compel an affiliate station to carry all network programs, is appropriate to assure the independence of the licensee and thereby promote diversity. In most respects these forms of control are not different from those exercised through the anti-trust laws, whose application to the mass media was upheld in *Associated Press* v. *United States*. Likewise, the financial resources of the licensee, his support by various groups in the community, and his personal character are relevant to his function as public agent or trustee, though not relevant to the exercise of his own right of expression through the use of radio and television facilities. Unless it appeared that some substantive impact of the regulation or some feature of its administration burdened rather than enlarged the system of freedom of expression the regulation would be immune to attack under the First Amendment.[17]

Regulations of the Federal Communications Commission designed to assure program balance would also, as a general proposition, not violate any mandate of the First Amendment. Such regulations require that a licensee present programs falling into different categories, such as news, education, politics, local talent, entertainment and the like. They are essential to assure that the licensee is carrying out his obligation as public trustee to secure the First Amendment rights of the listening public to hear. The distinction the Federal Communications Commission makes between a requirement that the licensee broadcast programs within its general categories, and control over the contents of a particular program, conforms exactly to the theory that the government can take measures to expand the variety of expression but may not censor the actual expression itself. There may be a close question as to whether any given action by the FCC does in fact promote diversity, or whether in the context of a particular situation specialization on the

---

[17]Associated Press v. United States, 326 U.S. 1 (1945). The chain broadcasting regulations were, of course, upheld in National Broadcasting Co. v. United States, discussed *supra*.

part of one station might not serve the purpose better. Within such limitations, however, the FCC is not abridging freedom of speech.

The most difficult problems arise when the government attempts to introduce greater diversity, particularly by compelling a licensee to present varied points of view on controversial issues, or by forcing him to grant access to persons whose interests are affected by a broadcast. These efforts are presently confined to the fairness doctrine and the equal time provision, but they could be greatly expanded. In general regulations of this nature add to the number of participants, increase diversity, and eliminate discrimination in the use of broadcast facilities, without controlling the content of the expression. They are therefore prima facie justified under the First Amendment. Serious questions may arise, however, when the limiting conditions prescribed by the First Amendment are applied in this area. The controls may in fact operate to reduce the amount of controversial discussion, at least as the broadcasting industry is now structured, and they provide the basis for intensive informal influence of government officials on private expression. Particularly difficult issues arise in according fair representation to minority or even individual points of view. But they cannot be avoided; ignoring them is a greater violation of the First Amendment than a rough but practical solution. On all such matters the judicial judgment under the First Amendment must turn largely on the circumstances of the particular case.

All in all, the fundamental principles that govern the control of radio and television are not too hard to formulate. *Red Lion* has laid a firm foundation. If the possibilities now opened up are exploited the implementation of those principles will pose more difficult problems. Nevertheless the guiding doctrines are available. Whether as a practical matter broadcasting facilities will ever be available on a wide scale to minority groups and people without funds is, of course, another question.

Federal Communications Commission v. Pacifica Foundation, 438 U.S. 726 (1978)

[This case concerns a broadcast by a radio station owned by Pacifica Foundation of a monologue by the comedian George Carlin that satirizes American attitudes toward "Filthy Words." A father heard the broadcast while driving with his son, and sent a complaint to the Federal Communications Commission. The FCC granted the complaint, and warned that it might in the future impose sanctions if such complaints were repeated. It also stated that the FCC is empowered to regulate such broadcasts on the basis of a statute that forbids the use of "any obscene, indecent, or profane language by means of radio communications." In a subsequent order, the Commission stated that it did not intend to absolutely prohibit such broadcasts, but that the initial order was intended to apply to the facts of the case, that is, a broadcast in the afternoon, when children are likely to be listening to the radio. The U.S. Court of Appeals reversed the FCC, though each judge had different reasons.

The U.S. Supreme Court reversed the Appeals Court, thus upholding the FCC's position. The opinions on the Court differed considerably, however. Justice Stevens wrote an opinion consisting of parts I, II, and III, and a part IV, which itself had three parts, A, B, and C. Parts I, II, and III of this opinion deal with the background of the case, and with the questions of statutory interpretation. Part IV, which addresses the constitutional issues, is reprinted below. Justices Burger and Rehnquist joined Justice Stevens' opinion.

Justices Powell and Blackmun accepted parts I, II, III, and part IV C, of Stevens' opinion, and this made a majority of the Court to uphold the FCC. However, Justices Powell and Blackmun rejected the constitutional views expressed in A and B of part IV. Their opinion has been reprinted below.

Justice Stewart wrote a dissenting opinion that was accepted by Justices Brennan, Marshall, and White. He held that the Court need not address the constitutional issues, as the statutes involved should be interpreted to prohibit only "indecent" language that is also "obscene." As all parties agreed that there was no sexual appeal to the monologue, and, hence, that it was not obscene, Justice Powell concluded that there was no statutory authority for the FCC to act in this case. As this opinion addresses only the narrower question of statutory interpretation, it is not reprinted.

Justices Brennan and Marshall joined Justice Powell in holding that the FCC lacked statutory authority to act. Justice Brennan went further and wrote an opinion prompted by his strong objections to the constitutional views expressed by the majority. Justice Marshall joined in this dissent, which is reprinted below.

Citations have been edited and footnotes renumbered.]

Opinion of Mr. Justice Stevens

IV

Pacifica makes two constitutional attacks on the Commission's order. First, it argues that the Commission's construction of the statutory language broadly encompasses so much constitutionally protected speech that reversal is required even if Pacifica's broadcast of the "Filthy Words" monologue is not itself protected by the First Amendment. Second, Pacifica argues that inasmuch as the recording is not obscene, the Constitution forbids any abridgment of the right to broadcast it on the radio.

A. The first argument fails because our review is limited to the question whether the Commission has the authority to proscribe this particular broadcast. As the Commission itself emphasized, its order was "issued in a specific factual context." 59 FCC 2d, at 893. That approach is appropriate for courts as well as the Commission when regulation of indecency is at stake, for indecency is largely a function of context—it cannot be adequately judged in the abstract.

The approach is also consistent with *Red Lion Broadcasting Co., Inc. v. FCC*, 395 U.S. 367. In that case the Court rejected an argument that the Commission's regulations defining the fairness doctrine were so vague that they would inevitably abridge the broadcasters' freedom of speech. The Court of Appeals had invalidated the regulations because their vagueness might lead to self-censorship of controversial program content. *Radio Television News Directors Association v. United States*, 400 F. 2d 1002, 1016 (CA7 1968). This Court reversed. After noting that the Commission had indicated, as it has in this case, that it would not impose sanctions without warning in cases in which the applicability of the law was unclear, the Court stated:

> We need not approve every aspect of the fairness doctrine to decide these cases, and we will not now pass upon the constitutionality of these regulations by envisioning the most extreme applications conceivable, United States v. Sullivan, 332 U.S. 689, 694 (1948), but will deal with those problems if and when they arise. 395 U.S., at 396.

It is true that the Commission's order may lead some broadcasters to censor themselves. At most, however, the Commission's definition of indecency will deter only the broadcasting of patently offensive references to excretory and sexual organs and activities.[1] While some of these references may be protected, they surely lie at the periphery of First Amendment concern. . . . The danger dismissed so summarily in *Red Lion*, in contrast, was that broadcasters would respond to the vagueness of the regulations by refusing to present programs dealing with important social and political controversies. Invalidating any rule on the basis of its hypothetical application to situations not before the Court is "strong medicine" to be applied "sparingly and only as a last resort." *Broadrick v. Oklahoma*, 413 U.S. 601, 613. We decline to administer that medicine to preserve the vigor of patently offensive sexual and excretory speech.

B.   When the issue is narrowed to the facts of this case, the question is whether the First Amendment denies government any power to restrict the public broadcast of indecent language in any circumstances.[2] For if the government has any such power, this was an appropriate occasion for its exercise.

The words of the Carlin monologue are unquestionably "speech" within the meaning of the First Amendment. It is equally clear that the Commission's objections to the broadcast were based in part on its content. The order must therefore fall if, as Pacifica argues, the First Amendment prohibits all governmental regulation that depends on the content of speech. Our past cases demonstrate, however, that no such absolute rule is mandated by the Constitution.

The classic exposition of the proposition that both the content and the context of speech are critical elements of First Amendment analysis is Mr. Justice Holmes' statement for the Court in *Schenk v. United States*:

> We admit that in many places and in ordinary times the defendants in saying all that was said in the circular would have been within their constitutional rights. But the character of every act depends upon the circumstances in which it is done. . . . The most stringent protection of free speech would not protect a man in falsely shouting fire in a theatre and causing a panic. It does not even protect a man from an injunction against uttering words that may have all the effect of force. . . . The question in every case is whether the words used are used in such circumstances and are of such a nature as to create a clear and present danger that they will bring about the substantive evils that Congress has a right to prevent. 249 U.S. 47, 52.

---

[1] A requirement that indecent language be avoided will have its primary effect on the form, rather than the content, of serious communication. There are few, if any, thoughts that cannot be expressed by the use of less offensive language.

[2] Pacifica's position would of course deprive the Commission of any power to regulate erotic telecasts unless they were obscene under Miller v. California, 413 U.S. 15. Anything that could be sold at a newstand for private examination could be publicly displayed on television.

We are assured by Pacifica that the free play of market forces will discourage indecent programming. "Smut may," as Judge Leventhal put it, "drive itself from the market and confound Gresham," 556 F. 2d, at 35; the prosperity of those who traffic in pornographic literature and films would appear to justify his skepticism.

Other distinctions based on content have been approved in the years since *Schenk*. The government may forbid speech calculated to provoke a fight. See *Chaplinsky* v. *New Hampshire*, 315 U.S. 568. It may pay heed to the "'commonsense differences' between commercial speech and other varieties." *Bates* v. *State Bar*, 433 U.S. 350, 381. It may treat libels against private citizens more severely than libels against public officials. See *Gertz* v. *Robert Welch, Inc.*, 418 U.S. 323. Obscenity may be wholly prohibited. *Miller* v. *California*, 413 U.S. 15. And only two Terms ago we refused to hold that a "statutory classification is unconstitutional because it is based on the content of communication protected by the First Amendment." *Young* v. *American Mini Theatres*, 427 U.S. 50, 52.

The question in this case is whether a broadcast of patently offensive words dealing with sex and excretion may be regulated because of its content.[3] Obscene materials have been denied the protection of the First Amendment because their content is so offensive to contemporary moral standards. *Roth* v. *United States*, 354 U.S. 476. But the fact that society may find speech offensive is not a sufficient reason for suppressing it. Indeed, if it is the speaker's opinion that gives offense, that consequence is a reason for according it constitutional protection. For it is a central tenet of the First Amendment that the government must remain neutral in the marketplace of ideas. If there were any reason to believe that the Commission's characterization of the Carlin monologue as offensive could be traced to its political content—or even to the fact that it satirized contemporary attitudes about four letter words[4]—First Amendment protection might be required. But that is simply not this case. These words offend for the same reasons that obscenity offends.[5] Their place in the hierarchy of First Amendment values was aptly sketched by Mr. Justice Murphy when he said, "such utterances are no essential part of any exposition of ideas, and are of such slight social value as a step to truth that any benefit that may be derived from them is clearly outweighed by the social interest in order and morality." *Chaplinsky* v. *New Hampshire*, 315 U.S. 568, 572.

Although these words ordinarily lack literary, political, or scientific value, they are not entirely outside the protection of the First Amendment. Some uses of even the most offensive words are unquestionably protected. . . . Indeed, we may

---

[3]Although neither Mr. Justice Powell nor Mr. Justice Brennan directly confronts this question, both have answered it affirmatively, the latter explicitly, and the former implicitly by concurring in a judgment that could not otherwise stand.

[4]The monologue does present a point of view; it attempts to show that the words it uses are "harmless" and that our attitudes toward them are "essentially silly." . . . The Commission objects, not to this point of view, but to the way in which it is expressed. The belief that these words are harmless does not necessarily confer a First Amendment privilege to use them while proselytizing, just as the conviction that obscenity is harmless does not license one to communicate that conviction by the indiscriminate distribution of an obscene leaflet.

[5]The Commission stated: "Obnoxious, gutter language describing these matters has the effect of debasing and brutalizing human beings by reducing them to their mere bodily functions. . . ." 56 FCC 2d, at 98. Our society has a tradition of performing certain bodily functions in private, and of severely limiting the public exposure or discussion of such matters. Verbal or physical acts exposing those intimacies are offensive irrespective of any message that may accompany the exposure.

assume, *arguendo*, that this monologue would be protected in other contexts. Nonetheless, the constitutional protection accorded to a communication containing such patently offensive sexual and excretory language need not be the same in every context.[6] It is a characteristic of speech such as this that both its capacity to offend and its "social value," to use Mr. Justice Murphy's term, vary with the circumstances. Words that are commonplace in one setting are shocking in another. To paraphrase Mr. Justice Harlan, one occasion's lyric is another's vulgarity. Cf. *Cohen v. California,* 403 U.S. 15, 25.[7]

In this case it is undisputed that the content of Pacifica's broadcast was "vulgar," "offensive," and "shocking." Because content of that character is not entitled to absolute constitutional protection under all circumstances, we must consider its context in order to determine whether the Commission's action was constitutionally permissible.

C. We have long recognized that each medium of expression presents special First Amendment problems. *Joseph Burstyn, Inc. v. Wilson,* 343 U.S. 495, 502–503. And of all forms of communication, it is broadcasting that has received the most limited First Amendment protection. Thus, although other speakers cannot be licensed except under laws that carefully define and narrow official discretion, a broadcaster may be deprived of his license and his forum if the Commission decides that such an action would serve "the public interest, convenience, and necessity." Similarly, although the First Amendment protects newspaper publishers from being required to print the replies of those whom they criticize, *Miami Herald Publishing Co. v. Tornillo,* 418 U.S. 241, it affords no such protection to broadcasters; on the contrary, they must give free time to the victims of their criticism. *Red Lion Broadcasting Co., Inc. v. FCC,* 395 U.S. 367.

The reasons for these distinctions are complex, but two have relevance to the present case. First, the broadcast media have established a uniquely pervasive

---

[6]With respect to other types of speech, the Court has tailored its protection to both the abuses and the uses to which it might be put. See, e.g., New York Times v. Sullivan, 376 U.S. 254 (special scienter rules in libel suits brought by public officials); Bates v. State Bar, 433 U.S. 350 (government may strictly regulate truthfulness in commercial speech). See also Young v. American Mini Theatres, 427 U.S. 50, 82 n. 6 (Powell, J., concurring).

[7]The importance of context is illustrated by the Cohen case. That case arose when Paul Cohen entered a Los Angeles courthouse wearing a jacket emblazoned with the words, "Fuck the Draft." After entering the courtroom, he took the jacket off and folded it. *Id.*, at 19 n. 3. So far as the evidence showed, no one in the courthouse was offended by his jacket. Nonetheless, when he left the courtroom, Cohen was arrested, convicted of disturbing the peace, and sentenced to 30 days in prison.

In holding that criminal sanctions could not be imposed on Cohen for his political statement in a public place, the Court rejected the argument that his speech would offend unwilling viewers; it noted that "there was no evidence that persons powerless to avoid [his] conduct did in fact object to it." *Id.,* at 22. In contrast, in this case the Commission was responding to a listener's strenuous complaint, and Pacifica does not question its determination that this afternoon broadcast was likely to offend listeners. It should be noted that the Commission imposed a far more moderate penalty on Pacifica than the state court imposed on Cohen. Even the strongest civil penalty at the Commission's command does not include criminal prosecution.

presence in the lives of all Americans. Patently offensive, indecent material presented over the airways confronts the citizen, not only in public, but also in the privacy of the home, where the individual's right to be let alone plainly outweighs the First Amendment rights of an intruder. . . . Because the broadcast audience is constantly tuning in and out, prior warnings cannot completely protect the listener or viewer from unexpected program content. To say that one may avoid further offense by turning off the radio when he hears indecent language is like saying that the remedy for an assault is to run away after the first blow. One may hang up on an indecent phone call, but that option does not give the caller a constitutional immunity or avoid a harm that has already taken place.[8]

Second, broadcasting is uniquely accessible to children, even those too young to read. Although Cohen's written message might have been incomprehensible to a first grader, Pacifica's broadcast could have enlarged a child's vocabulary in an instant. Other forms of offensive expression may be withheld from the young without restricting the expression at its source. Bookstores and motion picture theaters, for example, may be prohibited from making indecent material available to children. We held in *Ginsberg* v. *New York*, 390 U.S. 629, that the government's interest in the "well being of its youth" and in supporting "parents' claim to authority in their own household" justified the regulation of otherwise protected expression. *Id.*, at 640 and 639.[9] The ease with which children may obtain access to broadcast material, coupled with the concerns recognized in *Ginsberg*, amply justify special treatment of indecent broadcasting.

It is appropriate, in conclusion, to emphasize the narrowness of our holding. This case does not involve a two-way radio conversation between a cab driver and a dispatcher, or a telecast of an Elizabethan comedy. We have not decided that an occasional expletive in either setting would justify any sanction or,

---

[8]Outside the home, the balance between the offensive speaker and the unwilling audience may sometimes tip in favor of the speaker, requiring the offended listener to turn away. See Erznozik v. Jacksonville, 422 U.S. 205. As we noted in Cohen v. California: "While this Court has recognized that government may properly act in many situations to prohibit intrusion into the privacy of the home of unwelcome views and ideas which cannot be totally banned from the public dialogue . . . , we have at the same time consistently stressed that 'we are often "captives" outside the sanctuary of the home and subject to objectionable speech.'" 403 U.S., at 21.
The problem of harassing phone calls is hardly hypothetical. Congress has recently found it necessary to prohibit debt collectors from "plac[ing] telephone calls without meaningful disclosure of the caller's identity"; from "engaging any person in telephone conversation repeatedly or continuously with intent to annoy, abuse, or harass any person at the called number"; and from "us[ing] obscene or profane language or language the natural consequence of which is to abuse the hearer or reader." Consumer Credit Protection Act, Amendments, Pub. L. 95–109, 91 Stat. 877.

[9]The Commission's action does not by any means reduce adults to hearing only what is fit for children. Cf. Butler v. Michigan, 352 U.S. 380, 383. Adults who feel the need may purchase tapes and records or go to theatres and nightclubs to hear these words. In fact, the Commission has not unequivocally closed even broadcasting to speech of this sort; whether broadcast audiences in the late evening contain so few children that playing this monologue would be permissible is an issue neither the Commission nor this Court has decided.

indeed, that this broadcast would justify a criminal prosecution. The Commission's decision rested entirely on a nuisance rationale under which context is all-important. The concept requires consideration of a host of variables. The time of day was emphasized by the Commission. The content of the program in which the language is used will also affect the composition of the audience,[10] and differences between radio, television, and perhaps closed-circuit transmissions, may also be relevant. As Mr. Justice Sutherland wrote, a "nuisance may be merely a right thing in the wrong place—like a pig in the parlor instead of the barnyard." *Euclid* v. *Ambler Realty Co.*, 272 U.S. 365, 388. We simply hold that when the Commission finds that a pig has entered the parlor, the exercise of its regulatory power does not depend on proof that the pig is obscene.

The judgment of the Court of Appeals is reversed.

Appendix

The following is a verbatim transcript of "Filthy Words" prepared by the Federal Communications Commission.

"Aruda-du, ruba-tu, ruba-tu. I was thinking about the curse words and the swear words, the cuss words and the words that you can't say, that you're not supposed to say all the time, cause words or people into words want to hear your words. Some guys like to record your words and sell them back to you if they can, (laughter) listen in on the telephone, write down what words you say. A guy who used to be in Washington knew that his phone was tapped, used to answer, Fuck Hoover, yes, go ahead. (laughter) Okay, I was thinking one night about the words you couldn't say on the public, ah, airwaves, um, the ones you definitely wouldn't say, ever cause I heard a lady say bitch one night on television, and it was cool like she was talking about, you know, ah, well, the bitch is the first one to notice that in the litter Johnie right (murmur) Right. And, uh, bastard you can say, and hell and damn so I have to figure out which ones you couldn't and ever and it came down to seven but the list is open to amendment, and in fact, has been changed, uh, by now, ha, a lot of people pointed things out to me, and I noticed some myself. The original seven words were, shit, piss, fuck, cunt, cocksucker, motherfucker, and tits. Those are the ones that will curve your spine, grow hair on your hands and (laughter) maybe, even bring us, God help us, peace without honor (laughter) um, and a bourbon. (laughter) And now the first thing that we noticed was that the word fuck was really repeated in there because the word motherfucker is a compound word and it's another form of the word fuck. (laughter) You want to be a purist it doesn't really—it can't be on the list of basic words. Also, cocksucker is a compound word and neither half of that is really dirty. The word—the half sucker that's merely suggestive (laughter) and the word cock is a half-way dirty word, 50%

---

[10] Even a prime time recitation of Chaucer's Miller's Tale would not be likely to command the attention of many children who are both old enough to understand and young enough to be adversely affected by passages such as, "And prively he caughte hir by the queynte." G. Chaucer, *The Miller's Tale* 1.3276 (c. 1386).

dirty—dirty half the time, depending on what you mean by it. (laughter) Uh, remember when you first heard it, like in 6th grade, you used to giggle. And the cock crowed three times, heh (laughter) the cock—three times. It's in the Bible, cock in the Bible. (laughter) And the first time you heard about a cock-fight, remember—What? Huh? Naw. It ain't that, are you stupid? man. (laughter, clapping) It's chickens, you know, (laughter) Then you have the four letter words from the old Anglo-Saxon fame. Uh, shit and fuck. The word, shit, uh, is an interesting kind of word in that the middle class has never really accepted it and approved it. They use it like crazy but it's not really okay. It's still a rude, dirty, old kind of gushy word. (laughter) They don't like that, but they say it, like, they say it like, a lady now in a middle-class home, you'll hear most of the time she says it as an expletive, you know, its out of her mouth before she knows. She says, Oh shit oh shit, (laughter) oh shit. If she drops something, Oh, the shit hurt the broccoli. Shit. Thank you (footsteps fading away) (papers ruffling)

"Read it! (from audience)

"Shit! (laughter) I won the Grammy, man, for the comedy album. Isn't that groovy? (clapping, whistling) (murmur) That's true. Thank you. Thank you man. Yeah. (murmur) (continuous clapping) Thank you man. Thank you. Thank you very much, man. Thank, no, (end of continuous clapping) for that and for the Grammy, man, cause (laughter) that's based on people liking it man, yeh, that's ah, that's okay man. (laughter) Let's let that go, man. I got my Grammy. I can let my hair hang down now, shit. (laughter) Ha! So! Now the word shit is okay for the man. At work you can say it like crazy. Mostly figuratively, Get that shit out of here, will ya? I don't want to see that shit anymore. I can't *cut* that shit, buddy. I've had that shit up to here. I think you're full of shit myself. (laughter) He don't know shit from Shinola. (laughter) you know that? (laughter) Always wondered how the Shinola people felt about that. (laughter) Hi, I'm the new man from Shinola. (laughter) Hi, how are ya? Nice to see ya. (laughter) How are ya? (laughter) Boy, I don't know whether to shit or wind my watch. (laughter) Guess, I'll shit on my watch. (laughter) Oh, *the* shit is going to hit *de* fan. (laughter) Built like a brick shit-house. (laughter) Up, he's up shit's creek. (laughter) He's had it. (laughter) He hit me, I'm sorry. (laughter) Hot shit, holy shit, tough shit, eat shit, (laughter) shit-eating grin. Uh, whoever thought of that was ill. (murmur laughter) He had a shit-eating grin! He had a what? (laughter) Shit on a stick. (laughter) Shit in a handbag. I always like that. He ain't worth shit in a handbag. (laughter) Shitty. He acted real shitty. (laughter) You know what I mean? (laughter) I got the money back, but a real shitty attitude. Heh, he had a shit-fit. (laughter) Wow! Shit-fit. Whew! Glad I wasn't there. (murmur, laughter) All the animals—Bull shit, horse shit, cow shit, rat shit, bat shit. (laughter) First time I heard bat shit, I really came apart. A guy in Oklahoma, Boggs, said it, man. Aw! Bat shit. (laughter) Vera reminded me of that last night, ah (murmur). Snake shit, slicker than owl shit. (laughter) Get your shit together. Shit or get off the pot. (laughter) I got a shit-load full of them. (laughter) I got a shit-pot full, all right. Shit-head, shit-heel, shit in your heart, shit for brains, (laughter) shit-face, heh (laughter) I always try to think how that could have originated; the first guy that said that. Somebody got drunk and fell in some shit, you know. (laughter) Hey, I'm shit-face. (laughter) Shit-face, *today*. (laughter) Anyway, enough of that shit. (laughter) The big one, the word fuck that's the one that hangs them up the most. Cause in a lot of cases that's the very act that hangs them up the most. So, it's natural that the word would, uh, have the same effect. It's a great word, fuck, nice word, easy word, cute word, kind of. Easy word to say. One syllable, short u. (laughter) Fuck. (Murmur) You know, it's easy. Starts with a nice soft sound fuh ends with a *kuh*. Right? (laughter) A little something for everyone. Fu*ck* (laughter) Good word. Kind of a proud word, too. Who are you? I am FUCK. (laughter) FUCK OF THE MOUNTAIN. (laughter) Tune in again next week to FUCK OF THE MOUNTAIN. (laughter) It's an interesting word too, cause it's got a double kind of life—personality—dual, you know, whatever the right phrase is. It leads a double life, the word fuck. First of all, it means, sometimes, most of the time, fuck. What does it mean? It means to make love. Right? We're going to make love, yeh, we're going to fuck, yeh, we're going to fuck, yeh, we're going to make love. (laughter) We're really going to fuck, yeh, we're going to make love. Right? And it also means the beginning of life, it's the act that begins life, so there's the word hanging around with words like love, and life, and yet on the other hand, it's also a word that we really use to hurt each other with, man. It's a heavy. It's one that you save toward the end of the argument. (laughter) Right? (laughter) You finally can't make out. Oh, fuck you man. I said, fuck you. (laughter, murmur) Stupid fuck. (laughter) Fuck you and everybody that looks like you. (laughter) man. It would be nice to change the movies that we already have and substitute the word fuck for the word kill, wherever we could, and some of those movie cliches would change a little bit. Mad fuckers still on the loose. Stop me before I fuck again. Fuck the ump, fuck the ump, fuck the ump, fuck the ump, fuck the ump. Easy on the clutch Bill, you'll fuck that engine again. (laughter) The other shit one was, I don't give a shit. Like it's worth something, you know? (laughter) I don't give a shit. Hey, well, I don't take no shit, (laughter) you know what I mean? You know why I don't take no shit? (laughter) Cause I don't give a shit. (laughter) If I give a shit, I would have to pack shit. (laughter) But I don't pack no shit cause I don't give a shit. (laughter) You wouldn't shit me, would you? (laughter) That's a joke when you're a kid with a worm looking out the bird's ass. You wouldn't shit me, would you? (laughter) It's an eight-year-old joke but a good one. (laughter) The additions to the list. I found three more words that had to be put on the list of words you could never say on television, and they were fart, turd and twat, those three. (laughter) Fart, we talked about, it's harmless. It's like tits, it's a cutie word, no problem. Turd, you can't say but who wants to, you know? (laughter) The subject never comes up on the panel so I'm not worried about that one. Now the word twat is an interesting word. Twat! Yeh, right in the twat. (laughter) Twat is an interesting word because it's the only one I know of, the only slang word applying to the, a part of the sexual anatomy that doesn't have another meaning to it. Like, ah, snatch, box and pussy all have other meanings, man. Even in a Walt Disney movie, you can say, We're going to snatch that pussy and put him in a box and bring him on the airplane. (murmur, laughter) Everybody loves it. The twat stands alone, man, as it should. And two-way words. Ah, ass is okay providing you're riding into town on a religious feast day. (laughter) You can't say, up your *ass*. (laughter) You can say, stuff it! (murmur) There are certain things you can say it's weird but you can just come so close. Before I cut, I, uh, want to, ah, thank you for listening to my words, man, fellow, uh, space travelers. Thank you man for tonight and thank you also. (clapping, whistling)"

Mr. Justice Powell, with Mr. Justice Blackmun, Concurring

I join Parts I, II, III, and IV(C) of Mr. Justice Stevens' opinion. The Court today reviews only the Commission's holding that Carlin's monologue was indecent "as broadcast" at two o'clock in the afternoon, and not the broad sweep of the Commission's opinion. . . . In addition to being consistent with our settled practice of not deciding constitutional issues unnecessarily, . . . this narrow focus also is conducive to the orderly development of this relatively new and difficult area of law, in the first instance by the Commission, and then by the reviewing courts. . . .

I also agree with much that is said in Part IV of Mr. Justice Stevens' opinion, and with its conclusion that the Commission's holding in this case does not violate the First Amendment. Because I do not subscribe to all that is said in Part IV, however, I state my views separately.

I

It is conceded that the monologue at issue here is not obscene in the constitutional sense. . . . Nor, in this context, does its language constitute "fighting words" within the meaning of *Chaplinsky* v. *New Hampshire*, 315 U.S. 568 (1942). Some of the words used have been held protected by the First Amendment in other cases and contexts. . . . I do not think Carlin, consistently with the First Amendment, could be punished for delivering the same monologue to a live audience composed of adults who, knowing what to expect, chose to attend his performance. . . . And I would assume that an adult could not constitutionally be prohibited from purchasing a recording or transcript of the monologue and playing or reading it in the privacy of his own home. Cf. *Stanley* v. *Georgia*, 394 U.S. 557 (1969).

But it also is true that the language employed is, to most people, vulgar and offensive. It was chosen specifically for this quality, and it was repeated over and over as a sort of verbal shock treatment. The Commission did not err in characterizing the narrow category of language used here as "patently offensive" to most people regardless of age.

The issue, however, is whether the Commission may impose civil sanctions on a licensee radio station for broadcasting the monologue at two o'clock in the afternoon. The Commission's primary concern was to prevent the broadcast from reaching the ears of unsupervised children who were likely to be in the audience at that hour. In essence, the Commission sought to "channel" the monologue to hours when the fewest unsupervised children would be exposed to it. . . . In my view, this consideration provides strong support for the Commission's holding.

The Court has recognized society's right to "adopt more stringent controls on communicative materials available to youths than on those available to adults." *Erznoznik v. City of Jacksonville,* 422 U.S. 205, 212 (1975). . . . This recognition stems in large part from the fact that "a child . . . is not possessed of that full capacity for individual choice which is the presupposition of First Amendment guarantees." *Ginsberg v. New York, supra,* at 649–650 (Stewart, J., concurring in result). Thus, children may not be able to protect themselves from speech which, although shocking to most adults, generally may be avoided by the unwilling through the exercise of choice. At the same time, such speech may have a deeper and more lasting negative effect on a child than an adult. For these reasons, society may prevent the general dissemination of such speech to children, leaving to parents the decision as to what speech of this kind their children shall hear and repeat:

> *Constitutional interpretation has consistently recognized that the parents' claim to authority in their own household to direct the rearing of their children is basic in the structure of our society.* "It is cardinal with us that the custody, care and nurture of the child reside first in the parents, whose primary function and freedom include preparation for obligations the state can neither supply nor hinder." Prince v. Massachusetts [321 U.S. 158, 166 (1944)]. *The legislature could properly conclude that parents and others, teachers for example, who have this primary responsibility for children's well-being are entitled to the support of laws designed to aid discharge of that responsibility.* Ginsberg v. New York, 390 U.S. 629, 639 (1968).

The Commission properly held that the speech from which society may attempt to shield its children is not limited to that which appeals to the youthful prurient interest. The language involved in this case is as potentially degrading and harmful to children as representations of many erotic acts.

In most instances, the dissemination of this kind of speech to children may be limited without also limiting willing adults' access to it. Sellers of printed and recorded matter and exhibitors of motion pictures and live performances may be required to shut their doors to children, but such a requirement has no effect on adults' access. See *Ginsberg v. New York, supra,* at 634–635. The difficulty is that such a physical separation of the audience cannot be accomplished in the broadcast media. During most of the broadcast hours, both adults and unsupervised children are likely to be in the broadcast audience, and the broadcaster cannot reach willing adults without also reaching children. This, as the Court emphasizes, is one of the distinctions between the broadcast and other media to which we often have adverted as justifying a different treatment of the broadcast media for First

Amendment purposes. . . . In my view, the Commission was entitled to give substantial weight to this difference in reaching its decision in this case.

A second difference, not without relevance, is that broadcasting—unlike most other forms of communication—comes directly into the home, the one place where people ordinarily have the right not to be assaulted by uninvited and offensive sights and sounds. . . . Although the First Amendment may require unwilling adults to absorb the first blow of offensive but protected speech when they are in public before they turn away, . . . a different order of values obtains in the home. "That we are often 'captives' outside the sanctuary of the home and subject to objectionable speech and other sound does not mean we must be captives everywhere." *Rowan* v. *Post Office Dept.*, 397 U.S. 728, 738 (1970). The Commission also was entitled to give this factor appropriate weight in the circumstances of the instant case. This is not to say, however, that the Commission has an unrestricted license to decide what speech, protected in other media, may be banned from the airwaves in order to protect unwilling adults from momentary exposure to it in their homes.[11] Making the sensitive judgments required in these cases is not easy. But this responsibility has been reposed initially in the Commission, and its judgment is entitled to respect.

It is argued that despite society's right to protect its children from this kind of speech, and despite everyone's interest in not being assaulted by offensive speech in the home, the Commission's holding in this case is impermissible because it prevents willing adults from listening to Carlin's monologue over the radio in the early afternoon hours. It is said that this ruling will have the effect of "reduc[ing] the adult population . . . to [hearing] only what is fit for children." *Butler* v. *Michigan*, 352 U.S. 380, 383 (1957). This argument is not without force. The Commission certainly should consider it as it develops standards in this area. But it is not sufficiently strong to leave the Commission powerless to act in circumstances such as those in this case.

The Commission's holding does not prevent willing adults from purchasing Carlin's record, from attending his performances, or, indeed, from reading the transcript reprinted as an appendix to the Court's opinion. On its face, it does not prevent respondent from broadcasting the monologue during late evening hours when fewer children are likely to be in the audience, nor from broadcasting discussions of the contemporary use of language at any time during the day. The Commission's holding, and certainly the Court's holding today, does not speak to cases involving the isolated use of a potentially offensive word in the course of a radio broadcast, as distinguished from the verbal shock treatment administered by respondent here. In short, I agree that on the facts of this case, the Commission's order did not violate respondent's First Amendment rights.

[11]It is true that the radio listener quickly may tune out speech that is offensive to him. In addition, broadcasters may preface potentially offensive programs with warnings. But such warnings do not help the unsuspecting listener who tunes in at the middle of a program. In this respect, too, broadcasting appears to differ from books and records, which may carry warnings on their faces, and from motion pictures and live performances, which may carry warnings on their marquees.

II

As the foregoing demonstrates, my views are generally in accord with what is said in Part IV(C) of Mr. Justice Stevens' opinion. . . . I therefore join that portion of his opinion. I do not join Part IV(B), however, because I do not subscribe to the theory that the Justices of this Court are free generally to decide on the basis of its content which speech protected by the First Amendment is most "valuable" and hence deserving of the most protection, and which is less "valuable" and hence deserving of less protection. . . . In my view, the result in this case does not turn on whether Carlin's monologue, viewed as a whole, or the words that comprise it, have more or less "value" than a candidate's campaign speech. This is a judgment for each person to make, not one for the judges to impose upon him.[12]

The result turns instead on the unique characteristics of the broadcast media, combined with society's right to protect its children from speech generally agreed to be inappropriate for their years, and with the interest of unwilling adults in not being assaulted by such offensive speech in their homes. Moreover, I doubt whether today's decision will prevent any adult who wishes to receive Carlin's message in Carlin's own words from doing so, and from making for himself a value judgment as to the merit of the message and words. Cf. *Young* v. *American Mini Theatres*, 427 U.S., at 77–79 (Powell, J., concurring). These are the grounds upon which I join the judgment of the Court as to Part IV.

Mr. Justice Brennan, with Mr. Justice Marshall, Dissenting

I agree with Mr. Justice Stewart that, under *Hamling* v. *United States*, 418 U.S. 187 (1974), and *United States* v. *12 200-ft. Reels of Film*, 413 U.S. 123 (1973), the word *indecent* in 18 U.S.C. § 1464 must be construed to prohibit only obscene speech. I would, therefore, normally refrain from expressing my views on any constitutional issues implicated in this case. However, I find the Court's misapplication of fundamental First Amendment principles so patent, and its attempt to impose *its* notions of propriety on the whole of the American people so misguided, that I am unable to remain silent.

---

[12]For much the same reason, I also do not join Part IV(A). I had not thought that the application *vel non* of overbreadth analysis should depend on the Court's judgment as to the value of the protected speech that might be deterred. . . . Except in the context of commercial speech, see Bates v. State Bar of Arizona, 433 U.S. 350, 380–381 (1977), it has not in the past. . . .

As Mr. Justice Stevens points out, however, . . . the Commission's order was limited to the facts of this case; "it did not purport to engage in formal rulemaking or in the promulgation of any regulations." In addition, since the Commission may be expected to proceed cautiously, as it has in the past, . . . I do not forsee an undue "chilling" effect on broadcasters' exercise of their rights. I agree, therefore, that respondent's overbreadth challenge is meritless.

I

For the second time in two years, see *Young v. American Mini Theatres*, 427 U.S. 50 (1976), the Court refuses to embrace the notion, completely antithetical to basic First Amendment values, that the degree of protection the First Amendment affords protected speech varies with the social value ascribed to that speech by five Members of this Court. . . . Moreover, as do all parties, all Members of the Court agree that the Carlin monologue aired by Station WBAI does not fall within one of the categories of speech, such as "fighting words," . . . or obscenity, that is totally without First Amendment protection. This conclusion, of course, is compelled by our cases expressly holding that communications containing some of the words found condemnable here are fully protected by the First Amendment in other contexts. . . . Yet despite the Court's refusal to create a sliding scale of First Amendment protection calibrated to this Court's perception of the worth of a communication's content, and despite our unanimous agreement that the Carlin monologue is protected speech, a majority of the Court[13] nevertheless finds that, on the facts of this case, the FCC is not constitutionally barred from imposing sanctions on Pacifica for its airing of the Carlin monologue. This majority apparently believes that the FCC's disapproval of Pacifica's afternoon broadcast of Carlin's "Dirty Words" recording is a permissible time, place, and manner regulation. *Kovacs v. Cooper*, 336 U.S. 77 (1949). Both the opinion of my Brother Stevens and the opinion of my Brother Powell rely principally on two factors in reaching this conclusion: (1) the capacity of a radio broadcast to intrude into the unwilling listener's home, and (2) the presence of children in the listening audience. Dispassionate analysis, removed from individual notions as to what is proper and what is not, starkly reveals that these justifications, whether individually or together, simply do not support even the professedly moderate degree of governmental homogenization of radio communications—if, indeed, such homogenization can ever be moderate given the pre-eminent status of the right of free speech in our constitutional scheme—that the Court today permits.

A. Without question, the privacy interests of an individual in his home are substantial and deserving of significant protection. In finding these interests sufficient to justify the content regulation of protected speech, however, the Court commits two errors. First, it misconceives the nature of the privacy interests involved where an individual voluntarily chooses to admit radio communications into his home. Second, it ignores the constitutionally protected interests of both those who wish to transmit and those who desire to receive broadcasts that many—including the FCC and this Court—might find offensive.

"The ability of government, consonant with the Constitution, to shut off discourse solely to protect others from hearing it is . . . dependent upon a showing

---

[13]Where I refer without differentiation to the actions of "the Court," my reference is to this majority, which consists of my Brothers Powell and Stevens and those Members of the Court joining their separate opinions.

that substantial privacy interests are being invaded in an essentially intolerable manner. Any broader view of this authority would effectively empower a majority to silence dissidents simply as a matter of personal predilections." *Cohen v. California*, 403 U.S. 15, 21 (1971). I am in wholehearted agreement with my brethren that an individual's right "to be let alone" when engaged in private activity within the confines of his own home is encompassed within the "substantial privacy interests" to which Mr. Justice Harlan referred in *Cohen,* and is entitled to the greatest solicitude. *Stanley v. Georgia,* 394 U.S. 557 (1969). However, I believe that an individual's actions in switching on and listening to communications transmitted over the public airways and directed to the public at-large do not implicate fundamental privacy interests, even when engaged in within the home. Instead, because the radio is undeniably a public medium, these actions are more properly viewed as a decision to take part, if only as a listener, in an ongoing public discourse. See Note, "Filthy Words, the FCC, and the First Amendment: Regulating Broadcast Obscenity," 61 *Va. L. Rev.* 579, 618 (1975). Although an individual's decision to allow public radio communications into his home undoubtedly does not abrogate all of his privacy interests, the residual privacy interests he retains vis-à-vis the communication he voluntarily admits into his home are surely no greater than those of the people present in the corridor of the Los Angeles courthouse in *Cohen* who bore witness to the words "Fuck the Draft" emblazoned across Cohen's jacket. Their privacy interests were held insufficient to justify punishing Cohen for his offensive communication.

Even if an individual who voluntarily opens his home to radio communications retains privacy interests of sufficient moment to justify a ban on protected speech if those interests are "invaded in an essentially intolerable manner," *Cohen v. California, supra,* at 21, the very fact that those interests are threatened only by a radio broadcast precludes any intolerable invasion of privacy; for unlike other intrusive modes of communication, such as sound trucks, "the radio can be turned off," *Lehman v. City of Shaker Heights,* 418 U.S. 298, 302 (1974)—and with a minimum of effort. As Judge Bazelon aptly observed below, "having elected to receive public air waves, the scanner who stumbles onto an offensive program is in the same position as the unsuspecting passers-by in *Cohen* and *Erznoznik* [*v. City of Jacksonville,* 422 U.S. 205 (1975)]; he can avert his attention by changing channels or turning off the set." . . . Whatever the minimal discomfort suffered by a listener who inadvertently tunes into a program he finds offensive during the brief interval before he can simply extend his arm and switch stations or flick the "off" button, it is surely worth the candle to preserve the broadcaster's right to send, and the right of those interested to receive, a message entitled to full First Amendment protection. To reach a contrary balance, as does the Court, is clearly, to follow Mr. Justice Stevens' reliance on animal metaphors, . . . "to burn the house to roast the pig." . . .

The Court's balance, of necessity, fails to accord proper weight to the interests of listeners who wish to hear broadcasts the FCC deems offensive. It permits majoritarian tastes completely to preclude a protected message from entering the homes of a receptive, unoffended minority. No decision of this Court supports such a result. Where the individuals comprising the offended majority may freely choose to reject the material being offered, we have never found their privacy interests of such moment to warrant the suppression of speech on privacy grounds. Compare *Lehman v. City of Shaker Heights, supra. Rowan v. Post Office Department*, 397 U.S. 728 (1970), relied on by the FCC and by the opinions of my Brothers Powell and Stevens, confirms rather than belies this conclusion. In *Rowan*, the Court upheld a statute, 39 U.S.C. § 4009, permitting householders to require that mail advertisers stop sending them lewd or offensive materials and remove their names from mailing lists. Unlike the situation here, householders who wished to receive the sender's communications were not prevented from doing so. Equally important, the determination of offensiveness *vel non* under the statute involved in *Rowan* was completely within the hands of the individual householder; no governmental evaluation of the worth of the mail's content stood between the mailer and the householder. In contrast, the visage of the censor is all too discernable here.

B. Most parents will undoubtedly find understandable as well as commendable the Court's sympathy with the FCC's desire to prevent offensive broadcasts from reaching the ears of unsupervised children. Unfortunately, the facial appeal of this justification for radio censorship masks its constitutional insufficiency. Although the government unquestionably has a special interest in the well-being of children and consequently "can adopt more stringent controls on communicative materials available to youths than on those available to adults," . . . the Court has accounted for this societal interest by adopting a "variable obscenity" standard that permits the prurient appeal of material available to children to be assessed in terms of the sexual interests of minors. *Ginsberg v. New York*, 390 U.S. 629 (1968). It is true that the obscenity standard the *Ginsberg* Court adapted for such materials was based on the then-applicable obscenity standard of *Roth v. United States*, 354 U.S. 476 (1957), and *Memoirs v. Massachusetts*, 383 U.S. 413 (1966), and that "we have not had occasion to decide what effect *Miller* [v. *California*, 413 U.S. 15 (1973)] will have on the *Ginsberg* formulation." . . . Nevertheless, we have made it abundantly clear that "under any test of obscenity as to minors . . . to be obscene 'such expression must be, in some significant way, erotic.'"

Because the Carlin monologue is obviously not an erotic appeal to the prurient interests of children, the Court, for the first time, allows the government to prevent minors from gaining access to materials that are not obscene, and are therefore protected, as to them.[14] It thus ignores our recent admonition that "speech that is neither obscene as to youths nor subject to some other legitimate proscription cannot be suppressed solely to protect the young from ideas or images that a legislative body thinks unsuitable for them." . . .[15] The Court's refusal to

---

[14]Even if the monologue appealed to the prurient interest of minors, it would not be obscene as to them unless, as to them, "the work, taken as a whole, lacks serious literary, artistic, political, or scientific value." Miller v. California, 413 U.S. 15, 24 (1973).

[15]It may be that a narrowly drawn regulation prohibiting the use of offensive language on broadcasts directed specifically at younger children constitutes one of the "other legitimate proscriptions" alluded to in Erznoznik. This is so both because of the difficulties inherent in

follow its own pronouncements is especially lamentable since it has the anomalous subsidiary effect, at least in the radio context at issue here, of making completely unavailable to adults material which may not constitutionally be kept even from children. This result violates in spades the principle of *Butler v. Michigan,* 352 U.S. 380 (1957). *Butler* involved a challenge to a Michigan statute that forbade the publication, sale, or distribution of printed material "tending to incite minors to violent or depraved or immoral acts, manifestly tending to the corruption of the morals of youth." *Id.,* at 381. Although *Roth v. United States, supra,* had not yet been decided, it is at least arguable that the material the statute in *Butler* was designed to suppress could have been constitutionally denied to children. Nevertheless, this Court found the statute unconstitutional. Speaking for the Court, Mr. Justice Frankfurter reasoned:

> The incidence of this enactment is to reduce the adult population of Michigan to reading only what is fit for children. It thereby arbitrarily curtails one of those liberties of the individual, now enshrined in the Due Process Clause of the Fourteenth Amendment, that history has attested as the indispensable conditions for the maintenance and progress of a free society. Butler v. Michigan, supra, at 383-384.

Where, as here, the government may not prevent the exposure of minors to the suppressed material, the principle of *Butler* applies *a fortiori.* The opinion of my Brother Powell acknowledges that there lurks in today's decision a potential for "'reduc[ing] the adult population . . . to [hearing] only what is fit for children,'" . . . but expresses faith that the FCC will vigilantly prevent this potential from ever becoming a reality. I am far less certain than my Brother Powell that such faith in the Commission is warranted, see *Illinois Citizens Committee for Broadcasting v. FCC,* 515 F.2d 397, 418–421 (CADC 1975) (statement of Bazelon, C.J., as to why he voted to grant rehearing en banc); and even if I shared it, I could not so easily shirk the responsibility assumed by each Member of this Court jealously to guard against encroachments on First Amendment freedoms.

In concluding that the presence of children in the listening audience provides an adequate basis for the FCC to impose sanctions for Pacifica's broadcast of the Carlin monologue, the opinions of my Brother Powell, . . . and my Brother Stevens . . . both stress the time-honored right of a parent to raise his child as he sees fit—a right this Court has consistently been vigilant to protect. . . . Yet this principle supports a result directly contrary to that reached by the Court. *Yoder* and *Pierce* hold that parents, *not* the government, have the right to make certain

---

adapting the Miller formulation to communications received by young children, and because such children are "not possessed of that full capacity for individual choice which is the presupposition of the First Amendment guarantees." Ginsberg v. New York, 390 U.S. 629, 649–650 (1968) (Stewart, J., concurring). I doubt, as my Brother Stevens suggests, . . . that such a limited regulation amounts to a regulation of speech based on its content, since, by hypothesis, the only persons at whom the regulated communication is directed are incapable of evaluating its content. To the extent that such a regulation is viewed as a regulation based on content, it marks the outermost limits to which content regulation is permissible.

decisions regarding the upbringing of their children. As surprising as it may be to individual Members of this Court, some parents may actually find Mr. Carlin's unabashed attitude towards the seven "dirty words" healthy, and deem it desirable to expose their children to the manner in which Mr. Carlin defuses the taboo surrounding the words. Such parents may constitute a minority of the American public, but the absence of great numbers willing to exercise the right to raise their children in this fashion does not alter the right's nature or its existence. Only the Court's regrettable decision does that.[16]

C. As demonstrated above, neither of the factors relied on by both the opinion of my Brother Powell and the opinion of my Brother Stevens—the intrusive nature of radio and the presence of children in the listening audience—can, when taken on its own terms, support the FCC's disapproval of the Carlin monologue. These two asserted justifications are further plagued by a common failing: the lack of principled limits on their use as a basis for FCC censorship. No such limits come readily to mind, and neither of the opinions comprising the Court serve to clarify the extent to which the FCC may assert the privacy and children-in-the-audience rationales as justification for expunging from the airways protected communications the Commission finds offensive. Taken to their logical extreme, these rationales would support the cleansing of public radio of any "four-letter words" whatsoever, regardless of their context. The rationales could justify the banning from radio of a myriad of literary works, novels, poems, and plays by the likes of Shakespeare, Joyce, Hemingway, Ben Johnson, Henry Fielding, Robert Burns, and Chaucer; they could support the suppression of a good deal of political speech, such as the Nixon tapes; and they could even provide the basis for imposing sanctions for the broadcast of certain portions of the Bible.[17]

In order to dispel the spectre of the possibility of so unpalatable a degree of censorship, and to defuse Pacifica's overbreadth challenge, the FCC insists that it desires only the authority to reprimand a broadcaster on facts analogous to those present in this case, which it describes as involving "broadcasting for nearly twelve minutes a record which repeated over and over words which depict sexual or excretory activities and organs in a manner patently offensive by its community's contemporary standards in the early afternoon when children were in the audience." Brief for the Federal Communications Commission 45. The opinions of

[16]The opinions of my Brothers Powell and Stevens rightly refrain from relying on the notion of "spectrum scarcity" to support their result. As Chief Judge Bazelon noted below, "although scarcity has justified *increasing* the diversity of speakers and speech, it has never been held to justify censorship." 556 F. 2d, at 29 (emphasis in original). See Red Lion Broadcasting Co. v. FCC, 395 U.S. 367, 396 (1969).
[17]See, *e.g.*, I Samuel 52:22: "So and more also do God unto the enemies of David, if I leave of all that pertain to him by the morning light any that pisseth against the wall."; II Kings 18:27 and Isaiah 36:12: "Hath he not sent me to the men which sit on the wall, that they may eat their own dung, and drink their own piss with you?"; Ezekiel 23:3: "And they committed whoredoms in Egypt; they committed whoredoms in their youth; there were their breasts pressed, and there they bruised the teats of their virginity."; Ezekiel 23:21: "Thus tho calledst to remembrance the lewdnes of they youth in bruising they teats by the Egyptians for the paps of thy youth." The Bible (King James Version).

both my Brother Powell and my Brother Stevens take the FCC at its word, and consequently do no more than permit the Commission to censor the afternoon broadcast of the "sort of verbal shock treatment," opinion of Mr. Justice Powell, *ante,* 187, involved here. To insure that the FCC's regulation of protected speech does not exceed these bounds, my Brother Powell is content to rely upon the judgment of the Commission while my Brother Stevens deems it prudent to rely on this Court's ability accurately to assess the worth of various kinds of speech.[18] For my own part, even accepting that this case is limited to its facts,[19] I would place the responsibility and the right to weed worthless and offensive communications from the public airways where it belongs and where, until today, it resided: in a public free to choose those communications worthy of its attention from a marketplace unsullied by the censor's hand.

II

The absence of any hesitancy in the opinions of my Brothers Powell and Stevens to approve the FCC's censorship of the Carlin monologue on the basis of two demonstrably inadequate grounds is a function of their perception that the decision will result in little, if any, curtailment of communicative exchanges protected by the First Amendment. Although the extent to which the Court stands ready to countenance FCC censorship of protected speech is unclear from today's decision, I find the reasoning by which my Brethren conclude that the FCC censorship they approve will not significantly infringe on First Amendment values both disingenuous as to reality and wrong as a matter of law.

My Brother Stevens, in reaching a result apologetically described as narrow . . . takes comfort in his observation that "[a] requirement that indecent language be avoided will have its primary effect on the form, rather than the content, of serious communication," . . . and finds solace in his conviction that "there are few, if any, thoughts that cannot be expressed by the use of less

[18]Although ultimately dependent upon the outcome of review in this Court, the approach taken by my Brother Stevens would not appear to tolerate the FCC's suppression of any speech, such as political speech, falling within the core area of First Amendment concern. The same, however, cannot be said of the approach taken by my Brother Powell, which, on its face, permits the Commission to censor even political speech if it is sufficiently offensive to community standards. A result more contrary to rudimentary First Amendment principles is difficult to imagine.

[19]Having insisted that it seeks to impose sanctions on radio communications only in the limited circumstances present here, I believe that the FCC is estopped from using either this decision or its own orders in this case . . . as a basis for imposing sanctions on any public radio broadcast other than one aired during the daytime or early evening and containing the relentless repetition, for longer than a brief interval, of "language that describes, in terms patently offensive as measured by contemporary community standards for the broadcast medium, sexual or excretory activities and organs." 56 FCC 2d, at 98. For surely broadcasters are not now on notice that the Commission desires to regulate any offensive broadcast other than the type of "verbal shock treatment" condemned here, or even this "shock treatment" type of offensive broadcast during the late evening.

offensive language." . . . The idea that the content of a message and its potential impact on any who might receive it can be divorced from the words that are the vehicle for its expression is transparently fallacious. A given word may have a unique capacity to capsule an idea, evoke an emotion, or conjure up an image. Indeed, for those of us who place an appropriately high value on our cherished First Amendment rights, the word *censor* is such a word. Mr. Justice Harlan, speaking for the Court, recognized the truism that a speaker's choice of words cannot surgically be separated from the ideas he desires to express when he warned that "we cannot indulge the facile assumption that one can forbid particular words without also running a substantial risk of suppressing ideas in the process." *Cohen v. California*, 403 U.S., at 26. Moreover, even if an alternative phrasing may communicate a speaker's abstract ideas as effectively as those words he is forbidden to use, it is doubtful that the sterilized message will convey the emotion that is an essential part of so many communications. This, too, was apparent to Mr. Justice Harlan and the Court in *Cohen*.

> We cannot overlook the fact, because it is well illustrated by the episode involved here, that much linguistic expression serves a dual communicative function: it conveys not only ideas capable of relatively precise, detached explication, but otherwise inexpressible emotions as well. In fact, words are often chosen as much for their emotive as their congnitive force. We cannot sanction the view that the Constitution, while solicitous of the cognitive content of individual speech, has little or no regard for that emotive function which, practically speaking, may often be the more important element of the overall message sought to be communicated. Id., at 25–26.

My Brother Stevens also finds relevant to his First Amendment analysis the fact that "adults who feel the need may purchase tapes and records or go to theatres and nightclubs to hear [the tabooed] words." . . . My Brother Powell agrees: "The Commission's holding does not prevent willing adults from purchasing Carlin's record, from attending his performances, or, indeed, from reading the transcript reprinted as an appendix to the Court's opinion." . . . The opinions of my Brethren display both a sad insensitivity to the fact that these alternatives involve the expenditure of money, time, and effort that many of those wishing to hear Mr. Carlin's message may not be able to afford, and a naive innocence of the reality that in many cases, the medium may well be the message.

The Court apparently believes that the FCC's actions here can be analogized to the zoning ordinances upheld in *Young v. American Mini Theatres, supra*. For two reasons, it is wrong. First, the zoning ordinances found to pass constitutional muster in *Young* had valid goals other than the channeling of protected speech. . . . No such goals are present here. Second, and crucial to the opinions of my Brothers Powell and Stevens in *Young*—opinions, which, as they do in this case, supply the bare five-person majority of the Court—the ordinances did not restrict the access of distributors or exhibitors to the market or impair the viewing public's access to the regulated material. . . . Again, this is not the situation here. Both those desiring to receive Carlin's message over the radio and those wishing to send it to them are prevented from doing so by the Commission's actions. Although, as my Brethren point out, Carlin's message may be disseminated or received by other means, this is of little consolation to those broadcasters and listeners who, for a host of reasons, not least among them financial, do not have access to, or cannot take advantage of, these other means.

Moreover, it is doubtful that even those frustrated listeners in a position to follow my Brother Powell's gratuitous advice and attend one of Carlin's performances or purchase one of his records would receive precisely the same message Pacifica's radio station sent its audience. The airways are capable not only of carrying a message, but also of transforming it. A satirist's monologue may be most potent when delivered to a live audience; yet the choice whether this will in fact be the manner in which the message is delivered and received is one the First Amendment prohibits the government from making.

III

It is quite evident that I find the Court's attempt to unstitch the warp and woof of First Amendment law in an effort to reshape its fabric to cover the patently wrong result the Court reaches in this case dangerous as well as lamentable. Yet there runs throughout the opinions of my Brothers Powell and Stevens another vein I find equally disturbing: a depressing inability to appreciate that in our land of cultural pluralism, there are many who think, act, and talk differently from the Members of this Court, and who do not share their fragile sensibilities. It is only an acute ethnocentric myopia that enables the Court to approve the censorship of communications solely because of the words they contain.

"A word is not a crystal, transparent and unchanged, it is the skin of a living thought and may vary greatly in color and content according to the circumstances and the time in which it is used." *Towne* v. *Eisner*, 245 U.S. 418, 425 (1918) (Holmes, J.). The words that the Court and the Commission find so unpalatable may be the stuff of everyday conversations in some, if not many, of the innumerable subcultures that comprise this Nation. Academic research indicates that this is indeed the case. See B. Jackson, *Get Your Ass in the Water and Swim Like Me* (1974); J. Dillard, *Black English* (1972); W. Labov, *Language in the Inner City: Studies in the Black English Vernacular* (1972). As one researcher concluded, "words generally considered obscene like *bullshit* and *fuck* are considered neither obscene nor derogatory in the [black] vernacular except in particular contextual situations and when used with certain intonations." C. Bins, "Toward an Ethnography of Contemporary African American Oral Poetry," *Language and Linguistics Working Papers* No. 5, at 82 (Georgetown University Press 1972). Cf. *Keefe* v. *Geanakos*, 418 F. 2d 359, 361 (CA1 1969) (finding the use of the word *motherfucker* commonplace among young radicals and protestors).

Today's decision will thus have its greatest impact on broadcasters desiring to reach, and listening audiences comprised of, persons who do not share the Court's view as to which words or expressions are acceptable and who, for a variety of reasons, including a conscious desire to flout majoritarian conventions, express themselves using words that may be regarded as offensive by those from different socio-economic backgrounds.[20] In this context, the Court's decision may be seen for what, in the broader perspective, it really is: another of the dominant culture's inevitable efforts to force those groups who do not share its mores to conform to its way of thinking, acting, and speaking. See *Moore* v. *East Cleveland*, 431 U.S. 494, 506–511 (1977) (Brennan, J., concurring).

Pacifica, in response to an FCC inquiry about its broadcast of Carlin's satire on "the words you couldn't say on the public airwaves," explained that "Carlin is not mouthing obscenities, he is merely using words to satirize as harmless and essentially silly our attitudes towards those words." 56 FCC 2d, at 96. In confirming Carlin's prescience as a social commentator by the result it reaches today, the Court evinces an attitude towards the "seven dirty words" that many others besides Mr. Carlin and Pacifica might describe as "silly." Whether today's decision will similarly prove "harmless" remains to be seen. One can only hope that it will.

---

[20] Under the approach taken by my Brother Powell, the availability of broadcasts *about* groups whose members comprise such audiences might also be affected. Both news broadcasts about activities involving these groups and public affairs broadcasts about their concerns are apt to contain interviews, statements, or remarks by group leaders and members which may contain offensive language to an extent my Brother Powell finds unacceptable.

Epilogue
Thomas I. Emerson

This book has taken as its point of departure the traditional theory of freedom of expression, assuming the basic soundness of that theory and its workability in a modern democratic society. It has not undertaken to reexamine the premises upon which the theory rests or to question its general viability under present-day conditions. Nevertheless recent attacks upon the fundamentals of the system, which have mounted in the last few years, prompt me to add a few words about these broader issues.

It is interesting to note that current challenges to the system of freedom of expression in the United States have not proceeded, to any significant extent, along lines taken by some of the classical left in the past. There has been very little argument that modern society, with its need to plan and control on an extensive scale, cannot be organized on the principle that every member can say anything he likes at any time. The reason for this is undoubtedly that no strong movement of the old left presently exists in this country and no radical program of planning and control is now being seriously put forward. However that may be, in the absence of current controversy over this aspect of the problem, I shall confine my remarks to the challenges which have been produced by the particular period of strain which now exists.

The attack from the right proceeds on traditional grounds. It is urged that present-day society is filled with tensions, divisions and potential conflict; that

From *The System of Freedom of Expression*, copyright © 1970 by Thomas I. Emerson. Reprinted by permission of Random House, Inc.

opposition to existing policies and institutions is widespread and tends more and more to take the form of open disregard for laws; that, in short, the society faces an imminent breakdown of all law and order. In such a period, it is said, society cannot tolerate speech that stirs discontent, inflames passions, and moves people to violent action. Quite the contrary, the argument runs, additional laws are necessary, not only to curb disorder, but to prevent it from happening by eliminating conduct that might lead to it. Hence the Federal Riot Control Act, the revival of the Subversive Activities Control Board, the withdrawal of Federal funds from universities which fail to punish student disruption, and similar measures are advocated. All such laws, as previously made clear, have a destructive impact on the system of freedom of expression.

There can be little doubt that concern over the widening conflict in our society is well founded. In recent years there has been a serious falling away of consensus, a polarization of viewpoints, an increasing inability to solve the problems of society without the compulsion of violence or other illegal action. Moreover, modern society is particularly vulnerable to disruption by small but determined groups, or even by angry individuals. Nevertheless the answer to the call for repressive measures remains, even in a time of acute tension, the orthodox one, reiterated many times in the preceding pages. Suppression of expression does not solve the underlying problems; on the contrary it frequently intensifies them. The rules supporting freedom of expression do not preclude the adoption of measures to control action. Nor, of course, do they preclude the taking of steps to remedy the basic ills that give rise to the conflict. Indeed the system of free expression facilitates efforts to proceed by orderly change. On the other hand repression has no stopping place. Once begun, it can quickly move all the way to a totalitarian system.

These are the premises upon which the system of freedom of expression is founded. They may prove unworkable if economic, political, and social conditions deteriorate to the point where our whole society collapses. If that occurs it is unlikely that firm adherence to the principles of free expression will be a material contributing cause. There is no reason, therefore, to abandon those principles beforehand. The choice is essentially between a system of freedom of expression and a police state.

The challenge from the left poses different issues. The charge from that quarter is not that the system of freedom of expression cripples society's efforts to defend itself from disruption but that it does not provide an adequate technique for effectuating urgent social change, and may indeed hamper it. The main exponent of this position has been Professor Herbert Marcuse. Other important figures in the New Left movement, both white and black, have expressed similar ideas. In the movement generally there seems to be a growing indifference to the theory or operation of the system of freedom of expression. This is not to say that the New Left is unanimous on these issues, or that there is majority support for the Marcuse position. But such attitudes are certainly widespread.[1]

---

[1] See, *e.g.*, Robert P. Wolff, Barrington Moore, Jr., and Herbert Marcuse, *A Critique of Pure*

The existence of these views in the New Left movement is a phenomenon of far-reaching consequence. In the past, proponents of social change in America have usually supported, though they may not have been the leading fighters for, the system of freedom of expression. Even radical political groups, with ties to totalitarian parties in other countries, have tended to accept most of the traditional theory. Were the incipient hostility of the New Left movement to progress, along with an increasing polarization of political forces, the future of the system of freedom of expression in the United States would indeed be dark.

To some extent, particularly in Professor Marcuse, the New Left opposition to the system of freedom of expression is based on the classic arguments regarding tolerance and the nature of government. Tolerance, at least to the degree embedded in the proposed system, is viewed as a lack of moral conviction, an absence of political direction, and an excuse for refusing to budge from the status quo. Government based on a balance of pluralistic forces is viewed with similar skepticism, and reliance is placed upon the ability of the state to represent the interests of all citizens fairly. These views are founded on philosophical premises quite different from those that underlie the system of freedom of expression, and will not be debated here. To some extent the New Left attitude, particularly in the young, may reflect a general distrust of all rational systems, or a lack of interest in them. This, again, is a philosophical position that will not be argued at this point. To some extent the hostility to freedom of expression may represent merely general disagreement with the main political, economic, and social institutions of our society. This is wide of the mark. The system of freedom of expression is not inevitably tied to existing institutions. It is applicable to any open society.

The more significant objections of the New Left movement, for our purposes, are those based upon the operation of the system of freedom of expression in our modern society, at this time of crisis. These objections raise more immediate issues, which are within the boundaries of this book. In essence the system of freedom of expression is seen as a wholly inadequate instrument for dealing with the urgent problems of the day and, more than that, as a tool of repression used by the Establishment to maintain the status quo. Freedom of expression is viewed as part of the paraphernalia of liberal institutions which in practice operate to the detriment of submerged groups and against social change.

The position that significant change cannot be achieved in the present society through reliance upon the system of freedom of expression has, of course, ominous implications for the future of the country. If that view is carried to the point of violent revolution, then obviously the system of freedom of expression will have been destroyed. Short of this ultimate tragedy, however, the system would continue to perform its function, though perhaps on a reduced scale. The system is an instrument for facilitating orderly change and the degree to which it operates well depends upon how it is used and how it is supported. When any group makes the political judgment that it must pursue other tactics, outside the system, that is usually a sign that the system has not been put to proper use by those who

Tolerance (Boston, Beacon Press, 1965); "Marcuse Defines His New Left Line," *The New York Times Magazine*, Oct. 27, 1968, p. 29.

participate in it, or that the dominant group in the society has failed to maintain the economic, political, and social conditions which permit the system to operate. But the occurrence of such events is not ground for either the dominant group, the challenging group, or any other part of society to abrogate the system. The system still provides the only method of avoiding resolution of the issues through force alone. Every effort must be made, despite previous failures, to continue use of the system as far as possible and to restore it to operating order. No one gains from scrapping it at the first sign of trouble.

The feeling on the part of the New Left that the system of freedom of expression operates actively against its interests, by enabling the Establishment to block change, rests on several grounds. The main contentions seem to be that (1) the system is actually a sham, in that really radical or deviant expression is not allowed, or if ostensibly allowed is punished by indirect methods including trumped-up criminal prosecutions; (2) the system is loaded in favor of the status quo, particularly through Establishment control of the mass media; and (3) the system is utilized to prolong discussion, focus on procedural complications, and assure delay, thereby allowing the Establishment to avoid the real issues and divert attention from the need for action. In all these ways, it is asserted, the system of freedom of expression is a meaningless sop, designed to siphon off protest and delude the populace into believing it has a participating voice. As the preceeding pages have demonstrated, these contentions are not without some factual foundation. Nevertheless they do not add up to the position that the system should be ignored, opposed, or discarded.

It is true that the system of freedom of expression has never worked ideally and that expression which challenges the foundations of the society has often been suppressed or harassed. But the developments recounted in earlier chapters reveal that, as it operates today, the system affords even the most radical expression a substantial measure of protection. Significant progress has been made. It cannot be concluded that the gap between theory and reality which still exists justifies writing off the system. Even though the principle is not fully realized in practice, the existence and growth of the principle are significant. The alternative would be no legal protection whatever.

The control of the mass media by a small group representing the dominant element of our society is, as previously pointed out, a major weakness in the present system of freedom of expression. It is not a problem we show much sign of solving in the near future. Yet again this state of affairs is not fatal to the system. No society that ever existed has afforded equal access to the means of communication to all its members or groups. The dominant group, whether through power of government or the forces of laissez-faire, has always had the loudest voice, and probably always will. The validity of the system does not depend on exact equality. In fact the effort to achieve such equality by government allocation, without any reliance upon laissez-faire factors, might jeopardize rather than better the system. In any event the essential element in the system is the right of the minority to express its views through such methods as are available to it. The history of the civil-rights movement, the peace movement, the black movement, and others in recent years indicates that minorities have found ways to be heard and minority viewpoints have not been kept out of the marketplace altogether. The problem of equality is a crucial one, but the remedy is betterment of the system, not abandonment. Again, the alternative would be worse.

The charge that the system of freedom of expression is often used simply to prolong debate and avoid action likewise has considerable support in fact. Of course, any system of communication and persuasion necessarily involves delay. The more complex the system becomes the more entangled it gets in procedural niceties. However, if those in positions of power use the system merely to block action they can expect to reap the whirlwind. The problem here is similar to that with which we began. The system by itself does not produce any particular result. It is an instrument to be used by groups in society for conducting their affairs without resort to force. If the system is not properly used it will ultimately collapse. Short of that catastrophe, however, all groups are likely to benefit as long as it is maintained. Once more, the remedy is to force proper use of the system, not write it off.

What has been said up to this point concerns the immediate or short-term factors involved in the attitude of the New Left to the system of freedom of expression. There are also longer-range considerations that should be taken into account. Any society, no matter how organized, must face the question of the extent it will allow its members freedom of expression. No political movement looking to the future can forever ignore this problem. It would be unfortunate, therefore, if the shortcomings of the present system were to cloud the fact that in the long run the question must be resolved. Nor can the importance of the gains achieved in the last half century be ignored. The principles, traditions, institutions and attitudes that have been built up are not without their worth. If the system broke down, the road back would be long and hard.

Underlying these challenges to the system from both the right and the left are some hard, unresolved questions. Can the system of freedom of expression survive the shift from the liberal laissez-faire to the mass technological society? As one surveys the record, the older features of the system—protection of individual expression against government infringement—seem to present the more solvable problem. It is true that the growth in the functions and powers of government, the gradual disappearance of looseness in the structures of control, and the greater vulnerability of the society as a whole, all add to the complications. But the development of new doctrine, more sensitive institutions, and better understanding give hope that the problem can be mastered. The more difficult task will come with the need to call on government for removal of distortions from the system and for affirmative promotion of its operations. Here the laissez-faire approach must be replaced by new principles, new techniques, and new ways of thought. This is the great challenge and the open question.

Bibliography

Barron, Jerome A. *Freedom of The Press For Whom? The Right of Access to Mass Media.* Bloomington: Indiana University Press, 1973.

Berger, Fred R. "Pornography, Sex and Censorship." *Social Theory and Practice* 4 (1977): 183–209.

Berns, Walter F. *The First Amendment and the Future of American Democracy.* New York: Basic Books, 1976.

Bosmajian, Haig A., ed. *Dissent: Symbolic Behavior and Rhetorical Strategies.* Boston: Allyn & Bacon, 1972.

Chafee, Zechariah, Jr. *Free Speech in the United States.* Cambridge, Mass.: Harvard University Press, 1941.

Clor, Harry M. *Obscenity and Public Morality: Censorship in a Liberal Society.* Chicago: University of Chicago Press, 1969.

Dworkin, Ronald. "The Rights of Myron Farber." *New York Review of Books* 25 (1978): 34–36.

Emerson, Thomas I. *The System of Freedom of Expression.* New York: Random House, 1970.

Emerson, Thomas I. *Toward a General Theory of the First Amendment.* New York: Random House, 1966.

Feinberg, Joel. "Limits to the Free Expression of Opinion." In *Philosophy of*

Law, ed. Joel Feinberg and Hyman Gross. Encino and Belmont, Calif.: Dickenson Publishing Company, 1975, pp. 135–51.

Frantz, Laurent B. "The First Amendment in the Balance." 71 *Yale Law Journal* 1424 (1962).

Friendly, Fred. *The Good Guys, the Bad Guys and the First Amendment.* New York: Random House, 1975.

Glass, Marvin. "Anti Racism and Unlimited Freedom of Speech: An Untenable Dualism," *Canadian Journal of Philosophy* VIII (1978): 559–575.

Halperin, Morton H., and Hoffman, Daniel N. *Top Secret: National Security and the Right to Know.* Washington, D.C.: New Republic Books, 1977.

Hart, Harold H., ed. *Censorship, For and Against.* New York: Hart Publishing Co., 1971.

Hook, Sidney. *Paradoxes of Freedom.* Berkeley: University of California Press, 1962.

Hughes, Douglas A., ed. *Perspectives on Pornography.* New York: St. Martin's Press, 1970.

Kalven, Harry, Jr. "The Metaphysics of the Law of Obscenity." In *The Supreme Court Review, 1959*, ed. Philip P. Kurland. Chicago: University of Chicago Press, 1960, pp. 1–45.

Kalven, Harry, Jr. *The Negro and the First Amendment.* Chicago: University of Chicago Press, 1966.

Krislov, Samuel. *The Supreme Court and Political Freedom.* New York: The Free Press, 1968.

Kristol, Irving. "Pornography, Obscenity, and the Case for Censorship," *New York Times Magazine,* March 28, 1971, p. 23.

Levy, Leonard. *Legacy of Suppression: Freedom of Speech and Press in Early American History.* Cambridge, Mass.: Harvard University Press, 1960.

Mander, Jerry. *Four Arguments for the Elimination of Television.* New York: William Morrow, 1978.

Meiklejohn, Alexander. "The First Amendment Is an Absolute." In *The Supreme Court Review, 1961*, ed. Philip B. Kurland. Chicago: University of Chicago Press, 1962, pp. 245–66.

Meiklejohn, Alexander. *Political Freedom: The Constitutional Power of the People.* New York: Oxford University Press, 1965.

Nimmer, Melville B. "The Meaning of Symbolic Speech Under the First Amendment." 21 *UCLA Law Review* 29 (1973).

Scanlon, Timothy. "A Theory of Freedom of Expression." *Philosophy and Public Affairs* 1 (1972): 204–26.

Shapiro, Martin. *Freedom of Speech: The Supreme Court and Judicial Review.* Englewood Cliffs, N.J.: Prentice-Hall, 1966.

Sheehan, Neil, et al. *The Pentagon Papers.* New York: Bantam Books, 1971.

Tussman, Joseph. *Government and the Mind.* New York: Oxford University Press, 1977.

Wolff, Robert Paul, Moore, Barrington Jr., and Marcuse, Herbert. *A Critique of Pure Tolerance.* Boston: Beacon Press, 1965, 1969.

KF 4770 .A75 F73